PRAISE FOR *MAKII*

MW01088407

'This readable, common-sense, evidence-based book acts as a "go to" guide for implementing hybrid ways of working. The helpful coaching questions and case study reflections was like having my own hybrid business mentor at my side. It tackles, head on, the frustrations that many remote and hybrid workers face when working within work patterns that are trying to cater for a variety of individual needs and circumstances. Considering the bigger picture of healthier working, Gary Cookson sets out a compelling case for hybrid working being at the core of best practice for better work–life balance.'
Sue Murkin, healthier worker consultant

'I thought everything that needed to be said about remote and hybrid working had been said but then I read this book. Honestly, it's a manager's anthology. It should be easy access on every manager's shelf; it really hits the nail on the head for a pragmatic way of looking at something that has been around for a long time but continues to vex many. It's not often you get this level of detailed insight into how other businesses manage their staff so grab that opportunity now it's here. It's not a book you read once and put away. Keep it on the top of the pile because you'll be reaching for it regularly.'
Alan Price, CEO, BrightHR

'Gary Cookson has done it again: a book so full of ideas and suggestions that there is no excuse for your organization not to consider hybrid working patterns. The world of work is constantly moving, and I appreciate how Gary helps us to navigate this reality. He encourages us to consider our context and lays out many considerations, nuances and consequences. This book is a checklist of conversations to have about hybrid working, which makes it a must-read for all modern thinking organizations.'
Michelle Parry-Slater, L&D Director, Kairos Modern Learning, and author of *The Learning and Development Handbook*

'Highlights the necessity for intentional implementation strategies to leverage the numerous benefits of hybrid working. Gary Cookson prompts us to redefine workweeks, optimize technology and spaces, foster connectivity, overcome isolation, embrace asynchronous working and provide essential support for staff, teams and managers. Through numerous and diverse case studies, thought-provoking questions and practical suggestions, the book serves as a comprehensive guide and must-read for navigating the complexities and unlocking the potential of modern hybrid work environments.'
Andy Lancaster, Chief Learning Officer and Consultant, Reimagine People Development

'Hybrid working is everywhere, but it doesn't always work. Packed with insightful illustrations, diverse and well-researched topics and real-world case studies, this book is essential reading for any leader committed to creating positive, people-oriented workplaces.'
Rob Baker, Founder and Chief Positive Deviant, Tailored Thinking, and author of *Personalization at Work*

'The workplace has for ever changed – for the better. Gary Cookson captures the intentionality needed to engage, move and evolve effectively through this new environment. His book gives tangible examples and a framework employers can use to make hybrid work a success.'
Steve Browne, Chief People Officer, LaRosa's and author of *HR on Purpose!!*, *HR Rising!!* and *HR Unleashed!!*

'Hybrid working, contrary to some claims, was not a pandemic blip after all, but has become one of the key ways organizations can attract, engage, retain and unleash talent. This book is the go-to for anyone wanting to understand how to make hybrid working actually work rather than costly trial and error. Hybrid working is itself very much a work in progress so few can lay claim to be an expert on the topic. That said, Gary Cookson is in a league of his own.'
Shakil Butt, HR and leadership consultant, and Founder, HR Hero for Hire

'Offers up-to-date practical approaches and insights on navigating hybrid working. An essential overview including case studies and useful guidance to improve outcomes for people and organizations.'
David D'Souza, Director of Profession, CIPD

'Perfectly captures the tensions, nuances and challenges of modern work. Through insightful case studies and progressive thinking, the book highlights the immense opportunities ahead and gives you the tools and awareness to navigate them successfully.'
Gethin Nadin, award-winning psychologist, bestselling author and *HR Magazine's* #7 HR Most Influential Thinker

'Challenges outdated assumptions about office life and the traditional work-week. It offers actionable processes to improve flexible working policies and eliminates the "fear" that people will not be working.'
James Dean, Founder, HRC Online

'Jam-packed with insightful and inspiring case studies, bringing to life the benefits and pitfalls of various working approaches, mixed with practical ideas on how to best approach achieving an effective hybrid working philosophy fit for your unique organizational needs. There isn't a single formula to what effective hybrid working looks like, but this is the book that will help you to define and shape an approach that is right for your organization, your leaders and your people.'
Nebel Crowhurst, Chief People Officer, Reward Gateway

Making Hybrid Working Work

A practical guide for business success

Gary Cookson

KoganPage

Publisher's note

Every possible effort has been made to ensure that the information contained in this book is accurate at the time of going to press, and the publishers and author cannot accept responsibility for any errors or omissions, however caused. No responsibility for loss or damage occasioned to any person acting, or refraining from action, as a result of the material in this publication can be accepted by the editor, the publisher or the author.

First published in Great Britain and the United States in 2025 by Kogan Page Limited

2nd Floor, 45 Gee Street
London
EC1V 3RS
United Kingdom

8 W 38th Street, Suite 902
New York, NY 10018
USA

www.koganpage.com

Kogan Page books are printed on paper from sustainable forests.

ISBNs

Hardback   978 1 3986 1934 0
Paperback   978 1 3986 1932 6
Ebook   978 1 3986 1933 3

British Library Cataloguing-in-Publication Data
A CIP record for this book is available from the British Library.

Library of Congress Cataloging-in-Publication Data
Names: Cookson, Gary (Human resources consultant), author.
Title: Making hybrid working work : a practical guide for business success
  / Gary Cookson.
Description: London ; New York, NY : Kogan Page, 2025. | Includes
  bibliographical references and index.
Identifiers: LCCN 2024032898 (print) | LCCN 2024032899 (ebook) | ISBN
  9781398619326 (paperback) | ISBN 9781398619340 (hardback) | ISBN
  9781398619333 (ebook)
Subjects: LCSH: Personnel management. | Telecommuting. | Flexible work
  arrangements.
Classification: LCC HF5549 .C72454 2025 (print) | LCC HF5549 (ebook) |
  DDC 658.3–dc23/eng/20240719
LC record available at https://lccn.loc.gov/2024032898
LC ebook record available at https://lccn.loc.gov/2024032899

Typeset by Integra Software Services, Pondicherry
Print production managed by Jellyfish
Printed and bound by CPI Group (UK) Ltd, Croydon CR0 4YY

'You're not writing another one' said my wife Katie.

'I like it because you put my name in the dedication,' said my daughter Poppy.

'Your Mum would have read this, but I don't think I will, though I am proud of you,' said my Dad.

'Will this help us understand what it is you actually do?' said my son and daughter Owen and Faye.

'Can I colour in the pictures?' asked my son William.

It is clear that my first book had an effect on those closest to me.

Here I am again though, and again I will dedicate this work to those mentioned above. For reminding me what is important.

CONTENTS

PART THREE
Help and support

FOREWORD

by Perry Timms MCIPD, FRSA,
Founder and Chief Energy Officer, PTHR,
No. 1 Most Influential Thinker in HR for 2022,
4 × Guest Professor, 2 × Author

Increasingly many of us – including the author Gary Cookson and I – are more interested in work.

I say *more* because we are seeing work as not just a *means to an end* economic transaction so we can live the **rest** of our lives as best we can; but more as a **part of** our lives and how we design and engineer them.

This is reason number one for you to read this book. Because you should be interested in work beyond the economic aspects of it. It's a big part of your life whatever kind of work you do. If you're not interested in work *specifically* where the **choice of location and working pattern** is part of the deal, read it anyway. It'll be more useful than you might think.

A crucial part of the design and engineering of work in the mid-2020s has become the concept of flexible – and more specifically for this book – **hybrid working**. And before I go any further, this book already helps bring more clarity to this *easy-to-use but still somewhat nebulous* categorization. So that's another reason why you should get this book.

Many people claim to be experts in hybrid working. Yet we're still in the early stages of this so that claim should be treated with caution. I've got over 20 years of working in what we'd now call hybrid, and I will not make such an assertion myself. I have my experiences and views, but I wouldn't claim hybrid working expertise.

Gary is different though and is as near to an expert as you can get; down to his experiences and curiosity but more his determination to help us all get **hybrid working to work.**

Gary has devoted his more recent years to exploring, experimenting and engaging with the concept of hybrid work in a way that sets him apart from almost anyone else in this area. His credibility is down to several things:

1   The fact that he is devoid of any bias and affiliation with the office space community. Some of the biggest objectors to *work from anywhere* seem to emanate from those with financial or professional interests in the office as the only/best place of work.

2 He has HR/people profession, culture, learning and performance at the heart of his practice and, again, isn't biased towards the HR-only view of hybrid work.

3 He seeks out those in emerging practices and embedded philosophies and experiments in the hybrid working arena.

4 He synthesizes not just smartly, but with an action orientation. Gary **wants** you to make hybrid work work by helping you with suggestions on how you could do that.

So that's reason number three to read this book.

Reason number four is the sheer volume of practical case studies in this book. So many sizes, sectors and types of work – admittedly lots based on knowledge and creative work – illustrate how people have and are experimenting with hybrid working. This gives you, as a reader, comfort that this is not sensationalist or overtly biased reporting but real-life probes of the working future when it comes to the location of where work is done.

Reason number five is back to the nature and construct of this book – the calls to action and suggestions. It's like the compass, map, satnav and gingerbread crumb trail to all you'd need to consider in setting your hybrid working plans, philosophies, and practical application of those. If – as the cliché goes – you're on a journey with hybrid working, this will make your plotting and experience of it much more Route 66 than Road to Nowhere.

My take on this entire topic though is what a foreword ought to be, else it's just endorsements. Pleased though I am to make those five reasons stand out for you.

As I said, I've over 20 years of hybrid working. In 1998, I took on a project role that meant I needed to be in a range of locations across the UK. If you're too young to know this, dial-up, phone-line-based internet was just beginning to normalize how we accessed the internet. There were no smartphones but early devices with internet browsing capability existed and were the thickness of a small religious textbook. I managed to work on trains, in hotels and in different offices with the primitive laptop device I was given with about a 60-minute battery.

I adapted well. My new manager in this project (also used to working on the go) was great in helping and shaping a trust-based relationship. Pioneering video conferencing was just being introduced and we connected that way for more formal meetings when we weren't in the same location.

When I moved into an OD/HR role in 2003, this continued but by then laptops were a bit better in battery life. Smaller, and able to become the work device that accessed it all.

Fast-forward to 2012 when I began a freelance working model in my enterprise, and work-from-anywhere was an easy transition for me. Co-working spaces were in their earlier stages of being, hotel lobbies and coffee shop working became a normative state and the 'ask a respectable looking stranger to keep an eye on your laptop while you go to the toilet' became an almost everyday thing.

When the Covid-19 pandemic hit and lockdowns happened, it needed zero adjustments on my part and the team I'd not long assembled. We were remote from the get-go; dispersed across geolocations and flexible in hours or work.

Suddenly, everyone was having to do that. And all at once I saw the pain, confusion, misunderstanding and clumsiness of how people applied themselves to a virtual and digitally connected way of working from their own homes.

I entered debates, discussions and even learning about what remote working now meant and into the emergence from lockdowns into newfound experiences and choices and that life-engineering I opened this foreword with. And the word hybrid became the nomenclature.

And then I saw the headlines and fear-based diktats. And some – but not that many with clear authority and devoid of bias – studies and research in this area.

I'll stop there because the rest of this story is picked up in the book.

But what I will say is this.

1 I'm not anti-office. I'm pro-choice.

2 I'm not oblivious to the fact that some people cannot choose where they work, but that doesn't mean I don't appreciate their work any less because I enter office-v-anywhere debates and show my preference for anywhere.

3 I'm aware that working from anywhere and hybrid is a complex phenomenon we don't know enough about yet. In terms of workplace/ team culture impacts; innovation; promotion; performance and fairness.

4 I'm aware some people have a (perhaps romanticized and nostalgic) view of the office as some congregation of faithful advocates that I've never experienced. But maybe that's just me. It's been a functional place with facilities, equipment and people. *The place of worship is not the religion* is a phrase I've used.

5 Office working isn't the inclusive nirvana we might have thought it was. Many people with disabilities, caring needs, childcare, pets, mental health challenges, lifestyle choices and so on do *not* see the office the same way you might because it serves you as it is. Working from anywhere and hybrid working opens new ways that bring more equity to work.

6 I love my work, but that's independent of where it gets done. When I've been part of a fabulous event, that's rarely because the room had nice fittings and decor but more about what we **did** in that space.

I am now able to urge everyone to not just think about my six perspectives but, instead, read Gary's book.

So that's the end of my foreword bar this urge:

Keep experimenting, including people and co-create anything you do that is linked to hybrid working. Don't fixate on numbers like 60 per cent or 40 per cent of the time in the office but do fixate on a broader range of value parameters: human, social, intellectual, natural plus material and financial value.

Hybrid working could significantly help us all be more prosperous and fulfilled in our work. Don't spoil it by thinking a ratio of in/out will solve things. It won't. And Gary's book will tell you why and how to avoid that trap.

Bravo Gary. Bravo Kogan Page. Bravo case study organizations. Bravo hybrid. Bravo to a more inclusive, fair, balanced, and prosperous form of working.

PREFACE

What this book is about

This book is a guide on how to make hybrid working work more effectively, whether you are a leader, a manager, a people professional or an employee.

Many people who work in a hybrid way have struggled. Many organizations have struggled with it too. They have sometimes not known how to give the right advice and support to make hybrid working work, not having the right experiences or expertise to draw upon to help.

This book is therefore a guide on how to deliver this support. It is a how-to guide on all aspects of setting up hybrid working, leading and developing hybrid teams, and enhancing the experience of those working in a hybrid way. It covers how to tackle the big organizational decisions needed, how to ensure the work itself is suitable and workable in a hybrid way, how to redesign tasks and jobs, how to manage individuals differently when not co-located with them all the time, how to use data better to manage the operations of the team, and how to ensure teams develop and perform effectively.

This book will help people professionals make significant contributions to making hybrid working work, by supporting leaders, managers, teams and individuals to adapt the work they do, the way they work together and the way the organization is designed. It will also help leaders and managers themselves to develop the confidence to do such things.

The enforced nature of remote working during the Covid-19 pandemic meant that the advantages of remote, and later hybrid, working were experienced alongside the disadvantages it can bring. It was not a true reflection of these working models.

However what it did do was force the world of work to confront some previously held, long-standing 'truths' – beliefs such as work is best done in five shifts of eight hours, across a 40-hour working week, that people needed to live close enough to their place of work to get there on any given day and that work had to be done in one specific location between specific times. These were all proven untrue and, in many cases, completely unworkable.

This meant that the world of work changed without anyone really planning for it to. Some form of hybrid working will become normal for many organizations, and therefore we could craft something bigger, something better, than either face-to-face working or remote working, something that brings together the best of both worlds but is somehow greater than the sum of its parts – hybrid working.

But hybrid working cannot be left to chance. Individuals, teams and organizations could succeed more through luck than judgement, but why take that risk? Hybrid working is more than just arbitrarily deciding that people can work some days remotely and other days on site, it requires a structured, considered approach to redefining what work is and how it is done. Left to chance, the significant advantages to all stakeholders would remain out of grasp.

This book is for those who want to take big, confident strides into the world of hybrid working. The book is also for those who are unsure about the future and what to do, and who want some practical guidance about what to do differently.

It has case studies and examples, from organizations based across the world, showing how individuals, teams, leaders, managers and organizations have adapted to hybrid working – both successfully and unsuccessfully. It draws on research that explores the scale of the challenges and holds many insights from leading thinkers on the world of work, alongside academic research that highlights what could be possible.

It explores the ways in which leaders and managers of hybrid teams need to think about job design, team relationships, individual management arrangements, using data to gather evidence and make decisions, solve problems and cope with the rise of, and embed the principles of, asynchronous working within the organization. It will also explore whether moves away from a standard five-day working week are possible, desirable and – on the assumption that they could be – how to make such things work in our organizations.

Many people professionals, and many leaders and managers in organizations, are heavily influenced by a growing sense and pace of change in the world of work. All this points towards the realization of having to do things differently – but many will have asked the question, where do we start?

We start here.

Who I am and why I wrote this

In my career, I've done hybrid working for over two decades now. I was an early proponent of remote and hybrid working, doing it long before the technology made it easy and before it became both fashionable and, in many cases, essential. I've been able to build remote and hybrid teams for a long time.

My business – EPIC – exists as a hybrid business, delivering services in a hybrid way since 2017 and via a four-day working week since 2022.

My first book, *HR for Hybrid Working*, was published in 2022. It focused on how we need to reimagine people practices for the world of remote and hybrid working. This book is an ideal companion to that, building on themes explored within that book and taking bigger steps into the world of hybrid working. It comes because of feedback about *HR for Hybrid Working*, and developments in the world of work since that was written. It also reflects the balance of questions I am asked and what I am regularly invited to speak on, write about and consult upon in organizations – how to get hybrid working to work better.

Who you are and why I hope you're here

You may be a leader or manager who has been wrestling with making hybrid working work and adopting a trial-and-error approach. You may be concluding that a one size fits all approach across your organization is unlikely to yield results for your team, but without any analysis and structured thinking and guidance to help you see how to do things differently within your context.

You may be a very senior leader at executive level in a medium or large organization with responsibility for large chunks of the organization. You may want insight into how you can deliver your main leadership and management responsibilities in diverse ways and give confidence to those leaders and managers who report to you. This book may help to give you a distinct perspective on what hybrid working really is.

Some of you will be stand-alone people professionals or working in small teams and from a predominantly generalist perspective. If that is you, you could have few people to share ideas with, gain innovative ideas from or sense check modern thinking in your context. Your CPD budget may not stretch as far as larger teams' budgets might. It is difficult for the lone practitioner to have confidence to try things in work in a new way. I hope to give you that and support you in trying out the things you see, hear and learn from other forms of learning.

Some of you will be people professionals in much larger organizations, who may have a specialism and may support leaders, managers and teams based in multiple locations and geographies. It will give you confidence too – your primary driver is to show the value add and efficiency of hybrid working, but you could be stuck with stakeholders who have different ideas and may be short of options for things to try or move towards. You have here a practical handbook to help them understand how the world of work has changed, quickly and drastically, and how the things they are used to may no longer work – but, crucially, what could take their place and how to get it right.

Some of you may be from organizations without people professionals – typically small and micro-sized organizations whose delivery of traditional people services is likely to be done by non-specialists. In a smaller organization you have a unique context within which to consider hybrid working but may not have access to the specialist guidance you need to make it work. Well, you do now.

How the book works

The book will begin with several chapters exploring the changing nature of work. It will look at how we define and understand hybrid working, and the current debates in organizations about it. It will explore some of the evidence for (and against) hybrid working and how we change the mindsets of those opposed to it. It will also explore how hybrid working is part of a wider shift away from traditional forms of working and how this needs to be factored into organizational thinking.

The main section of the book will look at how we make hybrid working work better, making the point that there is no one size fits all approach, and highlighting the need to be conscious and deliberate in how it is designed. It will give guidance on how to design hybrid working and how to keep this design as flexible as possible. This section will also explore how this leads to personalizing the employee experience and employment relationship, and the implications this has for real estate and technology. It will also examine how specific types of employees may need specific support.

The book's final part will look at how we need to help individuals to make the most of hybrid working and how this changes the nature of a team. It will look at how teams can be more effectively supported, and how leaders and managers need to develop new skills – and how to supply these.

Each chapter will have a similar structure (inspired at least partially by Michelle Parry-Slater's book *The Learning and Development Handbook*), and which many of you will be familiar with from *HR for Hybrid Working*:

- A shorter read – a few pages for the short-of-time reader who wants a quick flavour and summary of the chapter without getting into the detail behind it.

- A longer read – the detail you need if the shorter read has piqued your interest, and you want to go in-depth on the issues explored. This will also include research compiled for this book from experts, thought leaders and leading thinkers on the world of work, sharing their views on themes explored in relevant chapters.

- Case studies – stories from the front line, sharing what organizations have done, what worked and what did not. The majority of these are from named organizations. Some others will be from clients of EPIC, or other organizations, who prefer to remain anonymous for assorted reasons. In sharing these anonymous case studies some of the organizational characteristics may have been made more generic to further protect their anonymity.

- Case study reflections – the main learning points to consider from each case study.

- The action plan – in building your practices further, and planning for actions you need to take to move forward on the issues examined in the chapter.

Each of the three parts of the book will conclude with a Sketchnote illustration, superbly crafted and provided by Rachel Burnham, to summarize the main themes appearing in that chapter. There is also a summary Sketchnote in this section to give an overall route map for the book. Rachel's work will be familiar to those of you who have read *HR for Hybrid Working*.

There will be a References and further reading section at the end of each chapter – further and wider reading and much of the evidence behind the chapter, linking to leading thinkers and thinking on the subjects discussed to help you apply the learning from reading this.

I'd love to hear from you as you read the book and/or after you are finished. Track me down on social media – X/Twitter, Threads or LinkedIn – and let me know your thoughts and questions.

Happy reading.

Summary

Hybrid working is hard to define

It isn't:
'a fixed time and point in space'

e.g. 9-5 here

There is more than 1 way of hybrid working

It isn't: 1/size — 1/size

There are alternatives to:

Fixed hybrid working

Effective hybrid working can't be left to chance

Instead be intentional

Purpose
Culture
Support
Intent
Guidance — N E S
Task Requirements
Choice

Identify which tasks can be remote? And which are

Task — from... to... only here

Fixed time — Fixed location

Consider *flexibility* for jobs that may not be able to be hybrid

Helping individuals & teams to navigate hybrid working by:

Contracting to agree expectations
Regular check-ins
successes
challenges
clarity
Team charter
about what productivity looks like
learning — mix of methods

Making a success of hybrid working involves:

Back to the drawing board for organizational design and work processes

Investment in using technology is needed to:

to speed up workflows
reduce bottlenecks
speed up decision-making

Creating a variety of spaces on-site will be needed

Library
Touchdown
Hot-desking
Flex Spaces

Help employees to know which area is best for each type of task.

Effective managers are key – help them to adapt by:

1-to-1 Support
Mindset shift
group support
Manager
DATA

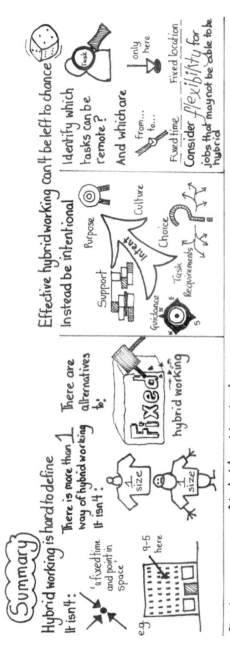

ACKNOWLEDGEMENTS

It would be remiss of me to not first thank you for buying and reading this book. Ultimately while I have enjoyed writing it, it has been written for you – so I hope you enjoy reading it and can use the thoughts within it.

My family again – my wife and four children primarily, but also my parents – have been instrumental in my whole life both personally and professionally, giving me inspiration, motivation and gratitude throughout the past two and a half decades. They have believed in me, even if not entirely sure what it is I do, and I am grateful again for their eternal support.

My publishers Kogan Page have believed in me and what I have wanted to say via their outlets. They have consistently supported me with both of my books and the work that has surrounded each. In particular I want to recognize the efforts of Chris Cudmore, Lucy Carter and Joe Ferner-Reeves.

Two people have made significant contributions to this book. Perry Timms's Foreword delighted me, as his stature within the people profession is beyond compare, and to have him read and comment on my work is something I still cannot quite believe. And Rachel Burnham's Sketchnote illustrations again perfectly capture the essence of each part and add a different dimension to reading. Without both Perry and Rachel this book would have been much less than it is.

Within this book there are numerous people whose contributions to examples and case studies have brought it alive. They have given their time and thoughts willingly and without hesitation. In the order they appear in this book: Melissa Sagastume, Sara Duxbury, Gail Hatfield, Andreia Trigo, Sarah Garner, Jessica Badley, Henry Stewart, Sarah Fern, Sasha Deepwell, Samantha Young, Neil Goodrich, Prodromos Mavridis, Alys Martin, Nicky Hoyland, Alan Price, Alex Holly, Jacqui Summons, Marc Weedon, Kate Bishop, Heather Barlow, Stuart Cavanagh, Fran Manca, Kelly Roskell, Kate Maddison-Greenwell, Anna Edmondson, Donna Nolan, Lee Pound, Ishbel Morren and Liz Dowling. In addition, there are others, who have requested anonymity, but for whose contributions I am also grateful.

Lots of other people who contributed random comments and quotes and to all those mentioned in the book (and all those not mentioned), thank you for making them. A few more people helped by giving their time to peer review some chapters for me as I went along – and this helped me polish what you have in front of you. In no order: Rebecca Francis-Davies, Selena Govier, Karen Sanders, Cheri Brenton, Sam Jenniges, Simone Fenton-Jarvis, Chris Nichols, Tamasin Sutton, Sharon Green, Tina Vale, Susie Phillips-Baker, Mary Hogan, Isabel Collins, Nicole Roberts, Mark Hendy, David Hayden, Rob Woollen, Daniel Taylor, Jenny Streeter, Rick Bradley, Jo Cook and Mark Sheppard.

Thank you again to many of my clients who have allowed me to anonymously use their experiences, and to my wider network for not just cheering me on along the way but for putting up with my constant mentions of how I'm doing and how it has been going while putting all this together. It is more exciting than I expected, authoring a book, and it is hard to keep that to myself.

PART ONE

The changing nature of work

1

What really is hybrid?

The shorter read

The world of work, and our expectations of it, have undoubtedly changed in recent years, a process accelerated by the Covid-19 pandemic. But the experiences we had during the enforced lockdowns were not true remote working – they were a knee-jerk reaction to an evolving crisis. Remote working can be much better than what many experienced then, but we do now have an understanding about what is possible with work because of this and our experiments with hybrid working since then.

Despite this, remote working remains popular among those who do it. Full-time remote working is much less popular, but equally full-time on-site working is not too popular either. Hybrid working seems, from available research, to be the most popular working arrangement among all those whose jobs allow for it.

The problem here is that there isn't a universally agreed definition of what hybrid working is, only what it isn't. Many want it, but they don't often know what it is that they do want. What most people do not want is to be told where and when they should work – flexibility matters to them, often more than many other things. But their experience of hybrid working is quite individual to each person.

But hybrid working is growing in both popularity and coverage – it is both sought after and valued by jobseekers and employees alike and is often equated to a significant pay increase if it can be achieved. It is how organizations do it where differences appear – some are formal in their approach, and others not. Some stipulate a percentage of working time to be spent on site, and others do not.

The problem with stipulating a percentage of working time to be spent on site is that it can often ride roughshod over individual circumstances and preferences. More significantly though it usually doesn't factor in the most appropriate way to do the tasks, and isn't a good start point for making hybrid working work.

Tensions are visible in some workplaces, between those who want to see more employees back on site for more (or all) of their working time and those who see that as a step back, and between those who can work in a hybrid way and those who cannot. This means we are at a crossroads and need to spend time embedding hybrid working practices and making them work more effectively. We also need to work on an inclusive approach so that those who cannot work in a hybrid way do not feel disadvantaged.

The advantages and disadvantages of hybrid working are well researched and well publicized but are also highly individual and contextual to organizational requirements and culture. The big debate often centres around its impact on productivity and performance. Research here shows that hybrid working is perceived by individuals to be highly beneficial to their own productivity and performance, but that managers often view it as neutral or slightly beneficial. What does seem clear is that very few organizations can point to a decrease in productivity and performance because of hybrid working. It is, at worst, neutral in most organizations.

The benefits of hybrid working can only be fully realized if it is done properly, with conscious, deliberate choices and thought. Otherwise, employees will feel disconnected, and confused about when to go on site or what for. Tensions will continue to rise, and there could be clashes between groups with opposing views. The entire employee experience has the potential to become a negative one if we don't get this right.

The wider consequences of not getting hybrid working right are worth thinking about too. There are implications for public health, local communities, transport, education, global society and connectedness, property prices, diversity and inclusion, and the wider environment.

But we also need to consider those whose jobs cannot be done in a hybrid way. This does not mean that they have no flexibility, indeed there are lots of examples of organizations providing flexibility in different ways. It is difficult, or perhaps impossible, to compare hybrid working jobs with non-hybrid working jobs. Perhaps we shouldn't. Perhaps we should work on personalizing the employment experience to everyone, irrespective of job function or role, so that each can have a tailored, individualized approach to work.

We have opportunities to ask and answer questions that will enable us to change the nature of work for all employees. Much of what we need to do can be achieved through making hybrid working work more effectively, but the potential is wider than just that.

Hybrid working isn't going away. Let's take the chance to make it work better.

The longer read

The new normal?

The world of work was already changing, but this change accelerated when the Covid-19 pandemic began. Many organizations had been experimenting with remote working, and some with what we now call hybrid working, but it took enforced lockdowns to accelerate this to a point where it became the norm for many.

The enforced nature of remote working meant that it brought with it many disadvantages as well as advantages. Those who had long-standing experience of remote working prior to 2020 knew these full well, but for the majority this was their first experience of working regularly anywhere other than on site.

It wasn't a true experience or reflection of what remote working could and should have been. But what it did do was force the confrontation of many wrongly held 'truths' about the world of work. Things like:

- The best way of working is five shifts of eight hours (usually Monday to Friday, 9 am to 5 pm).
- The optimum working week is around 40 hours long.
- That work must be done in one fixed location on site.
- That employees need to live close enough to their place of work to get there on any given day.

A survey by YouGov showed that prior to 2020, 68 per cent of UK employees never worked from home, 13 per cent did so the whole time and 19 per cent did so some of the time – what we would now call hybrid working (Smith,

2020). Strikingly though, of those who had never worked from home (68 per cent of the total), a massive 91 per cent said that they wanted to continue doing this for at least some of their time – a sign of how they recognized the plus points of hybrid working. This is also shown in the Insights Global Hybrid Working Report, which showed that while 22 per cent of people worked full-time on site, only 17 per cent wanted to do so, and 8 per cent of people worked fully remotely but 19 per cent wanted to do so (Brand, 2023a). This mismatch in current and preferred working arrangements is cited in many other pieces of research (see References and further reading at the end of this chapter) and appears to be widespread.

Hybrid working, therefore, was something that only a minority had experienced before the end of the enforced lockdowns and yet had gained traction as an extremely popular way of working. Most people had experienced enforced remote working, and/or had experienced mandated on-site working. These people were aware of the pros and cons of both styles of working and had reached a view that it may be possible to combine these by adopting hybrid working.

But did they know what they were wishing for? What really is hybrid working?

If you were to visit a stock image website and search for images of hybrid working, you wouldn't get anything sensible. Images of hybrid dogs, hybrid cars and hybrid plants are plentiful, but not hybrid working. Searching for images of working does bring back images of people working happily in offices, on other physical sites, and occasionally in a home environment using technology. But these three things together, no.

So, if stock image sites, which have images for everything, haven't got anything that shows us what it is, what chance do we have of really defining it and agreeing what it is?

Perhaps only by agreeing what it *isn't*.

The opposite of hybrid working involves a fixed point in time and space (a quote from one of my favourite programmes, the British science-fiction show *Doctor Who* – and I'm really pleased the quote's time has come). This is the equivalent of saying to someone that their work *must* be done in just one specific physical location in one specific time slot.

That's not hybrid working, but it is the only way we can define it – we agree what it isn't – a fixed point in time and space. And it isn't a popular concept either. You'll struggle to find many people who like working remotely all the time, and you'll struggle to find many people who like working on site all the time too. Most people prefer flexibility where they can get it.

But if we can't really define what hybrid working is, does that matter? A recurring theme in this book is that there is no one size fits all approach to hybrid working. How one organization, or indeed one individual, defines it will be different to another. This means that we must think about work differently. It is not just defined by where it takes place, or even when, but by what work is being done and the circumstances and environment around each individual.

Hybrid work is not, has never been, and can never be, the same for everyone.

Is hybrid growing in popularity?

It certainly seems to be. Research by Greenhouse cited in a People Management article suggested that 40 per cent of jobseekers would not apply for a job without hybrid working to suit their preferences, and that 77 per cent of employees would look for a new job if their current hybrid working arrangements were ceased (Mayne, 2023).

So, it seems popular, but is it widespread?

WFH Research shared in May 2023 that 59 per cent of employees worked all their time on site, 29 per cent were hybrid and 12 per cent fully remotely (Barrero, Bloom and Davis, 2021). However, this was a very wide-ranging sample including many jobs that would be considered front line and whose ability to work in a hybrid way was near-impossible, and excluded many jobs such as contractors, the self-employed and other groups for whom hybrid working could be a normal arrangement. The research concluded that among people who *can* work in a hybrid way, hybrid is extremely popular, and indeed suggested that it is the equivalent of an 8 per cent pay increase to be able to work in a hybrid way (Barrero, Bloom and Davis, 2021).

The ONS found that the level of remote and hybrid working has stayed relatively constant, between 25 per cent and 40 per cent, throughout the post-pandemic period – suggesting that it is resilient to the end of Covid-19 restrictions (i.e. when people didn't HAVE to work remotely any more) and global cost-of-living challenges too (ONS, 2023).

The CIPD's own research shows that 83 per cent of organizations have some form of hybrid working in place, though with different degrees of formality (CIPD, 2023a). The degree of formality will make a difference to how it works, and in a later chapter we will examine what advantages and disadvantages formal approaches bring. They also cite that the split of mandating a minimum number of days in the workplace is around 50-50 across all organizations (CIPD, 2023a). However, I would suggest that an arbitrary days of the week split is not a helpful starting point or indeed a helpful minimum expectation, without first examining the type of work being done and the requirements that the various tasks have. This will be examined further in Chapter 4.

What is the direction of travel?

The CIPD report that 20 per cent of organizations are looking to enable more hybrid working, via different methods such as new and better technology, manager training and on-site redesign (CIPD, 2023a). However, there is growing pressure in 40 per cent of organizations for employees to spend more time in the office, coming mostly from senior leaders who think that doing so improves collaboration, relationships and engagement (CIPD, 2023a). Added to this there remain tensions between those who can and those who cannot work in a hybrid way, with suggestions that the ability to do so creates an unfair situation. The tension goes both ways, as those who are not on site can often feel that they are excluded and isolated from what goes on there.

We sit, therefore, at a crossroads. Unless we can embed hybrid working practices and make them work more effectively, there is little to stop this pressure from building and becoming commonplace. If we liken this to Lewin's famous three-stage model of change, we have done the unfreezing, we have made the changes, but we are not refreezing to sustain what we have done. In the following two examples we see organizations that have had similar experiences going in opposite directions.

REDUCING REMOTE AND HYBRID WORKING

Company Y is a global market analyst firm based predominantly in Mumbai, India. They have 4,000 employees, with additional small outposts in global financial capitals. They are part of a larger US-owned group and have evolved different practices based on both the type of work they do and the prevailing culture within India. I spoke to an experienced manager, who has requested anonymity for both them and Company Y.

Prior to the Covid-19 pandemic Company Y was completely on-site-based, with very little – if any – remote working. Their offices remained closed for approximately two years, during which time Company Y became completely remote-based. Following the reopening of their offices in early 2022, Company Y once again became fully on-site-based for their India-facing businesses (but hybrid for non-India-facing businesses). They explained to their staff that this was based on business requirements. In the early days of getting people back on site, Company Y offered incentives and lots of innovative on-site benefits and activities, but now that they are nearing 100 per cent compliance with on-site presence, these are being significantly scaled back having served their purpose.

The person I spoke with was of the view that this is typical of the prevailing culture within India – in their experience Indian companies providing services to other Indian companies are very on-site- or office-focused and often anti-remote working. They believe that most managers are only comfortable when they can see and hear what their employees are doing. It is almost unheard of in Company Y for anyone with management responsibility to do any remote working. The experienced manager drew a distinction between such companies providing India-facing services, which are predominantly anti-remote working, and those companies who provide mostly international-facing services, where the culture is markedly different and largely more positive towards remote working.

In Company Y employees now can work remotely once a week but in practice this is discouraged. The experienced manager believes that working remotely limits promotion opportunities. Interestingly, on the day we spoke, the experienced manager was working remotely, due to their own manager being out of the office travelling. They believe that many employees would work remotely more often if they could, and the work itself is done via a screen so could easily be done from any location.

I asked the person what evidence had been provided by Company Y to back up their beliefs in the supremacy of on-site presence and they confirmed that none had been provided. Senior management had a belief that productivity and performance had suffered due to remote working, but no data confirmed this, and no improvement has been seen since the enforced return to being on site. Consequently, the experienced manager I spoke to feels that some employees are unhappy with the enforced full on-site presence and would not be surprised if some had left Company Y because of this. They also noted that the enforced on-site presence could have consequences for diversity and inclusion – those with caring responsibilities (primarily women) could be excluded from working successfully on site or indeed anywhere in Company Y, and that many more such people simply don't bother applying for jobs with Company Y, seeking hybrid and remote work elsewhere.

On this latter point, the experienced manager reported that the labour market within India is currently buoyant. Company Y is unconcerned by attrition or a lack of diversity in talent attraction, feeling that they can easily find replacement workers, and that those who are best suited to hybrid and remote working can easily find such jobs elsewhere. My own research supports this view, and within India there seems to be a real divergence between those companies who enforce on-site attendance, and those who promote hybrid and remote working. And workers are faced with a clear choice based on how they themselves prefer to work. It may, as the experienced manager I spoke with believed, take a whole generation before change is seen – when leaders who 'grew up' with the possibility and viability of remote working become the majority at the top of organizations.

INCREASING REMOTE AND HYBRID WORKING

Melissa Sagastume is the Director of HR at Outlook Amusements, who provide telephone and virtual psychic services. Their headquarters is in California in the US and they have around 150 employees.

Outlook had two offices – in California and Texas – until 2020 when they went fully remote due to the Covid-19 pandemic. Before then, there was no culture of remote working, with only selected employees able to do so. Those employees were mostly those who had relocated elsewhere and both they and Outlook wished to maintain the employment relationship. However, these instances were rare and not many employees were approved to do so.

Clearly the pandemic changed things, and the ending of the pandemic coincided with the expiry of leases on Outlook's offices, which they made a conscious decision not to renew. This was based on company performance being sustained via remote working. Outlook began using co-working spaces to tap into the desire for some employees to see each other on a semi-regular basis but found that this was so infrequently used as to be inefficient.

When Outlook gave up their two offices, they alerted employees that the company would be open to them relocating to certain states and continuing to work for the company – and this happened. It also meant that when recruiting, Outlook could target US-wide talent rather than those who lived within commuting distance of one of the offices.

Sagastume mentioned that because of different labour laws within US states, providing fair and equitable terms and conditions could have proved difficult, but a decision was made to use Californian labour laws – which tend to be more generous to employees than US federal law – as a guide in certain instances, regardless of where an employee was based.

Sagastume reported that all employee-related metrics are positive since the move to being fully remote, and that business performance remains positive too. The move has had a positive impact on talent attraction, in terms of quantity, quality and diversity of hire. To help maintain the culture and working relationships, monthly in-person social events are held in California and Texas, which are optional, and each quarter there are departmental meetings (plus associated socials) with travel and accommodation paid for by Outlook to encourage more people to attend. The company also hosts monthly virtual social events such as trivia contests, wellness events and the most popular of all – drag queen bingo, to allow any employee to attend, regardless of geographic area.

I asked Sagastume what their challenges had been, and she mentioned several:

- Spreading their employee base across multiple time zones proved tricky at first but they have found ways to work around this. Core meeting hours, etiquette about contacting people outside normal working hours and encouraging flexible working patterns have all helped here. This also varies by department and operational needs. The customer service department, for example, adapted more quickly because they already had a 24/7 schedule they worked around.

- Not having close working relationships and contact with colleagues could have led to conflict. Outlook conducts personality assessments for each person to help them understand better how they relate to others, how they best communicate and more. They are coached on how to relate better to their team, and managers are encouraged to think about how best to manage everyone based on their profile.

- Fully remote employees inevitably have a different interface with their personal lives and often need help managing that and obtaining the right support. Outlook are consciously working on that, through providing guidance on how to manage work–life balance more effectively.

- Asynchronous working is something Outlook employees have struggled to adapt to, and Sagastume is leading work to help with that. She is reviewing the technology that supports asynchronous working and helping individuals to learn more effective ways of working asynchronously.

- From a cultural perspective, Sagastume is keenly aware that those employees who were with Outlook when they were fully on site have a slightly different culture to those who have joined since Outlook became fully remote. The in-person social events are an attempt to merge these cultures.

Because of the above issues Sagastume believes that the move to fully remote working has not been 100 per cent successful but also believes that it could never have been. She believes that they are in a beta-testing version of what work is, and it will continue to evolve. Outlook did consider enforcing a return to on-site working but did not, because of fears of how it would adversely affect their employees. Now, they are happy with what they feel is a realistic option.

In the examples, both companies had been entirely on site until the Covid-19 pandemic and then, for a time, entirely remote. The decisions made when they didn't have to be entirely remote any more are quite different though and the direction of travel completely opposite.

What is worrying though is that many employees who can work in a hybrid way have not been consulted about how to best do so (CIPD, 2023a). There are many examples of organizations that have done so though, and many appear as case studies and examples in this book.

What will make hybrid work is being led by the task requirements – where, when and how a particular task is done. This will establish some clear boundaries and guidelines for how to create the best hybrid working arrangement. Overlaid upon that is consideration of the best environment and equipment to support the task requirements, the relative level of maturity and confidence of the team members doing it, and individual circumstances too. This creates a personalized model of employment, which we will examine in more detail in Chapter 5.

Given the crossroads that we are at, we inevitably see research that points out the advantages and disadvantages of both remote and on-site working. It is possible to form a firm belief in either viewpoint – many have. What seems likely though is that hybrid working, if done properly, will create something that is greater than the sum of its parts. Something better than either remote or on-site working have been or could be.

But what are the advantages and disadvantages commonly cited?

Why is hybrid working attractive?

There are many reasons why hybrid working seems to be attractive and popular among employees, but also for organizations.

Having partial or full control over when, where and how work is done can be a significant motivator, explained in many classical and modern motivational theories.

For individuals

I believe that the following advantages can be leveraged through effective hybrid working:

- Greater sense of well-being
- Improved engagement and motivation
- Improved work–life balance
- Greater financial well-being (primarily through saving money on commuting)
- Enhanced IT skills
- Positive impact on psychological contract, and more discretionary effort available through greater choice over when, where and how to work

For organizations

It is likely that the following advantages can be leveraged through effective hybrid working:

- Wider (from both geographic and diversity perspective) talent pools from which to recruit

- Increased flexibility to deliver services
- Boosts to talent attraction and retention

If one researches disadvantages of hybrid working, these are almost all expressed from an organizational viewpoint. Very few disadvantages for individuals themselves are cited. The most cited disadvantages are around the impact that hybrid working has on collaboration, culture and managerial effectiveness. All of these can be overcome and will be specifically addressed by this book.

Hybrid working can be beneficial for individuals, teams and organizations, but of course only if done carefully and with full recognition of the potential pitfalls.

If the right amount of thought and planning goes into hybrid working, then collaboration will naturally occur at more appropriate points. Consciously designing opportunities to work together, whether virtually or face-to-face, will strengthen team relationships. Teams are likely to develop more streamlined ways of communicating and decision making, and to support each other in more effective ways. All these things can aid productivity and performance.

As a result, organizations benefit. There are likely to be savings on office space, travel costs and expenses, and improvements in most employee-related measures such as engagement, absence and turnover. The organization itself could be seen as an employer of choice, as well as a responsible and sustainable organization within its community.

This all sounds good, but these can only be realized with proper planning and conscious, deliberate effort. If we leave things to chance we may succeed, but more through luck than judgement.

How does hybrid work affect productivity and performance?

This is an important question to consider when looking at whether hybrid working is working well or not. Let's start with some examples from CIPD and other research:

- Chinese online travel agent Ctrip did a nine-month trial involving 249 employees, whose job was to answer the phone and take bookings, a relatively routine, transactional kind of work that did not require high levels of team communication. These volunteers were randomly allocated to either WFH (working from home) four days per week or continue to work in the office. The homeworkers were 13 per cent more productive – a highly significant increase (CIPD, 2020).

- A survey of 501 financial services workers found that, among those who said they were as productive, or more productive, working from home during lockdown, 54 per cent cited fewer distractions and 52 per cent a quieter working environment (CIPD, 2020).

- A survey of 597 managers by the University of Birmingham showed that 60 per cent felt flexibility over where work was done increases both productivity and motivation, and 73 per cent felt giving flexibility over working hours increased productivity (Forbes et al, 2022).

- Thirty-eight per cent of organizations feel that increasing remote and hybrid working increases organizational productivity, with only 13 per cent feeling it had had a detrimental impact. This research also shows that year on year fewer organizations are feeling there is a detrimental impact on productivity (CIPD, 2023a).

- The 'Work After Lockdown' study asked workers to report whether they felt their own productivity had changed since before lockdown. Eighty-eight per cent said that they had got 'more done' or 'as much done' as in the office pre-lockdown, and just over one in ten felt they were 'doing less' (quoted in Mutebi and Hobbs, 2022).

There are a huge number of similar examples available in research and others will appear in this book. All these point to a growing realization that productivity has not been reduced by hybrid working (or even by fully remote working) and in many cases has seen an improvement. At worst, it can be said that hybrid working has a neutral effect on both productivity and performance.

What hybrid working (and, by extension, other forms of flexibility) does have is a significant positive effect on those who can make it work. The CIPD calculates that around 4 million employees have changed jobs due to a lack of such flexibility (CIPD, 2023a). Flexibility and remote working are regularly shown in various studies as important factors when choosing a new job.

It should be noted that most of the assessments about the impact of hybrid working on productivity and performance are self-reported but given that there is no commonly agreed definition of either, this may be the only way we can examine the issue.

An article in *Harvard Business Review* commented on some of the differences in perspectives as being useful to understand here, asking what counts as productivity. In the research, employees tended to include commuting time to on-site locations as part of their working day, so being able to use that as working time instead (or leisure time if that suited them) meant that they felt they were achieving more by working remotely. Managers, on the contrary, tend not to include commuting time to an on-site location as part of an employee's working day, so are more likely to measure what gets done as opposed to the time taken to do it (Bloom et al, 2023). This is an interesting point but again would most likely mean that remote and hybrid working has at worst, a neutral impact on productivity and performance.

That is not to say that hybrid working is perfect though.

Noting some challenges

There are challenges ahead and this book will tackle them as we work through the issues. Some of the notable challenges are:

- A study of UK-based remote workers by HowNow showed that 67 per cent felt disconnected from their colleagues, and 49 per cent felt this sense of disconnection was having a negative impact on how they viewed their job (Stringer, 2021). This is interesting but is based on those who work predominantly fully remotely. It tells us a lot about what organizations often get wrong with remote and hybrid working – they are leaving such things to chance. It also tells us a lot about what on-site working experiences need to focus on to overcome this drawback. We will explore how to do this in Chapters 9 and 10.

- Going on site to work (whether that is to the organizational office or perhaps some shared workspace) comes with its own challenges too. Individuals who have got used to working without noise and distractions at home can find that on-site workplaces and shared spaces are simply too noisy and distracting for them to be able to work (Brand, 2023b). This will be covered specifically in Chapter 6.

- Thirty-eight per cent of hybrid employees say that they do not know when or why to come on site, and only 28 per cent of organizations have clarified this (Microsoft, 2022). This is a big reason why many employees are reluctant to come on site – no-one wants to do that just to spend the whole day in virtual meetings or performing tasks better done remotely. This will be tackled in Chapters 4, 5 and 10.

- There are tensions between those who can and those who cannot hybrid, as well as tensions between those with different degrees of hybrid working (Buntine, 2021). We will address this partially in this chapter but also in Chapter 7.

- Senior leaders often have a very different perspective on remote and hybrid working than the rest of the organization and are proportionately more influential with their views than other employees. Changing mindsets is critical here, and this will be covered in Chapter 2.

- If not done correctly, individuals with hybrid working arrangements will see 'work extension', where work and life boundaries become blurred and employees feel pressure (whether real or imagined) to work more hours and be more available, possibly even working while sick (Mutebi and Hobbs, 2022). This is often a natural occurrence because of people feeling that being granted more empowerment somehow needs to be paid back by working longer or harder but is one that managers must keep an eye on. We will explore how in Chapters 8 and 9.

So, what if we didn't do hybrid working properly, or at all?

If we did not realize the benefits (as explored) of hybrid working, this could make people unhappy. This would have a consequential negative effect on organizational performance and, ultimately, the economy.

Not doing hybrid working, or perhaps not doing it properly, could have negative effects on individual health and well-being, particularly mental health. This could lead to strain on public health resources. The Covid-19 pandemic has shown us opportunities to change what we use public transport and our towns and cities for, and not fully implementing hybrid working would prevent us fully realizing some of the potential changes we could implement.

We have the ability with hybrid working to bring global society closer together given the ability to work from anywhere and at any time – and not doing that could slow down these positive international changes.

The CIPD points out that moving back to on-site working could increase discrimination against people with disabilities, long-term health conditions and those with caring responsibilities, as well restricting talent pools and diversity in organizations (CIPD, 2023a). This latter point is one that organizations would do well to consider. Remote and hybrid working often significantly expands the talent pool available to organizations and, given the tight labour markets in existence post-pandemic, this is not a risk many will want to take.

Remote and hybrid working, if done properly, will need an increase in training and support around IT skills and cybersecurity, and improved access to digital technologies, therefore minimizing digital exclusion (Mutebi and Hobbs, 2022). As a result, not doing hybrid working properly would sacrifice such opportunities, with consequential effects on the economy and society.

From an environmental perspective, hybrid working brings positive changes to air quality, waste, noise and light pollution that many in society will want to see achieved. Other research shows how city living is now becoming prohibitive to many (Daisley, 2023) so preventing proper hybrid working could exacerbate cost-of-living crises felt by many.

What might happen to your local area if hybrid working became the norm, or if it disappeared completely? There are a range of things to think about here. The local economy could benefit greatly from more people working and spending money in that area. House prices could increase if each household had a top-notch remote-working set-up. People working very remotely from their workplaces could be exposed to new ideas and ways of thinking, which could in turn benefit their local communities. Local communities themselves may become extensions of the workplace community. And if hybrid working stopped and everyone went back to on-site working, this could all fail to materialize. We must make it work better.

Seems like a no-brainer. But what about those who are not as fortunate in their working arrangements?

What about those who cannot do hybrid working?

As mentioned earlier in this chapter, there are significant portions of the workforce whose job roles mean that little, or likely no, hybrid working is possible. There is thus a danger of a two-tier workforce being created, and already we have examined evidence of tension between those who can and those who cannot do hybrid working.

There will always be work that needs to be done on site, and much of that at a fixed time too. There is the risk that such jobs are ignored when we are building our hybrid working approach, but this should not be the case. In roles where there is little flexibility on where work takes place, there should still be conversations about what flexibility there could be on when it needs to be done, and/or how.

Sara Duxbury is Global Head of Learning, Organization and Talent Development at the UK clothing retail organization All Saints, who featured in *HR for Hybrid Working* as a case study on how they had transformed their approach to L&D. I caught up with Duxbury to explore how they are adapting their approach to hybrid working now that Covid-19 restrictions are no longer present – particularly around how they approach flexibility for front-line customer-facing staff.

Duxbury advised that L&D remains entirely virtual, as this helps with their global workforce as well as those who have a hybrid arrangement in place. When full-day virtual sessions are arranged, all attendees are expected to be working from home, even if normally they would be shop based.

All Saints aim to treat their employees more maturely and give them boundaries within which there is considerable flexibility. Previously many shop-based employees had 8-hour per week contracts, but these have been replaced with 24-, 30- and 36-hour contracts, which are more helpful for budgeting incomes and people's livelihoods, as well as integration into All Saints culture. Each of these new contractual arrangements can be flexible in terms of when the work is done, based on individual preferences where possible.

For head office-based staff, All Saints have adopted a 60:40 office to home ratio. This was consciously done to avoid some roles being 100 per cent remote and creating a divide among their workforce, since some tasks are very location-specific. However, this is not enforced, and each team is free to work out how best to achieve this ratio. Indeed, many senior leaders have taken the opportunity to move to three- or four-day working weeks – and again this is consciously done to mirror the shorter working weeks that the shop-based employees have with their 24- or 30-hour contracts.

Within the shops, senior stylists can become virtual customer experience advisers. Previously this task was restricted to those working at the head office.

Those undertaking such split roles have the choice to do that virtual task from any location, though this does mostly take place from home due to greater investment in technology to be able to do so. And as artificial intelligence takes greater responsibility for delivering some services, it is possible that greater flexibility about work location may open for other staff too, particularly as they progress through their retail career.

As we can see from the example it is possible to factor in those whose roles cannot incorporate hybrid working into the overall approach. A useful way of working out what flexibility there could be is to ask some or all the following questions:

- Can we change where it needs to be done?
- Can we change when it needs to be done?
- Can we change how it needs to be done?
- Can we change who it needs to be done by?
- Can we outsource it?
- Can we move it to another team?
- Can we automate it?
- Can we stop doing it?

Involving employees in answering these questions is likely to improve engagement and understanding of the overall organizational approach, and to lessen the tensions felt between those who can and those who cannot do hybrid working.

There are, of course, other forms of flexibility beyond hybrid working and the CIPD reports that 65 per cent of organizations provide some form of this to their front-line workers – things like flexibility in start and finish times, self-rostering rotas and shift swaps (CIPD, 2023a). In addition to this, more forms of flexible working include compressed hours, term-time working, job-sharing and others – all of which may be feasible for those whose jobs do not allow hybrid working.

Advertising non-hybrid jobs as flexible by default may encourage early and easier conversations about such things and may open new talent pools for the organization to tap into, as well as aiding retention of talented employees who may otherwise seek to leave due to a lack of flexibility.

Other organizations containing a good proportion of roles that cannot do hybrid work have successfully implemented things like:

- Flexitime (managed within a shift rota)
- Casual or bank staff instead of regular shift work
- Fractional roles (as little as one day per week)
- Time off in lieu for accrued overtime
- Ability to work weekends instead of weekdays
- Split shifts
- Night shifts on request
- Extending operational hours to provide for different shifts
- Non-standard start and finish times
- Reduced working hours
- Multi-skilling to enable greater cover between roles
- Shift swapping via an app
- Greater notice of shift patterns
- Recruiting staff to work specific days (e.g. Saturdays) (McCartney, nd)

It can be possible, but one of the keys to this is understanding the experience of such employees and ensuring that leadership behaviours are conducive to these types of arrangements. These are things that we will examine in more detail in Chapters 7 and 8.

So, hybrid working is popular, beneficial to individuals, at worst neutral for organizations, and is growing in range and coverage. If we do not do it properly, there are potentially very big consequences. And it is possible to be inclusive in the way we achieve flexibility, even for roles that may not be able to work remotely.

It isn't going away. But we must make it work better than we have been.

In this chapter we will look at two companies who have been making headway with hybrid working but experiencing different challenges.

CASE STUDY ONE

The company is in the scientific research industry with around 200 staff operating on the East Coast of the US. The information in this case study comes from someone in their people team. Anonymity has been requested for both them and the organization.

This organization did hardly any remote working prior to the Covid-19 pandemic. Technology was there to support it, but culturally it was not encouraged. During the pandemic, their employees were considered essential workers throughout, so business continued during lockdowns and there was no furloughing of any staff. There were changes to how and where they worked though. Those who could work remotely – mostly the business support departments – did. However, a good proportion of employees – site security, scientists, technologists and laboratory technicians – could not. This was logical as they needed to use scientific equipment that remained in a fixed location, which could only be used at certain times, and needed constant guarding.

Even post-lockdowns, strict legislative and regulatory guidelines stipulate a fixed time, fixed location for many tasks performed in the organization. For affected departments and employees, they looked at other ways to offer flexibility. They introduced staggered start and finish times and had a weekly rolling schedule for fairness. They consciously became a lot more flexible on working times in general, with the focus on the work being done rather than when it was done. This was a big shift away from the earlier 9 am to 5 pm culture.

They also empowered managers to manage their teams and who came on site as they saw fit, and therefore who could work remotely. This meant some of the scientific departments could have people working remotely if they had work to do where they did not need to be on site – for example report writing.

Initially communication between departments became problematic, and there was some tension as people who were working remotely were needed by people on site. Their management team had to learn to work more effectively together to resolve such tensions and communication difficulties, making greater use of available technology to help them.

Their biggest problem came from the study directors department, as they all had desk-based jobs so could technically work remotely but had to supervise the work done by other people who were based on site all the time. The on-site staff were frustrated that the study directors were remote. These tensions were resolved by the study directors department coming on site more often to be visible to the on-site staff. Therefore, supervision itself became a more on-site experience.

Other frustrations came from those working on site towards those working remotely, as they felt the remote workers were getting people on site to do 'their job'. This was resolved by prompting managers to look at job roles and tasks requirements to ensure that there was cover in teams for the on-site work.

At time of writing, the approach is that unless there is a specific requirement to be on site for a particular task, the expectation is that the employee will work remotely. In practice, however, this means most employees are on site for two to three days a week, but this differs from team to team. By making a flexible working request, employees can request to be on-site-based for their entire time.

CASE STUDY TWO

Gail Hatfield is the Group People Director at Kimal Ltd, which provides specialist renal and cardiology equipment to social healthcare professionals and organizations. They have 550 employees globally, with around 300 of these based in the UK. In her previous job at Energy Systems Catapult, Hatfield provided a case study for *HR for Hybrid Working* and returns here to tell us how hybrid working is going at her new organization.

Prior to Hatfield joining Kimal, they had furloughed most of their UK staff during the various Covid-19 lockdowns, but quickly discovered that this meant that they could not continue to run their operations and undid much of this by adopting a hybrid approach to work, but without a great deal of forethought. Hatfield found that when she joined the organization they had muddled through somehow, making the best of what they had and knew.

This was hybrid out of necessity, and not through choice. It is a situation that was replicated in many organizations, with no formal approach or adjustments to any policies, except where Covid-19 restrictions imposed them.

As Hatfield arrived in the organization, she realized that Kimal needed to work out what they wanted from hybrid working.

She began by determining what tasks needed to be done at a specific, fixed, physical location. She then worked out which jobs predominantly comprised such tasks. Anyone who fell into that category needed to be mostly, if not entirely, site based.

From this point Kimal's line managers were given considerable autonomy to work things out for themselves, following some general principles – for example tasks that required close collaboration among multiple people needed to be done on site. Anything outside of the general principles was left to individuals to work out – they were given choice about where and when to work, if they got their work done.

Ideally, this adult–adult approach would work but, as we will see in other case studies and examples, this approach does not work well for everyone. In Kimal's case, many line managers needed a lot more support than this – they appreciated the general principles and the empowerment but were generally unsure of how to work things out. Hatfield realized this after several months of trying this approach. Her analogy is that of a pub garden – she says people need and want boundaries – for example 'how far can I go in this garden without my parents being concerned? Which toys and equipment am I safe to use and which not?' In the absence of boundaries, individuals and line managers came up with their own approaches and these had mixed results – hybrid wasn't as effective as it could have been.

In Kimal's case, this approach led to individuals regularly comparing themselves to others, and expressing doubts about whether their own ways of working were fair or effective – even though this adult–adult empowered approach should theoretically have done away with some concerns and comparisons.

What it did do was show a big distinction between whether people *want* to be on site or *need* to be on site. Teams were often choosing to come on site purely to socialize, and not because of the task requirements. Kimal's approach allowed for teams to be able to do that, but Hatfield wishes she had been clearer about the want versus need distinction at the outset. This type of clarity and guidance would have helped teams to consider hybrid working in a different way.

I asked Hatfield how hybrid working had affected managers and their teams. She commented that there had been some difficult conversations taking place, often around whether it is acceptable for people to combine childcare with working, and when a person's performance dips below acceptable levels. These have been the exceptions though, and performance and productivity are mostly unaffected – either way – by hybrid working.

What she has noticed is a difference in managerial attitudes driven by different levels of confidence in leading remote and hybrid teams. She says that debating remote versus hybrid versus on site is often a misleading debate – that the more appropriate debate to have is how to improve managerial capability and confidence in managing, regardless of employee location. This is something explored explicitly in a later chapter of this book.

Initially, Kimal did not provide guidance to individuals on how to make the best use of their home working space, nor did they make any attempts to remodel their on-site working spaces. However, they have now taken steps to do both, recognizing that people and teams need guidance and need to be provided with the most appropriate space and equipment for their tasks.

Addressing the fairness issue, Kimal have realized that there is no one size fits all approach to hybrid working and allow individuals, being led by the task demands, to craft their own approach. However, to address inequities among their workforce, particularly for those whose job cannot involve any element of remote or hybrid working, they have been supplementing salary levels as a way of compensating for having to work in a fixed location at a fixed time.

I also asked about moving away from the traditional working week and this is something Kimal have begun to experiment with – there are exploratory conversations happening within teams about moving to a four-day working week. Around half of their workforce are on fixed-time working, but for the half that are not there is scope for considerable flexibility. Successful hybrid working can often lead to movements away from the traditional working week, and vice versa – the two are often intertwined, so this is interesting to note and something that will be explicitly explored in Chapter 3. Kimal are making other moves here to overcome talent attraction issues – they are faced with a very low supply of the skills they need and are actively trying to entice people back into work by offering them different working arrangements, and more. Hatfield commented that people are often enticed back into work having retired previously, by changing what work is – making it a more social, more casual activity. Hybrid, and moves to different working patterns, are a help with that but not the only thing that will help.

Summing up, Hatfield is quietly pleased with how Kimal's move to hybrid working has gone. They have learnt lessons along the way and know more now about what their workforce and managers need to make it work more effectively. They know that there is no one size fits all approach, but that appealing to individual employees and being led by the requirements of the task will create something unique and personal to those circumstances. They have realized that hybrid working is, at worst, having a neutral impact on productivity and performance but that the positives can easily be seen in improvements in engagement, retention and more. Being led by task requirements also gives them a head start with workforce planning and a better insight into their future business requirements.

Case study reflections

In the scientific organization case study, the following points are worth further consideration:

- Sometimes what sustains a 9 am to 5 pm on-site-based culture is custom and practice and the view that 'we've always done it this way'. It can take a significant event (such as a pandemic) to confront this.
- Many jobs that need to be predominantly on site will have aspects to them that are asynchronous and can be done any time, any place. This instantly gives some flexibility to play with.
- Giving managers the freedom to examine task requirements in their teams and work out the best-fit hybrid approach for that team is likely to yield very good results.
- Consider those operating other stages of a process and whether the interface between an on-site part of that process and a remote part of that process is more effective if done on site or not.
- Having a remote-first approach and asking people to make business cases via flexible working requests to be on site full time is an interesting reframing of the current debates around hybrid working.

In the Kimal case study, the following points are worth bringing out and reflecting on here:

- There really is no one size fits all approach to hybrid working. Gail Hatfield experienced, within the space of a few months, two very different approaches in different organizations. Each approach is highly contextual to each organization and its needs and requirements.

- Many organizations will have adopted rules and ways of working during the Covid-19 lockdowns that are not appropriate any more, and need updating – but the rigidity of some of these could be a barrier.

- Hybrid working by necessity is a very common situation, but hybrid working can only be effective if given careful and conscious thought and deliberation.

- Being led by the task requirements is a strong starting point (see Chapter 5) as it gives an insight into the way the organization needs to work. This in turn would enable more informed decisions to be made about real estate, technology and more.

- Treating employees like adults – and giving them autonomy – as a general principle is admirable, but bear in mind that some people require more guidance – and boundaries – than this.

- Comparisons between individual and team working arrangements are in some ways inevitable; however, equality and fairness are not the right things to consider here. Instead, consider equity and the equitableness of working arrangements compared to individual circumstances.

- Distinguishing between whether people *want* or *need* to be on site is an important step in understanding people's working preferences and individual arrangements. It will also help us to understand the mindsets of those with strong views on hybrid working (see Chapter 2). When building hybrid working arrangements, we should consider both in turn.

- Managerial capability and confidence are among the biggest barriers to making hybrid working work and will shape cultural aspects too (see Chapters 2 and 8).

- We must recognize that hybrid working requires dedicated, bespoke workspaces. We can create or provide guidance on these (see Chapter 6) so that it is not left to chance.

- Making hybrid working work is something that can enable different working arrangements, and vice versa. We will explore this more in Chapter 3.

- Finally, it seems that the benefits of hybrid working far outweigh any drawbacks, with little or no data to suggest it is detrimental to the way organizations work or perform.

The action plan

If you are wanting to make hybrid working approaches more effective in your organization, here are some things you may want to reflect upon:

- How can you challenge accepted truths and beliefs about work that are wrongly held and shared in your organization?
- How can you find out what your employees feel about any current hybrid working arrangements?
- What would potential job applicants to your organization say about its current hybrid working arrangements?
- How will your organization define what hybrid working really is for itself, teams or its employees? How much does it matter if it doesn't define it?
- What proportion of jobs in your organization COULD adopt hybrid working, and what proportion cannot? What desire is there to change this?
- What advantages and disadvantages would there be to having a formal approach to hybrid working in your organization?
- What advantages and disadvantages would there be to stipulating a minimum amount of on-site time for your employees?
- How can you properly examine the requirements that each task in each job has for when, where and how it is done?
- What lessons can you learn and apply from previous change management programmes about how to embed and sustain a change such as hybrid working arrangements?
- How can you encourage constructive debate about the advantages and disadvantages of hybrid working arrangements among your organization?
- How can you collect and utilize data and other evidence around how hybrid working affects productivity and performance?
- What is the capability of your managers to effectively manage a remote or hybrid team? If they fixate on where work is done, how much is this masking a different issue?

- What role do you see your hybrid working arrangements having on the wider economy, communities and environment in general?

- How can you build flexibility by default into roles where hybrid working arrangements are not possible?

- What would happen if you had a remote-first approach in your organization, and those wishing to work on site had to justify that?

- How will you encourage healthy debate about the nature of work itself within your organization?

References and further reading

Barrero, J M, Bloom, N and Davis, S J (2021) Why working from home will stick, National Bureau of Economic Research Working Paper 28731, https://wfhresearch. com/wp-content/uploads/2023/06/WFHResearch_updates_June2023.pdf (archived at https://perma.cc/L4GW-9YNF)

Bloom, N et al (2023) Research: Where managers and employees disagree about remote work, *Harvard Business Review*, 5 January, www.hbr.org/2023/01/research-where-managers-and-employees-disagree-about-remote-work (archived at https://perma.cc/93B8-LZB3)

Brand, A (2023a) 70% of UK hybrid workers never want to return to the office full time, according to new research, *HR Review*, 17 March, www.hrreview.co.uk/hr-news/strategy-news/70-of-uk-hybrid-workers-never-want-to-return-to-the-office-full-time-according-to-new-research/151582 (archived at https://perma.cc/Z9P9-9QZ8)

Brand, A (2023b) Bosses confirm offices are failing to adapt to hybrid working, *HR Review*, 30 January, www.hrreview.co.uk/hr-news/bosses-confirm-offices-are-failing-to-adapt-to-hybrid-working/150467 (archived at https://perma.cc/4F6E-CA6H)

Buntine, M (2021) Insights from local authorities on hybrid working, Timewise, May, www.timewise.co.uk/article/insights-local-authorities-hybrid-working/ (archived at https://perma.cc/ULY8-XTBU)

Cholteeva, Y (2023) Seven in 10 companies globally have mandated return to the office, study reveals, *People Management*, 30 May, www.peoplemanagement. co.uk/article/1824486/seven-10-companies-globally-mandated-return-office-study-reveals (archived at https://perma.cc/FF65-RV7N)

CIPD (2020) Working from home: Assessing the research evidence, September, www.cipd.co.uk/knowledge/fundamentals/relations/flexible-working/working-from-home-evidence-after-lockdown (archived at https://perma.cc/P9G5-YEWY)

CIPD (2022) Working trends post-pandemic

CIPD (2023a) Flexible and hybrid working practices in 2023, 25 May, www.cipd. org/en/knowledge/reports/flexible-hybrid-working-2023/ (archived at https:// perma.cc/76ZE-WMWJ)

CIPD (2023b) Flexible and hybrid working: Principality Building Society, 25 May, www.cipd.org/en/knowledge/case-studies/flexible-hybrid-working-principality/ (archived at https://perma.cc/A4TP-RUNZ)

CIPD (nd) Flexible and hybrid working: Scottish water, www.cipd.org/en/knowledge/ case-studies/flexible-hybrid-working-scottish-water/ (archived at https://perma.cc/ C4LN-5AWZ)

Daisley, B (2023) Culture is feeling part of something, Make Work Better, 18 May, https://makeworkbetter.substack.com/p/culture-is-feeling-part-of-something (archived at https://perma.cc/NHL7-X3A9)

Forbes, S, Birkett, H, Evans, L and Chung, H (2022) Flexible Working and the Future of Work: Managing employees since COVID-19. Retrieved from Equal Parenting Project, United Kingdom.

Gartner (2023) Gartner forecasts 39% of global knowledge workers will work hybrid by the end of 2023, 1 March, www.gartner.com/en/newsroom/press-releases/2023-03-01-gartner-forecasts-39-percent-of-global-knowledge-workers-will-work-hybrid-by-the-end-of-2023 (archived at https://perma.cc/XSM6-YZC5)

Geddes, L (2023) What have the past three years taught us about hybrid working? The Guardian, 10 March, www.theguardian.com/business/2023/mar/10/ what-have-the-past-three-years-taught-us-about-hybrid-working (archived at https://perma.cc/FS7W-V99V)

Hi Bob (nd) The advantages of the hybrid work model, www.hibob.com/guides/ hybrid-working-model-advantages/ (archived at https://perma.cc/26GT-E4Q3)

McCartney, C (nd) Flexible working in front line roles: What is possible? CIPD, https://community.cipd.co.uk/cipd-blogs/b/cipd_voice_on/posts/flexible-working-in-front-line-roles-what-is-possible (archived at https://perma.cc/6E8L-B2ZU)

Mayne, M (2023) Majority of employees ready to walk if companies do not embrace hybrid working, report reveals, People Management, 19 June, www. peoplemanagement.co.uk/article/1826848/majority-employees-ready-walk-companies-not-embrace-hybrid-working-report-reveals (archived at https:// perma.cc/J9Q5-SFEN)

Microsoft (2022) Great expectations: Making hybrid work work, 16 March, www. microsoft.com/en-us/worklab/work-trend-index/great-expectations-making-hybrid-work-work (archived at https://perma.cc/9ZJE-M9YE)

Mutebi, N and Hobbs, A (2022) The impact of remote and hybrid working on workers and organisations, POST, UK Parliament, 17 October, https://post. parliament.uk/research-briefings/post-pb-0049/ (archived at https://perma.cc/ WLP6-GC7D)

O'Connor, S (2023) The ability to work from home does not just benefit the elite, *Financial Times*, 9 May, www.ft.com/content/44e81232-9b25-4f4a-91ab-4462978dc204 (archived at https://perma.cc/B8P3-6BJV)

ONS (2022) Is hybrid working here to stay? Office for National Statistics, 23 May, www.ons.gov.uk/employmentandlabourmarket/peopleinwork/employmentandemployeetypes/articles/ishybridworkingheretostay/2022-05-23 (archived at https://perma.cc/26YE-HQME)

ONS (2023) Characteristics of homeworkers, Great Britain: September 2022 to January 2023, Office for National Statistics, 13 February, www.ons.gov.uk/employmentandlabourmarket/peopleinwork/employmentandemployeetypes/articles/characteristicsofhomeworkersgreatbritain/september2022tojanuary2023 (archived at https://perma.cc/XGN7-3E2Z)

Smith, M (2020) Most workers want to work from home after COVID-19, YouGov, 22 September, www.yougov.co.uk/topics/economy/articles-reports/2020/09/22/most-workers-want-work-home-after-covid-19 (archived at https://perma.cc/42CM-DVKG)

Stringer, G (2021) British workforce is disconnected and lonely – yet majority want to continue WFH in some capacity, HowNow, 17 March, www.gethownow.com/return-to-work-report/ (archived at https://perma.cc/P67G-VMUE)

Stutzman, F (2023) LinkedIn, 28 March, www.linkedin.com/feed/update/urn:li:activity:7046458413077168128/ (archived at https://perma.cc/4K23-2E8P)

Tsipursky, G (2023) New study shows managers are changing their minds about the hybrid work model, *CEOWORLD Magazine*, 21 March, www.ceoworld.biz/2023/03/21/new-study-shows-managers-are-changing-their-minds-about-the-hybrid-work-model/ (archived at https://perma.cc/2RXG-NKPN)

Warrington, J and Chan, S P (2023) Staff turn on home working as four in ten say it has negative impact, *The Telegraph*, www.telegraph.co.uk/business/2023/05/09/staff-turn-on-home-working-four-in-ten-say-negative-impact/ (archived at https://perma.cc/7X4P-ZHUZ)

2

Is hybrid working?

The shorter read

Is hybrid work working? The answer to that question depends on how you want it to work and the measures you are judging the impact by. It isn't always about performance and productivity, and many organizations have no way of measuring whether it is working or not – and are OK with that.

Hybrid work can work, but only if we want it to. If we leave it to chance, it is unlikely to work, but with conscious and intentional effort, it usually will. There is certainly the groundswell of opinion among the global workforce that they want it to work, but they are also telling us what isn't working now – about on-site experiences, team relationships, mutual expectations and more.

One of the problems we face is that many leaders want to prioritize on-site working, for reasons they sometimes struggle to clearly articulate. Mandating a certain portion of working time to be on site may sound sensible and even reasonable but applies a one size fits all approach to hybrid working, which may ride roughshod over not just individual circumstances but the nature of the work being done too.

The available research shows that there are significant benefits from spending a portion of working time on site, so this should be done. But *when and how and why* matter, and it is these questions that organizations are often failing to address effectively. Working this out is critical to making hybrid working work and leveraging those benefits. Planned and organized hybrid that accounts for the type of work and individual preferences is more effective than mandated hybrid, which could do neither.

If left to chance, hybrid often falls foul of status quo bias, and gives rise to difficulties with collaboration and communication, impacting on culture. Everyone working in a hybrid way needs effective training, guidance and support on how to do so properly. Beyond that, there are significant organization design challenges to be overcome too – this reshapes what work is.

What about the risk to culture? While hybrid working can deteriorate organizational culture, it will only do so if no one is paying culture any attention. Similarly, it can impact relationships at work, but only if we pay those little attention either.

Team cultures are often more straightforward to establish and maintain in hybrid environments, and this can come at the expense of wider organizational culture, which may remove some of the unifying nature it can have. Careful balance is needed in how to encourage and nurture both, with neither being to the exclusion of the other.

Physical workplaces can embody but never entirely represent organizational culture. The physical environment matters to people, but only when they know what the organizational purpose is first, how they are expected to behave, and what the value is that they create for the organization. For the physical workplace to be successful, several things must be done to consciously redesign it and, even then, expectations must be set about how it is used and how people are to interact within it. I believe that the average employee simply wants the physical workplace to be functional for the tasks they do within it – but have we got that?

Some good news comes from our ability to create and maintain cultures remotely from our personal lives, and we could apply many lessons learnt from such experiences. Beyond this there are several things we need to do to create the right kind of culture in our organizations. Most of this is centred around being more intentional and more explicit about what we do and how we do it – organizational purpose, relationship-building, creating cross-organizational connectedness, clarity on communication channels, role modelling from leaders and more.

We still have big challenges with some people who are opposed to hybrid working, and some of this comes from pre-existing biases with other bits stemming from fear of the unknown and what that could do to their role. We must work to overcome all of these by providing the right training, guidance and support, and by consciously challenging unhelpful mindsets.

The longer read

Is hybrid work working?

The answer to this important question depends on how you choose to measure it in your organization. That could be about performance or productivity, it could be about revenue or profits, or about engagement and well-being, or anything else that matters to your organization. As we will see in this chapter, there are lots of ways to measure the impact of hybrid working and your organizational context is what makes the difference. What's important here though is knowing this at the outset and having some baseline measure to be able to track the impact, which means you must consciously decide: a) to measure the impact and b) how to do that. This further raises the question about whether we should measure the impact and whether it matters if we don't. In our previous chapter we talked about how hybrid working seems to have at worst, a neutral impact on productivity – but do we measure on-site working in the same way? We don't – so why should we obsess about measuring the impact of hybrid working? Anecdotal evidence certainly suggests that presenteeism was a big problem for many organizations when fully on site, and indeed was almost accepted practice. We knew that that element of on-site working didn't work. What about other aspects?

One other point stands out, before we get into looking at how organizations are measuring the impact. Hybrid working can work, but only if you want it to. This is a variation on the saying that you get out what you put into things. Hybrid working is the same. If you leave it to chance, if you don't make efforts to make it work, then it won't work. If you want it to work, if you make conscious, deliberate choices to help, then it will work.

The problem in many organizations now is that there isn't clear agreement about whether all stakeholders want hybrid working to work.

Hybrid work remains popular, as we saw in our last chapter. Very few people want to remain fully remote, but very few want to be fully on site either. Research by Unispace found three main reasons for the latter point, suggesting it is a mix of not wanting to spend time commuting, not wanting to spend money on commuting, or working on site, and not really seeing what point there is in being on site when their work can be done remotely

(Unispace, 2023). The final point is the one that organizations really must think about. Clearly having an on-site location close to an individual's home address, or paying for some or all of their transportation costs and food/drink while there would address the first two points, but these are likely to be infeasible for most. But determining the purpose of on-site presence is a very good start point. People don't want to come on site to do work they would be better suited doing remotely – such as sitting in virtual meetings for parts or all of their day. But this means we must be purposeful about what we use the on-site location for, as well as how we design it.

Andreia Trigo is Chief Executive of Enhanced Fertility, a company that provides personalized fertility diagnostics and care to customers globally. Enhanced Fertility has only eight employees – half of these are based in Portugal, and the other half in the UK. All employees have the flexibility to work globally.

Enhanced Fertility was founded in late 2020 in the middle of the Covid-19 pandemic and is very much a product of its time. They began as 100 per cent remote because restrictions needed them to be, and designed their services to be completely accessible from any location in the world, again because they needed to. However, they have retained this ethos despite the easing of restrictions.

The organization promotes accessibility as one of their main aspects, and therefore prioritizes digital forms of communication for both customers and employees. They also value individual autonomy in terms of both when and where work is done, and enable their employees to work wherever they wish in the world, and whenever they wish.

With the eight employees being geographically dispersed, managing working across time zones takes some proactive scheduling. Trigo are not rigid on working times and give people as much flexibility as possible, managing them on outputs and outcomes rather than when they are working. Sensible decisions are encouraged about how and when is best to collaborate with each other, given working across time zones.

To help with collaboration, the organization provides weekly virtual get-togethers, and a host of asynchronous tools such as WhatsApp and Trello. These are supplemented by organized annual in-person events for the entire organization – focusing on team building, relationships and strategy development – and smaller, more ad hoc in-person working when two or more people attend events together or want to meet up. Co-working spaces are used occasionally for such things and to allow employees to work around other people even if not from the same organization. When someone joins the organization, there is a mix of online and in-person shadowing, attendance at in-person events and more, to enable them to settle in quicker before moving to their own remote working pattern.

Trigo outlined some of the advantages that this approach brings Enhanced Fertility. She feels her employees are more loyal, more engaged and deliver higher levels of performance, enjoying the autonomy and flexibility they are given. Having a globally dispersed organization means that Enhanced Fertility can, and do, recruit from anywhere in the world, giving access to a wider skills pool. Employees report that they are happy with being able to work anywhere in the world too, with some spending extended periods of time visiting family in other countries while continuing to work. She has slight concerns about people working too many hours or at unhealthy times, but stresses that she lets people make their own decisions about this.

Trigo also notes that the average age of the employees is low, lower than anywhere she has worked previously, and she feels that this has a bearing on how they view the world of work. Many of them are of what she calls 'the Covid generation' and have to some degree grown up being used to handling an increased number of transactions and interactions online, to building relationships virtually via social media and messaging apps, and not necessarily missing the 'noise' of the office as much as some others might.

In the example, we see how Enhanced Fertility are measuring the impact of their approach, and the benefits that they can see.

While we know that remote working can allow people to achieve better work–life balance, this isn't always the case and individuals need guidance and boundaries to be set; otherwise, if left to their own devices, there is the temptation for their work habits to become unhealthy. Hybrid working can address this by creating structure and giving those boundaries to employees, but again only if the on-site experience (as well as the remote experience) is one that is consciously designed to work that way. And this needs to be achieved without forcing people to work in any specific location for any portion of their time – research shows that 42 per cent of organizations that mandate a return to an on-site location experience higher turnover, and

29 per cent are struggling to recruit (Unispace, 2023). Many organizations find it incredibly difficult to explain why their employees need to be on site.

However, one doesn't have to go far to find examples of senior leaders in organizations talking publicly about why on-site working needs to be prioritized, or examples of organizations that are mandating near or full on-site presence. Some organizations have considered incentivizing people to be on site, and others have appealed to people's sense of morality. Dell has only asked employees who live within one hour of the on-site location to be there three days a week (Machell, 2023), whereas others have adopted a blanket approach to all staff.

None of the above approaches are guaranteed to be effective, since they strike at the heart of what makes remote and hybrid working popular – the ability to organize work and life so that a fair balance is achieved. Since that is highly individual, a blanket mandate is naturally perceived by many employees as a threat, whether intended that way or not. Careful thought is clearly needed.

Organizations must consider what they want their staff doing when on site. Spending large parts of a day doing things that could be done from the comfort of one's own home seems irrational. Somehow, we must harness the best of what on-site work has to offer – connection with other people, relationship-building and social bonding.

Microsoft comments that the employee mindset has changed – that the 'worth-it' equation has irrevocably altered since the Covid-19 pandemic, and that only organizations that create flexible and well-being-focused cultures will be able to build thriving and growing organizations (Microsoft, 2022). This seems very true – our view of what work is has changed, but organizational culture has not always caught up with that. Furthermore, Microsoft research shows that 52 per cent of employees are likely to move job to one that offers more hybrid or remote working in the next year, and that remote and hybrid jobs get 2.6 times more views and three times more applicants compared to fully on-site roles (Microsoft, 2022).

But is this people just wanting something that is good for them but not for the organization? The University of Leeds found that employees who had a hybrid arrangement had stronger job satisfaction and engagement, higher self-reported levels of performance and better work–life balance – and this stemmed from including some on-site working rather than being fully remote (Davis et al, 2022). However, what this research also showed was that the amount of on-site working needed to generate these improvements was not specified – this reinforces points made elsewhere in this book that there is no one size fits all approach to hybrid working. Mandating a specific number of days on site is arbitrary and needs to be based on the work being done alongside individual circumstances, with appropriate boundaries in place within which employees can exercise choice. Training and coaching to do all this effectively is also critical, but sadly often lacking.

Leaders who feel that being on site is a key influencer on how their employees feel and interact are likely correct. However, the context for this matters, and the amount of time needed to achieve this influence is not defined. The University of Leeds research showed that allowing flexibility and choice is more likely to achieve this than a mandate to be on site for a specific time, but that only a minority of workers had this type of choice and flexibility (Davis et al, 2022). Therein lies some of the risk mentioned earlier about people wanting to change jobs – it is choice they are seeking, not necessarily remote or mandated hybrid working. If employees have greater choice about where, when and how they work, allowing them to blend remote and on-site working in a way that suits them and their work, it is likely that all related indicators will improve in a way that fully remote, or fully on site, or mandated hybrid, could not achieve.

Still, though, we see some leaders and organizations attempting to herd employees back on site more and more, despite the evidence showing empowered hybrid working achieves much more. Why is this?

There is perhaps a status quo bias that is affecting the thinking of some people when it comes to remote and hybrid working, making them cling to the idea of traditional on-site working simply because it is what they have always known. Research from before and during the Covid-19 pandemic revealed a stigma towards remote workers, which has perhaps lessened since then but not disappeared completely (Mutebi and Hobbs, 2022). This view will be explored further in a later part of this chapter. What else could be the reason for the mandated returns to on-site working?

Is it about collaboration? Twenty-six per cent of organizations in one piece of research cited difficulty with interaction and collaboration because of remote working (Mutebi and Hobbs, 2022). This suggested some sense of disconnect between individuals and their organizations and colleagues. Similarly, a 2020 CIPD report did reinforce this by showing 36 per cent struggling with reduced interactions and collaboration. However, it also discovered that 43 per cent found that remote and hybrid work improved those things (CIPD, 2020). This suggests a   split in how collaboration is viewed in organizations, perhaps by those at different levels too. Some organizations have clearly made it work, and others have not. What is causing this difference?

Some research suggests that the organizations that were already managing results and outcomes instead of hours have coped better with the shift to remote and hybrid working (Delaney, 2022). While this will have helped, I believe it is how organizations have approached what hybrid is and what it means that is making a difference to how it works. Just because people in an organization can work in a hybrid way and seem to be coping OK with that, doesn't mean that it is the most effective way of working. In fact, it probably isn't. And that may be why some senior leaders want to return to on-site working.

That, though, is perhaps the wrong way of solving this problem. The wrong debate to have.

Left to chance, hybrid is unlikely to work unless, ironically, by chance. What hybrid working needs to work is effective training and guidance for employees, teams and leaders on how to work effectively in remote, hybrid and on-site modes – asynchronously and synchronously. This is more than mandating hybrid approaches. It is more than writing policies and procedures or redesigning the on-site experience. It is a fundamental shift in what work, and our experience of it, is. All the things mentioned in this paragraph will be helpful, but as the University of Leeds research points out, this is a whole system design challenge – 'an opportunity to step back and question why things have been done the way they have and to fundamentally rethink and improve what it means to "go to work" – this is challenging, daunting and risky, but ultimately exciting and potentially transformative!' (Davis et al, 2022).

As with many significant organizational changes, the bigger challenge is cultural. Changing mindsets, changing systems, changing the way people do things and the way they act. Ironically, one of the charges levelled at hybrid working is that it destroys culture, but I think if we are to make it work, we must consciously redesign culture in our organizations.

What is culture and why does it matter?

There is no universally agreed definition of organizational culture and yet almost all people will know what we mean when we talk about it. It is all the things that make a place unique. We often think of a common understanding of behaviours, mindsets, interactions, decisions and more. Culture matters so much that various sources estimate around 70 per cent of organizational change initiatives fail due to a lack of understanding of organizational culture. This is sometimes viewed as an urban myth, but there is something in it that speaks to the importance of organizational culture.

Various pieces of research show the impact that a strong culture has. It can impact revenue growth, retention, well-being and engagement, and returns to stakeholders (Talent Intelligence, 2022).

Organizational culture existed prior to the Covid-19 pandemic. During that pandemic though, culture wasn't given much thought, as the priorities for organizations and individuals lay elsewhere – quite understandably. In some organizations the lack of conscious focus on their culture will have led to some cultural deterioration – much like if you leave a tarmacked road without any conscious upkeep and repair over a few years it will deteriorate. For some leaders, this was taken as proof that remote working had a negative impact on culture, but that isn't the case. What has a negative impact on culture is leaving it alone and not focusing on it.

What we have in front of us over the next few years is a unique opportunity to reshape, remake organizational culture – to give it the focus it needs and leverage the positive benefits that a great culture can give us. And whether that's remote, hybrid or on site makes no difference to that. All it takes is conscious effort.

Does hybrid work affect culture?

'Distributed work doesn't kill company culture. It reveals it' (Herd, 2023). This quote from Chris Herd, founder of Firstbase, on social media resonates a lot with the points I am making in this chapter. For distributed work, substitute remote and/or hybrid work, and you'll see what I mean.

As many as two-thirds of organizations may be struggling to maintain morale and culture because of remote and hybrid working (Brower, 2021), but as mentioned above the cause for this is not remote and hybrid working – it is the lack of conscious and intentional effort around the culture.

Unfortunately, there is, as we have examined, no one size fits all approach to maintaining culture but left to chance, it will be affected by remote and hybrid working. Herd's point above is a valid one because it shows the effect well. Hybrid working holds up a mirror to organizational culture. Left to chance, the glare from that reflection will erode culture, but the beauty of the reflection is that it shows you what areas need work, what areas are working well and where the blind spots might be.

There may be a connection between those organizations that feel that culture is affected by hybrid working and those that have failed to grasp the opportunity it gives them, and have therefore left it all to chance.

Even the UK's Chancellor of the Exchequer offered an opinion about the effect of remote and hybrid working on organizational culture, commenting that remote work offers exciting opportunities but that he worried 'about the loss of creativity when people are permanently working from home and not having those water-cooler moments where they bounce ideas off each other' (Race, 2023).

Forty-three per cent of leaders say that relationship building is the greatest challenge in hybrid work (Microsoft, 2022). This could be because of fewer opportunities for informal conversation and social interaction. Employees who have thriving relationships with their immediate team members report better well-being, higher productivity and greater loyalty to their employer. Those with thriving relationships with other teams report even higher levels of these aspects. And yet, for remote workers only 50 per cent say that they have or are encouraged to build these types of relationships (Microsoft, 2022).

What matters in building relationships is proximity, and we should see this as an emotional concept rather than a physical closeness. We become close to those we interact with frequently, and this builds empathy, understanding and connections on multiple levels. Proximity can come from being physically close to someone, for example seeing them in person. Proximity can also come from virtual connections and simply feeling close to someone through shared goals, shared likes and dislikes, shared ways of thinking. Research has shown that quality communication and team identification aid emotional proximity within a team, and while it can be difficult to replicate in-person socialization and connections, the technology used to enable remote and hybrid working gives opportunities to innovate and do things differently (Mutebi and Hobbs, 2022).

Organizations, and their leaders, must establish a clear purpose to the on-site elements of hybrid working. They must prioritize and focus on in-person collaboration, socialization opportunities and other things that can be difficult to achieve when working remotely. This means rethinking the physical space to make these things occur more naturally, and experimenting with different ways of bringing people together to find something that works for all concerned. Otherwise, hybrid working can and will erode organizational culture – at least for the whole organization, but not necessarily for each team.

Team versus organizational culture

As relationships with immediate team members really matter to remote and hybrid workers, we clearly must work on and prioritize those. We will look in a later chapter at some ways to do that, but we must also guard against the risk that each team becomes siloed from the rest of the organization. This could happen with each team being given licence to work out the best way of hybrid working for its team members and the culture it needs to enable the best from its team members.

The danger, therefore, is that each team culture becomes so dominant within that team that it precludes any awareness or conscious mirroring of organizational culture. And while organizations are, of course, conglomerations of teams with different characteristics, the organization itself must still have a culture otherwise it may as well not exist. As we will see in the case studies for this chapter, this is a likely occurrence and while there are positives to it, allowing team cultures to override organizational culture gives more credence to the views held by some leaders that hybrid working damages organizational culture. If we allow team culture to be dominant, we make it easy for such views to become solidified 'truths' within the organization, leading to a mandate to be mostly or fully on site.

We could adopt many techniques to combat this but consciously co-locating individual workers alongside those from other teams on their on-site days is one thing that could help, as opposed to bringing whole teams on site and seating them together on those days.

Organizations based in multiple geographies and time zones have a range of helpful experiences in this – they've been challenged to create a strong corporate culture while also allowing local microcultures to thrive. Royal DSM, a Dutch health and nutrition company, cited in *Harvard Business Review*, now treats their culture as a flotilla of independently piloted ships rather than a single tanker (HBR, 2022).

Is culture linked to being on site?

To answer this question, we could start by examining the role that a physical workplace can play in creating and revealing organizational culture. There are many organizations that have deliberately created bright, vibrant and varied workplaces even prior to the Covid-19 pandemic, and who see these workplaces as an embodiment of their culture. For a good example do a quick search and look at the Wrexham, UK-based Moneypenny's offices – there are many more examples like this but Moneypenny no doubt feel that the physical workplace they have created reveals, and enhances, their organizational culture.

The physical workplace is clearly a critical asset, and most businesses own or lease one that suits the needs they had when they set it up. But in almost all cases, this was prior to the mass increase in remote and hybrid working. And while culture can be represented in the style, layout and overall look and feel of a physical building, it is not confined to that building. It never has been, and never could be.

What physical workplaces do achieve though is ensuring that employees feel connected to the wider purpose and values of the organization, and to each other, by deliberately creating an environment in which these things are visible, encouraged and hard to ignore. That again though is not unique to the physical workplace – the ability to do those things isn't confined to having a specific location that embodies it.

But for many other organizations that have not consciously designed a workplace that embodies their culture, they may find that mandating employees back on site for part or all of their time is not going to solve any cultural issues. It may simply move them to a different place. Research from the University of Leeds showed that the office was still being used for solo work, with perhaps 60 per cent of tasks being individual-focused and only 20 per cent requiring in-person interactions (Davis et al, 2022). This means we must look at the balance of tasks an individual needs to undertake before looking at what percentage of their time they could and should spend on site.

There are significant benefits to be reaped from having some on-site presence though. Leeds research suggested that this improves connections between employees, and helps build a stronger social network. However this is only a significant improvement for people whose jobs require such things, as it supports an improved information flow and informal collaboration (Davis et al, 2022). To make this work regardless of job we perhaps need to revisit the success that many leaders and teams had during the enforced Covid-19 lockdowns, where check-ins on a social level and team bonding were given a higher priority and worked because of that. That was almost entirely virtual and happened without a fixed physical location, showing that although a fixed physical location can be helpful for such benefits, they can be achieved virtually too. But if it can be done properly, the physical location can be beneficial and outweigh the downsides (often related to cost and time) of travelling there.

But what does properly mean? If the number of days on site doesn't appear to be a major factor, what is? Leeds research talks about purposeful presence, whereby time on site is coordinated so that individuals (in their example, new starters) are on site when key colleagues are too (Davis et al, 2022). There were opportunities when fully on site to connect informally with people from other teams – cafeteria queues, lifts, corridors and the like – but this was because of conscious workplace design. The same type of conscious effort will enable our organizations to achieve similar things for their hybrid workforces. Indeed, there are many organizations that have only ever been 100 per cent remote, and they have managed to build successful cultures with intentional effort.

To make the most of the on-site space that we have, we must think about how we can encourage people to work strongly and creatively together when at a fixed physical location. Eighty-eight per cent of employees in a Gallup survey reported having a mix of independent and collaborative tasks – the key is therefore to coordinate the collaborative tasks to be done on site, leaving the independent tasks to be done remotely (Harter, 2023).

Many organizations and employees report that on-site working is harmful to productivity if people spend most of their time collaborating, socializing, mentoring and more (Tsipursky, 2023). This points to us having to reframe what productivity means but also reach consensus in our organizations about what our on-site physical locations are to be used for. On site has a key role to play, but it is not everything. A *Harvard Business Review* article states that mandating employees back on site drove connectedness, flexibility and engagement down (HBR, 2022).

We can only really leverage the benefits of on-site working if we are intentional about it. When we talk about demographic characteristics in a later chapter we will see, again, how this matters more than ever. If we leave on-site working to chance, few if any of the benefits will be achieved. We must be intentional about remote working, on-site working and therefore hybrid working, if we are to create and maintain the culture we want our organizations to have.

Lessons from our personal lives about culture

We will shortly look at what we need to be intentional about in the workplace (whether remote or on site), but the good news is that most of us already have the required skill set and mindset from things we have done in our personal lives.

If you consider your extended family, or your close friendship circle, there is a high chance that you maintain those relationships largely remotely with only sporadic, but planned, in-person gatherings. There is an equally high chance that you are strongly connected to these people despite only seeing them occasionally, and it is because of what you do when you do meet in person that large times spent away from them doesn't reduce the connection you have.

When you meet with these groups it is for planned occasions with set (or largely understood) objectives, agendas and structures to guide the interactions. It isn't left to chance. In between those times, you maintain relationships often asynchronously, using technology and catching up with individuals either in person or virtually.

You have a culture in your extended family or close friendship circle that isn't written down anywhere but everyone in it understands and could describe. And there isn't a fixed physical on-site location where either of those groups 'exists'. You've never needed one, and never will. You have a hybrid life and you've never really thought about how much on-site time or remote time is needed to keep this hybrid life going.

We will examine some of this again in our final chapter on how to support teams, but the principles here apply across the entire organization. We must be intentional about organizational culture, and some of the following things would help, based on how our extended family and close friendship groups also tend to operate.

Scheduling events where people can socialize is very helpful – if you didn't have these in the diary well in advance with your family or close friendship groups, they'd likely not happen spontaneously. But when they do happen, they strengthen bonds and help new people within those groups to develop good relationships. They also likely take place at various locations and not one specific location, and the logistics involved are likely a democratic process too.

Being clear about the unique nature of the group and what people value about it (perhaps its purpose or values) is something to clarify and share. In your personal social groups, you'll see this happening on social media when people share photos, check-ins, emotions and what they enjoyed about getting together with the other people in that group. It helps new people in those groups to see what they could find useful and enjoyable about being in that group.

How to create culture in hybrid teams and organizations

As mentioned, there is a need to be more intentional. Teams and the entire organization need to make things explicit that in a more traditional on-site culture may have been unwritten rules. In our final chapter we will examine more of what this means for teams specifically, but in this part, we will look at helpful things for organizations.

From a company values perspective, an employee's awareness and connections to these really matters. This could be tested at recruitment stage and discussed openly during onboarding and induction stages too, so that employees feel comfortable being able to express important aspects of their identity that match closely to the organizational values.

Employees need to see how their role contributes to the organization, and that the value they create comes from what they do, not where they do it. Virgin Money, cited in *Harvard Business Review*, uses an app to allow employees to pinpoint what they value most in their work, and structure a discussion with their managers about how to adjust their roles and the rhythm of how work gets done, to better deliver that value (HBR, 2022).

Purpose matters greatly to employees, and in hybrid settings it is more critical. Without being fully on site to sense the energy and shared purpose that can come from being co-located with team members, it can deteriorate and be overtaken by a sense of isolation. Thus, organizations must be intentional about articulating their purpose – this must be explicitly explained at regular intervals to employees, so that each employee knows how their work is connected to that purpose, and how the team's work connects with those of other teams to create added value. In turn, this should help with accountability, in that individuals and teams can be held accountable to the wider organizational purpose via performance management discussions.

Teams need to be connected explicitly to other teams, and individuals likewise with other individuals from other teams. In our case studies in this chapter, you'll see examples of cross-organizational groups being created to consciously create opportunities to meet with and collaborate with individuals from other teams, and this is to be encouraged. I've done this in the past in my hybrid working organizations, often on themes that matter to the organization (for example the design of a new office building, or changes to service delivery), and they've always worked well. Lisa Murphy, Director of Limelite, introduced me to the concept of dynamic governance, or sociocracy, which has overlapping project teams that report into each other. While this has limitations, it has big advantages in the focus it gives to relationship building and how it brings employees organically into contact with people from other parts of the organization. In a hybrid working organization these principles may be very helpful.

The cross-organizational groups can then be supplemented by internal social media channel discussions that allow for more employees to get involved – again this is something I've done to good effect in previous organizations to enable remote employees to feel like they had a voice, such as when the organization was redesigning its performance management systems.

Using internal social media is a great way to encourage cross-organizational networks and relationships to build. Sharing company news and updates and allowing or even encouraging comments and debate is helpful. I've done this when sharing news of a merger via Yammer. One well-known food manufacturer in the UK now does all its internal communications via social media such as TikTok and Instagram, with the feeling that it allows employees based in different places to more easily find out what is going on in the organization and interact with others more easily too. Internal social media is also effective for finding out what employees have in common, such as shared pastimes, shared likes and more – connections can be built across the organization more easily based on these.

There is a risk of communication overload or channel overload, so the organization needs to make it explicit which methods or channels are used for what purpose. There should be clear and widely shared expectations for how and where organizational information is going to be shared, and whether any or what kind of response may be needed from employees. Teams may well develop preferences for their own communications, but organizational-level communication should be consistent in terms of where and how to find it – and in particular no internal communications should be restricted to on-site methods only.

Thought Exchange mentions the power of swag, which is also interesting – as an excellent way to remind employees who may not be on site all the time who they work for. They recommend branding some of the equipment employees may use when working remotely (Gangnes, 2022).

Subject to logistics, bringing the entire company together at least once a year for an entire company event can be extremely powerful. Logistically this could prove impractical but even virtually this could be extremely useful at creating clarity of organizational purpose and reinforcing aspects of corporate culture.

Culture can therefore be created in remote and hybrid organizations, but only through careful, deliberate actions. But one of our biggest challenges is to change the mindset of those who are opposed to hybrid working.

What is behind the mindset of those opposed to remote and hybrid working?

Earlier in this chapter we mentioned status quo bias, and this is likely behind many views about remote and hybrid working, as are vested interests. The changes to the world of work can be perceived as a threat to what people know, are comfortable with or are invested in. This may mean they overlook the evidence that supports how beneficial remote and hybrid working can be, and may become fixated on the familiar and traditional approach of on-site working – believing on site is the only environment suitable for productivity (Tsipursky, 2023). Many leaders are afraid that productivity and performance reduces in remote and hybrid environments, despite opposing views from most employees.

As we have discussed earlier, this focus on productivity is narrow. There are multiple indicators that need to be reviewed, like different pieces of a jigsaw, and many leaders have not been given the guidance and support to enable this to be a comfortable approach. It also strikes at the very heart of what some leaders believe leadership to be about. As GP Strategies points out, 'if individuals were productive, distributive decision making increased, and they were able to hold themselves and their teams accountable, how does that shape the role of the leader?' (Clark, 2021). If leaders don't have to have sight of employees for those employees to be productive, what could be left for the leaders to do?

Leadership used to be a very sensory experience. Leaders could see people, hear people and, in some unfortunate cases, even smell their people. But remote and hybrid working can be likened to losing one of your senses – you must rely on different signals and evidence to be able to live a normal life, but it can be done. Many leaders relied upon being able to see when someone was productive or when they were struggling, but now must pick up signals that tell them about those things in different ways.

Some leaders will only be able to view productivity through that original lens, or only be able to manage people in one way – when they can see them. Some will only have experienced this way of leading and managing and cannot fully empathize with different points of view. To this, I would suggest that if we examined the average demographic of leaders who are opposed to hybrid working versus the average demographic of their employees, we would see that those leaders are more male, more white, older, wealthier and more likely to have fewer young children, than the people who report to them. They have likely benefited from traditional ways of on-site and less-flexible working, and almost certainly will have entered the world of work when remote working – and indeed things like social media and any technology that administers one's life – were far less prevalent. That affects how they see the world, and the world of work. Learning new skills and new mindsets could be something that hasn't been explored with them or could be viewed negatively by them.

These types of beliefs are a form of confirmation bias. Someone with a confirmation bias would ignore any information that may contradict their belief (such as the vast range of evidence that shows how popular and effective hybrid working is) and only look for information that confirms that belief. They have a view of how things should work and would stick with that view even if changes happen that offer a better situation. With the enforced nature of remote working during the Covid-19 pandemic bringing with it many disadvantages (and therefore not being a true experience of what remote working could be) it has served to confirm in many leaders' minds that remote working could never work, and that hybrid working could never work either. We have a problem if that view is held and expressed by the most senior people in an organization.

Research has determined that more senior leaders usually have less day-to-day contact with employees than middle and first-line managers do, and therefore cannot as easily see how many aspects are enhanced by remote and hybrid working (Kowalski and Ślebarska, 2022). The ability of very senior leaders to see the whole picture is therefore often limited and biased as a result.

Some of the beliefs have been reinforced by difficulties people may have had operating in a remote or hybrid environment. Difficulties with technology that impact communication and collaboration, as well as difficulties with managing work–life balance, and difficulties effectively managing performance. While these are real difficulties, do you remember the paraphrased quote from Chris Herd earlier in this chapter about hybrid working revealing culture? That's applicable here. What this experience shows is that the way those leaders were doing those things wasn't flexible enough to cope with change, and that the leaders, the individuals and teams needed much more guidance, help and support to be able to cope with the change than they were given. Remember also that an estimated 70 per cent of changes fail because of a lack of cultural awareness and alignment? That's why some leaders feel hybrid working isn't working – but it's because the effort hasn't been made. If it had been, it could have worked.

How to change mindsets

A theme running through this chapter is the need to be intentional with making hybrid working work, and to give people the required help, guidance and support they need. Training managers is a good start point – we shouldn't assume that managers are doing well. They may, through trial and error, have coped, but most will need some structured support to be able to manage a hybrid team. Research suggests though that only 28 per cent of organizations plan to do this, despite an acknowledgement that lots of things could suffer if left to chance (Mutebi and Hobbs, 2022). When organizations do provide this type of training for managers, it can result in an 18 per cent increase in productivity (Navarra, 2022). In a later chapter we will look specifically at what types of things could be included in this training, but without training we take a big risk.

We could also explore what is stopping the changing of mindsets. A helpful tool to use here would be Kurt Lewin's force field analysis. This may show that it is a lack of data, or a lack of trust, or possibly status quo bias, that is holding leaders back and will give us something to work with.

Mindsets themselves though can be tricky things to change, but consciously holding certain beliefs at the forefront of a leader's mind will help them to change their reticence about hybrid working. This would involve us regularly challenging them and reminding them of certain things, such as:

- The technology can aid innovation and collaboration, not stifle it.
- Remote and hybrid working can enable us to access greater diversity of thought and characteristics irrespective of working location.
- People want to collaborate in different ways, not just when on site.
- Everyone is different, with different needs, environments and ways of working. The work they do is different too, and we should craft something that makes the most of that.

- They have a responsibility to engage all team members regardless of where they are working, or when, to ensure inclusive decision making.
- We don't need to 'solve' hybrid working straight away – we can evolve it as we go along and learn from things that do and do not work.
- Hybrid working can be used to remind people that they are part of a larger organization, and using different forms of virtual and in-person communications can enhance this.
- What matters is the organizational purpose and how it delivers this to its stakeholders. That can be done in lots of different ways, not simply when on site.

Is this easier said, than done, though? In later chapters we will explore more of how we do this on a practical level.

In this chapter we will examine how two different organizations have been implementing and seeing the impact of hybrid working.

CASE STUDY ONE

Sarah Garner is the Head of People and Organisational Development at Wealden District Council. Wealden has around 450 staff and provides a range of services typical for a local authority to a region in East Sussex in the UK.

A significant number of these 450 staff are long-serving, and many have only ever worked for Wealden. This has created a more traditional and static culture with limited exposure to new practices or thinking, and quite admin heavy as a result. The Covid-19 pandemic was therefore a challenge and the organization had to deliver radical change at pace. They did so with success though, and remote working became normal at that point.

During the Covid-19 pandemic, the Leadership Team at Wealden had to ensure delivering essential services and support for businesses and the most vulnerable in the area while also choosing to focus on staff well-being. Staff well-being has continued to be the focus since. In assessing the impact of remote and hybrid working, leaders at Wealden look first at the impact on staff well-being before they look at anything else. Alongside the needs of the service, well-being is balanced over the need for any member of staff to come on site and has resulted in extremely high engagement survey results, which show that staff feel very well looked after.

The Chief Executive of Wealden Council is described by Garner as a low-control CEO, someone who likes to empower people to make their own decisions and encourages them to experiment. When the organization introduced its hybrid working approach, the CEO encouraged people to be on site two days a week but provided little else in the way of guidance – the aim was that teams would find a way to make this work. However, in the early days, most managers found this an impossible ask – every service, and every individual, had different needs.

For its first year, Wealden's hybrid working approach was not working, and there was disagreement within the organization about the principles needed to make it work more effectively. Intentional and deliberate decision making was needed, and this was apparent when Garner joined the organization.

Garner felt the organization had done a lot of positive and often innovative things. She cites as examples additional payments made to remote and hybrid workers to cover increases in energy and broadband costs, and a full revamp of Wealden's offices to provide more hot-desking and touchdown spaces, with standardized equipment across spaces to make it easier to work seamlessly in different spaces.

However, she also noticed some negatives arising from the approach and its inherent disagreements. While enforced remote working and a focus on individual and team wellness had brought teams very close together, enhancing their ways of working, it had created an unfortunate silo effect. Cross-organizational activities, beyond the regular whole-organization briefings from the Leadership Team, had almost dried up. The empowerment given to service managers to work out their own hybrid approaches meant that services were becoming increasingly fragmented.

Wealden had created a very comprehensive hybrid working process, accompanied by guidance for both managers and staff. Garner ensured there was sufficient leadership development for those managing hybrid teams and expected to deliver services in a hybrid way. This development focused on how to create accountability, how to make decisions based on principles, and how to encourage collaboration and partnership working. She also worked to create leadership communities of practice so that thinking and practice could be shared more easily across the organization to overcome silo thinking.

Garner's view about the silo working effects of remote and hybrid working tap into some organization design and development aspects. She feels that these types of issues were perhaps embedded in some teams and services already, and were bubbling away but not as visible, prior to remote and hybrid working. Remote and hybrid working therefore gave visibility to and a platform for addressing these issues and created a burning platform for Wealden to address otherwise invisible cultural blind spots. She commented that hybrid working forces the right kinds of conversations to happen and improves organization design and culture if it is done deliberately and intentionally. Similarly, she felt that hybrid working made the strengths and weaknesses of the Leadership Team more visible, showing them where their blind spots were and forcing them to address the way they worked and behaved together. On the latter point, Leadership Team meetings are now much more intentional – not just reading and approving papers, which can be done asynchronously, but are more discussion- and debate-focused. Hybrid working has therefore changed meeting structures and purposes for the better at Wealden.

Garner was positive about the overall effects of hybrid working in a general sense. Wealden have prioritized staff well-being and all indicators related to this are improved because of their hybrid working approach, but Garner also reports no negative changes to any measure that matters to the organization. She feels it does aid productivity, but the organization has only anecdotal evidence of this. Also anecdotally, she feels hybrid working improves collaboration, team dynamics and organizational culture, but only when done 'well' – tellingly, she says that all of these can suffer if hybrid working isn't working well.

Wealden has met with some very strong resistance from a small number of staff who do not want to work on site at all. To a large degree this is being worked around by managers who, Garner feels, do not know how to (or whether to) deal with it. Interestingly there is no obvious problem created by or exacerbated by this behaviour, and as usual in Wealden the overriding concern is around staff welfare. Consequently, Garner's team have consciously changed their own skill sets and mindsets to enable them to better support managers with such difficult situations, and to encourage personalized, individualized relationships between managers and their staff that are fully cognizant of individual circumstances and preferences.

Garner reports no explicit tensions between those who can and those who cannot work in a hybrid way. She feels that there is a very strong sense of pride among the entire Wealden workforce, and this is seen more obviously in front-line roles where remote working is not possible. She believes this overcomes many of the potential tensions that could otherwise arise and works hard to promote this sense of pride within the organization.

The organization has made big decisions around pay and rewards, and faces some around real estate. From a pay and rewards perspective, the global cost-of-living crisis has changed many staff and job applicants' views. People are more easily able to, and willing to, work out the costs to them of fully remote, fully on site and hybrid, and are comparing overall reward packages to determine which method of working they prefer. Wealden has addressed differentials through a comprehensive pay review in which all posts were benchmarked against the market median, and developed a new salary scale. Its pay policy is to remain at, or above, local public sector median pay rates.

From a real estate perspective, Wealden intends to lease out parts of its headquarters to get full occupancy and usage from it. This is expected to be to other public service organizations that will be of use to Wealden's own customers when coming on site (for example medical services). This changes what its buildings are used for, becoming more of a one-stop-shop for many types of public service. It also changes the requisite culture within the building, as multiple organizations can be homed within the Council's headquarters. This will likely have a surprisingly positive effect on the Council's revenue streams. Wealden has decisions to make about the long-term strategic direction it takes here.

CASE STUDY TWO

Jessica Badley is the Director of People and Resources at the British Society for Rheumatology (BSR), a membership organization based in London with around 40 staff and several thousand subscribed members all over the UK. Prior to the Covid-19 pandemic, there had been no remote working in BSR, except in emergency situations. There was little technology to enable it or a culture to support it, and the organization had a very traditional Monday to Friday, 9 am to 5 pm, office-based way of working. This obviously changed rapidly during that pandemic.

When the pandemic receded, BSR tried to get their employees back into the office two days a week but met with a lot of strong resistance. The decision to bring people back on site was driven by the need to make use of their building, which they owned. People began to leave because of the enforced two days on site. This was, in Badley's view, entirely understandable. BSR's work is UK-based and requires its staff to be mobile within the UK, and so forcing people to have a fixed London base when its staff had suddenly realized the effectiveness of having no fixed base seemed illogical at best.

Badley spent time talking to each individual employee, and the feedback was that the two-day on-site requirement felt arbitrary, with little understandable rationale from a service-delivery perspective and was not working for anyone. In addition, she uncovered that each employee was doing a different two days on site, and so the building occupancy levels remained very low. This meant the goal for bringing people back on site was not being achieved. Badley then consulted with each employee, including all managers, about how best to make hybrid working work, and concluded that trust was key to this and to allow each team to work out its own hybrid working pattern.

Each team is now encouraged to plan out what it wants to do when on site, with in-person meetings and collaboration through anchor days, away days and social activities given a high priority and facilitated across the organization to allow different teams to come together.

Linked to this, BSR have been trialling a reduced working week of 31.5 hours, which is a general reduction of half a day. Again, this is worked out separately by each team, with the team and its members challenged to work out how to deliver their service and maintain or improve productivity while reducing hours. The resulting 'spare' half day varies by team.

All organizational performance measures have either improved or stayed the same, and BSR no longer struggles to recruit to any vacant posts. People-related metrics have also improved.

Like Wealden District Council, BSR has solved the low occupancy rates in their building by leasing out whole floors. This creates an income stream for them, which is welcomed. They have revamped what remains so that there are more collaborative spaces, more hot desks and no fixed settings.

Badley confesses to being bemused that some people, often senior leaders in organizations, have a mindset that on-site work is best, and that people are best when on site. In BSR she has been able to show otherwise, though this has not been without challenges.

She has learnt that people need more guidance on using technology than just being shown *how* to use it. She comments that there is often a cultural aspect to using technology and cites Microsoft Teams as an example – people need to know when and why to use it, what it is best for and when to use other media. People also need to establish etiquette around response times, available times and what these mean – along with circumstances that could vary these. Leaders needed to be held accountable for role modelling these behaviours and needed help on how to build trust and empowerment with their team members. Badley is confident that the current hybrid working approach delivers all these things for BSR.

To help with maintaining organizational culture, Badley has consciously been building communities of peer practice, such as managers' networks. She reports that these are working very well both virtually and in person, and even as hybrid events. The managers' network and other similar networks at different levels in the organization help, in Badley's view, improve organizational culture and collaboration and prevent silo working. In this she reinforces what Sarah Garner said in Wealden District Council, that hybrid working can make organizational culture deteriorate if left to chance, and team cultures can prevail, but that conscious and deliberate effort can improve both.

Case study reflections

In the first case study, Wealden District Council, the following points are worthy of consideration:

- The quote earlier in this chapter from Chris Herd about hybrid working exposing or revealing organizational culture rings very true here. The issues it has forced Wealden to address were already there pre-pandemic and pre-hybrid working. They have not been created because of hybrid working. Hybrid working gives an opportunity to address them.

- It is possible to measure the impact of hybrid working using many different measures, and often what matters most to the organization is what gets measured. In this case, staff well-being matters most – and measured on that, hybrid working has been successful for this organization.

- As with other examples, hybrid working has lots of anecdotal evidence of improved productivity but rarely anything tangible. However, there is also no evidence of any reduced performance or productivity measures.

- Autonomy and empowerment are important for managers and individuals to feel that they can craft something that works for them. However, the organization must give some guidance, some boundaries, to avoid potential chaos. There must be an intentional approach, leaving little to chance.

- Team culture is relatively easy to establish and maintain in a hybrid working environment, but this can come at the cost of cohesive organizational culture. Conscious, deliberate action is needed to maintain this organizational culture otherwise it could deteriorate over time.

- People professionals need to develop a strong organizational development skill set and mindset to be able to support their organizations through the decisions needed to make hybrid working work.

- Personalized, individualized relationships between managers and staff can get the best from all parties.

- Fostering and encouraging a sense of pride in the work people do can reduce tensions between those with different working arrangements.

- Hybrid working offers opportunities to review how work is rewarded, but care must be taken with this.

- Hybrid working also offers opportunities to create more revenue streams and change the nature of some local communities. Long-term strategic, and deliberate, decisions are needed to make this work well, though.

In the second case study, the British Society for Rheumatology, the following points are also worthy of consideration:

- It can be possible for organizations to completely pivot their way of working from traditional Monday to Friday, 9 am to 5 pm, office-based to radically different models and patterns.

- If employees are mandated to work on site, they are likely to need a stronger reason than making good use of the building.

- Thinking about ways to get employees closer to customers may mean that maintaining a fixed on-site presence is not the most appropriate thing to do any more.

- Talking to employees as individuals is likely to reveal a whole host of different and valid reasons to work in a particular way but is also likely to drive up engagement.

- Empowering teams to work things out for themselves can be risky, as we saw with Wealden, but in different circumstances can work well. Challenging teams to find ways to improve productivity with the 'carrot' of reduced hours for the same pay can create innovation.

- Revamping the office to encourage the right kind of working is critical, and it is likely that multiple-occupancy buildings are increasing in popularity as a way of improving occupancy and generating income.

- Giving leaders, teams and individuals more than just technical training on hybrid working technology and practices is vital if it is to work more effectively.

- Consciously creating opportunities to maintain and enhance organizational culture can be effective at preventing its deterioration.

The action plan

If you are wanting to improve how hybrid working is working in your organization, here are some things you may want to reflect upon:

- How do you want to measure the impact of hybrid working, and does everyone in your organization agree with and understand that?

- What view do your senior leaders have on hybrid working versus on-site working, and how fixed is that view?

- How will you ensure that the on-site experience becomes a positive, valuable one for all?

- What are the respective attractions for your organization of mandated hybrid versus empowered/flexible hybrid?

- What evidence do you have of hybrid working's impact on collaboration and communication in your organization?

- How will you start the debate about wholesale organizational system changes because of hybrid working?
- How would you describe the culture in your organization, and what impact does hybrid working have on that?
- What type of effort is required to maintain your organizational culture (irrespective of hybrid working or not)?
- What does hybrid working, in its current state, reveal about your organizational culture, and how do you feel about that?
- How will you help employees to build proximity to their teammates and others in the organization?
- What things will you do to establish the organizational purpose more firmly among hybrid workers?
- How will you avoid team cultures overriding organizational culture?
- What role does your physical workplace play in organizational culture? What role *could* it play?
- How can you encourage easy collaboration and socialization when people are working on site?
- What lessons can you apply from managing your own personal social networks that would help you in creating the same sense of community in your organization?
- How will you ensure that teams connect to other teams?
- What challenge do you need to make to status quo bias in your organization?
- What evidence can you provide that would change the mindsets of those opposed to hybrid working?

References and further reading

Bloom, N et al (2023) Research: Where managers and employees disagree about remote work, *Harvard Business Review*, 5 January, www.hbr.org/2023/01/research-where-managers-and-employees-disagree-about-remote-work (archived at https://perma.cc/L2ZB-6SAJ)

Brower, T (2021) How to sustain company culture in a hybrid work model, *Forbes*, 7 February, www.forbes.com/sites/tracybrower/2021/02/07/how-to-sustain-company-culture-in-a-hybrid-work-model/ (archived at https://perma.cc/NJ4H-NFCY)

Cholteeva, Y (2023) Is hybrid work good for everyone's wellbeing? People Management, 15 June, www.peoplemanagement.co.uk/article/1826471/hybrid-work-good-everyones-wellbeing (archived at https://perma.cc/H3XT-H4KY)

CIPD (2020) Embedding new ways of working: Implications for the post-pandemic workforce, September

CIPD (2023) Flexible and hybrid working practices in 2023, 25 May, www.cipd.org/en/knowledge/reports/flexible-hybrid-working-2023/ (archived at https://perma.cc/V8M6-F5XN)

Clark, L (2021) Leader mindsets: New ways of thinking for a new hybrid world, GP Strategies, 11 August, www.gpstrategies.com/blog/leader-mindsets-for-a-hybrid-world/ (archived at https://perma.cc/LMW9-5H82)

Dale, G (2023a) Autonomy, choice and the potential hybrid push-back, hrgem, 28 February, www.hrgemblog.com/2023/02/28/autonomy-choice-and-the-potential-hybrid-push-back/ (archived at https://perma.cc/X253-LWTA)

Dale, G (2023b) Reasons your CEO wants you back in the office, hrgem, www.hrgemblog.com/2023/05/11/reasons-your-ceo-wants-you-back-in-the-office/ (archived at https://perma.cc/Z5NG-VC8T)

Davis, M C et al (2022) Where is your office today? New insights on employee behaviour and social networks, University of Leeds, October, https://futureworkplace.leeds.ac.uk/wp-content/uploads/sites/86/2022/10/Where-is-your-office-today-Oct-2022-2.pdf (archived at https://perma.cc/KZ9B-DT2Q)

Delaney, K J (2022) How to shift mindset and practices for hybrid work, Charter, 1 May, www.charterworks.com/robert-pozen-hybrid-work-remote-how-to-shift-mindset-and-practices/ (archived at https://perma.cc/C8Y9-RBMR)

Gangnes, J T (2022) Building culture in a remote & hybrid workplace, ThoughtExchange, 29 April, thoughtexchange.com/blog/building-culture-in-a-remote-hybrid-workplace/ (archived at https://perma.cc/89V8-VKQL)

Hall, R (2024) Four-day week made permanent for most UK firms in world's biggest trial, *The Guardian*, 21 February, www.theguardian.com/money/2024/feb/21/four-day-week-made-permanent-for-most-uk-firms-in-worlds-biggest-trial (archived at https://perma.cc/B6BW-UMY8)

Hancock, B, Schaninger, B and Weddle, B (2021) Culture in the hybrid workplace, McKinsey & Company, 11 June, www.mckinsey.com/capabilities/people-and-organizational-performance/our-insights/culture-in-the-hybrid-workplace (archived at https://perma.cc/J57K-R3XY)

Harter, J (2023) How important is time in the office? Gallup, 2 March, www.gallup.com/workplace/468599/important-time-office.aspx (archived at https://perma.cc/T7AX-DS2V)

HBR (2022) Revitalizing culture in the world of hybrid work, *Harvard Business Review*, November–December, www.hbr.org/2022/11/revitalizing-culture-in-the-world-of-hybrid-work (archived at https://perma.cc/96L4-8V7B)

Herd, C (2023) LinkedIn, 27 June, www.linkedin.com/feed/update/urn:li:activity:7079594317454950400/ (archived at https://perma.cc/FHV6-MYHQ)

HR Zone (nd) How do you maintain culture in a hybrid workplace? www.hrzone.com/community/blogs/terkel/how-do-you-maintain-culture-in-a-hybrid-workplace (archived at https://perma.cc/Q34N-YCBC)

Kowalski, G and Ślebarska, K (2022) Remote working and work effectiveness: A leader perspective, *International Journal of Environmental Research and Public Health*, 19 (22), https://doi.org/10.3390/ijerph192215326 (archived at https://perma.cc/8J32-9NDH)

Machell, M (2023) Return to the office: What employers are doing to incentivise in-office work, *HR*, 16 June, www.hrmagazine.co.uk/content/news/return-to-the-office-what-employers-are-doing-to-incentivise-in-office-work (archived at https://perma.cc/3CYN-DL4J)

Microsoft (2022) Great expectations: Making hybrid work work, 16 March, www.microsoft.com/en-us/worklab/work-trend-index/great-expectations-making-hybrid-work-work (archived at https://perma.cc/45YR-ULTZ)

Mitel (2023) The rising mental and monetary costs of remote and hybrid work in 2023, 20 March, www.mitel.com/blog/the-rising-mental-and-monetary-costs-of-remote-and-hybrid-work (archived at https://perma.cc/ZGE9-Y6SY)

Mutebi, N and Hobbs, A (2022) The impact of remote and hybrid working on workers and organisations, POST, UK Parliament, 17 October, https://post.parliament.uk/research-briefings/post-pb-0049/ (archived at https://perma.cc/JUG8-7GDW)

Navarra, K (2022) In hybrid work, don't rely on just one aspect of productivity, SHRM, 9 October, www.shrm.org/resourcesandtools/hr-topics/employee-relations/pages/in-hybrid-work-dont-rely-on-just-one-aspect-of-productivity.aspx (archived at https://perma.cc/BN5E-Y88K)

Parker, K (2023) About a third of U.S. workers who can work from home now do so all the time, Pew Research Center, 30 March, www.pewresearch.org/short-reads/2023/03/30/about-a-third-of-us-workers-who-can-work-from-home-do-so-all-the-time/ (archived at https://perma.cc/6FAY-8MYX)

Prodoscore (nd) Hybrid and remote employee monitoring software, www.prodoscore.com/solutions/remote-and-hybrid-work/ (archived at https://perma.cc/6258-Z3L9)

Race, M (2023) Chancellor Jeremy Hunt: Office working should be 'default', BBC News, 17 May, www-bbc-co-uk.cdn.ampproject.org/c/s/www.bbc.co.uk/news/business-65621081.amp (archived at https://perma.cc/8RMN-YGAQ)

Talent Intelligence (2022) How to sustain organizational culture in a hybrid work model, www.talentintelligence.com/how-to-sustain-organizational-culture-in-a-hybrid-work-model/ (archived at https://perma.cc/UN77-X86Q)

The Access Group (2023) A Hybrid Working Nation: How it's working out, https://pages.theaccessgroup.com/A-hybrid-working-nation-how-its-working-out.html (archived at https://perma.cc/PRM5-VBDQ)

Tsipursky, G (2021) The psychology behind why some leaders are resisting a hybrid work model, *Fortune*, 9 June, www.fortune.com/2021/06/08/return-remote-work-hybrid-model-surveys-covid/ (archived at https://perma.cc/J342-U5LD)

Tsipursky, G (2023) The forced return to the office is the definition of insanity, *Fortune*, 26 June, www.fortune.com/2023/06/26/forced-return-to-office-is-the-definition-of-insanity-remote-hybrid-work-careers-gleb-tsipursky/amp/ (archived at https://perma.cc/8DQ6-D26F)

Unispace (2023) Returning for Good, www.unispace.com/returning-for-good (archived at https://perma.cc/3VWV-P8FB)

Wood, J (2022) Hybrid working: Why there's a widening gap between leaders and employees, World Economic Forum, 20 December, www.weforum.org/agenda/2022/12/hybrid-working-remote-work-office-senior-leaders/ (archived at https://perma.cc/F2G5-JW3B)

Workplace (nd) Five ways to build culture in a hybrid workplace, Meta, https://en-gb.workplace.com/blog/hybrid-workplace-culture (archived at https://perma.cc/FY9U-E8F8)

3

Working 9 to 5?

The shorter read

In this chapter we will explore what a reduced working week could mean for hybrid working, and vice versa, as well as what it means for individuals, organizations and society at large. There is certainly momentum building behind the idea of moving away from the traditional five-day working week.

Seen in a wider context, the current exploration of moves to reduce the working week is part of a much longer-term trend dating back over 150 years and reflects changes within society and work during the Industrial Revolution and thereafter. History is not so much repeating itself, as continuing – and in the modern world, fixed times and locations of work, particularly Monday to Friday, 9 am to 5 pm, are often incompatible with the demands of family and society. We must change something, and not be restrained by status quo bias.

Experiences of making remote and hybrid working work can help us when considering how to make this change. Being more conscious and deliberate about designing how, when and where work is done enables more effective remote and hybrid working, but also enables a reduction in the working week – if we want it to. Leaving it to chance won't make it happen.

There are of course many alternatives to the traditional working week, and some more palatable than others for certain jobs and organizations. All have their advantages and disadvantages. We must work alongside employees to find the approach that suits the organizational and individual context best – but this is something we should already be doing to enable more effective hybrid working too.

There are many challenges to overcome, but with proper planning and transparent discussions and decision making this can be done. The benefits are obvious for individuals, but recent research has shown very few, if any, adverse effects for organizations. The potential drawbacks come into sharp focus for many very easily, but again through intentional action these can be overcome.

We must be flexible, as we must with hybrid working. We must be innovative and creative – again we will be doing this with making hybrid working work too. It can be done – if we want it to.

There are bigger considerations too – doing this properly could lead to significant environmental and societal benefits, furthering many causes. The challenges are there, but the benefits are there to be realized too. Taken in a wider historical context, this isn't the biggest change humans have had to cope with. We can do this.

The longer read

The death of the traditional five-day working week?

In 2022, 61 UK-based organizations covering nearly 3,000 employees took part in the world's largest organized trial of a four-day working week. At the end of this, 92 per cent of these organizations said they would continue with it beyond the trial (although some said they would tweak it to suit them even better), and many individual employees in the trial said they would only return to a traditional five-day working week if incentivized with a significant pay increase (Cave, 2023). Most of the businesses saw no drop in productivity during the trial, with 46 per cent seeing productivity improving. However, benefits were seen in lots of areas including staff well-being, turnover, attendance, organizational efficiency and more (Hall, 2024).

Does this mean that the traditional five-day working week is dying out? And is this aided, or harmed, by moves to increase the amount of remote and hybrid working that is being done? In this chapter we will explore why momentum seems to be building behind a move away from the traditional five-day working week, what alternatives there are and how to make it work alongside effective remote and hybrid working.

How did we end up working five days a week anyway?

The now traditional five-day working week is not as old or established a concept as many would think. In most developed economies it is around 100 years old as a standard arrangement. Its origins lie deeper though, and are intertwined with the story of homeworking too.

I spoke with a leading historian in the UK (who wishes to remain anonymous), to get some insight into what had driven society to adopt a five-day working week in the first place.

They believe that homeworking has been complicated by both feudalism and capitalism across the centuries. Using the UK as an example, they explained how in places like Lancashire and Yorkshire, families tended to all live and work in the same home, all working for the same family business as one unit. This was changed in the 18th century as the Industrial Revolution began – many family businesses were heavily disrupted by new technology and automation, forcing many to seek employment in new factories and mills that sprung up in (and led to the huge growth of) towns and cities. The owners of these factories and mills needed to introduce standardized hours so that their overheads were manageable and opening and running the buildings was regulated and efficient – so they introduced six-day working weeks, with only Sunday being a non-working day.

They explained that the move to reduce working hours and days was largely a political one, the result of campaigns and class-based action, which employers resisted. The reductions were not easy to come by.

The concept of 'Saint Monday' is something they explained to me also. This was a phenomenon in both the UK and US, where excesses of alcohol and other substances on an employee's one day off on Sunday resulted in large amounts of absenteeism, and presenteeism, on Mondays. Unauthorized time off work on Mondays led to an increase in demand for and take-up of leisure pursuits, aiding the campaigns for more time off. Many employers then countered this trend by giving Saturdays off (either the afternoon or the full day) for leisure pursuits, creating the weekend as we now know it. This is also the main reason why many UK football matches traditionally have Saturday afternoon kick-offs.

Allowing Saturdays and Sundays off meant that both Jewish and Christian workers could worship on their respective holy days, and time was created for leisure pursuits also. This model caught on and became standard practice in the years following the First World War, aided by changes in legislation driven by safety concerns.

The insights from the historian are interesting. They pose some interesting points for us to consider with regard to hybrid working too. Remote and hybrid working creates the possibility that some households will have multiple family members working in the same location, albeit for different employers – a not too dissimilar situation to the pre-industrial time. It also means there could be a move away from workers grouped together in cities and large towns in the same location working standardized hours. Both are things we will explore further in later chapters. Remote and hybrid working has brought employee well-being to the fore in employers' thoughts, and addressing these by creating more leisure time for employees is a natural response – repeating the rationale for introducing a five-day working week in the first place.

Is history repeating itself? It certainly seems so, after a break of over half a century. Seen in a longer-term context, the move away from a traditional five-day working week is part of a wider trend to reduce the working week and working day, from a height of six 12-hour days in the 1850s, to five 8-hour days by the 1950s. A good piece of research that shows this data is available from Our World in Data (Giattino, Ortiz-Ospina and Roser, 2020). The campaigns that led to these changes were based largely on worker health and safety, and to provide workers (at that time being mostly men) with more time to recover from the working week and therefore be better husbands and fathers. Sound familiar?

The traditional five-day working week, with eight-hour days, based in one on-site location, is based on the premise that whoever does that has someone else at home, unpaid, doing the childcare, housework, cooking and more. That really isn't the case for most households any more, and as society has evolved, we need the working week to evolve also. That involves remote and hybrid working to help us to cope with the demands we have on our time and energy, but also perhaps changing the working week itself.

In the Icelandic public sector steps have already been taken to address this. Publicly reported as working four days a week, Iceland's public sector journey has involved reducing the number of hours worked each week – moving from 40 hours to 35 hours, but with no reduction in pay (Veal, 2021). That isn't a four-day working week but is still an impressive reduction, especially when set alongside reported claims that productivity has at least remained the same, if not improved. In Iceland, as no adverse effects have been noticed, these arrangements are now being made permanent. What isn't clear though is whether this impact is because of improvements in productivity or more intensive and harder working (which will negate the intended benefits of reducing working hours). Could the rest of the world follow suit? Perhaps – the Scottish Government launched its own trial of four-day week working for public services in 2024.

It is worth recalling that around 25 per cent of the UK workforce (and a similar percentage worldwide) have never worked a five-day week, so the amount of change needed to make this work could be less than first thought (Otte, 2023). For the rest who do though, the prospect of a reduced working week may feel too good to be true. For organizations that have not yet been involved in any trial the changes may feel too complex to work through, even if they agree with the principle. We must look for ways to make this easier.

This is where effective remote and hybrid working could really help. In this book we talk about redesigning job tasks to allow for more asynchronous and efficient ways of working – doing those things could enable a reduced working week. Personalizing the employee experience would ensure that everyone has the most productive way of working for them – and that is unlikely to be the traditional five-day working week for many. This is also covered later in the book.

Proper planning is needed to make this change work, as we will see in our case studies for this chapter. In the UK pilot, some organizations had been planning for this change for over a year. A good way of approaching whether the change is desirable and feasible is not to ask 'why should we reduce the working week?' but 'why do we need to retain a five-day week?'. Approaching it from this perspective is likely to provoke interesting debate, particularly when combined with some of the things we explore in this book about making hybrid working work better and improving the employee experience. It will force people in organizations to justify why a five-day working week is the most appropriate arrangement – and many won't be able to.

For the same reasons, we shouldn't fixate on a four-day week. Just because the trials have all focused on that, doesn't mean that it is the most appropriate arrangement. The focus, as it is with hybrid working when done effectively, is about improving performance, ways of working and personalizing work. A four-day week could be the method for getting there, but so could many others. We should focus on the outcome we want and not the method to achieve it.

Alternative options to a traditional five-day working week that could be explored include, but are not limited to:

- A four-day week
- A nine-day fortnight

- A floating seven to eight hours that can be taken each week when an employee needs to
- No set hours at all
- Earlier finishes on set days (e.g. Fridays)
- Annualized hours
- Reduced hours but not reduced days
- Counting days/weeks in results not hours (Ingram, 2023)

Each of these has advantages and disadvantages that need to be explored. The key is to position the move away from the traditional working week as an efficiency project – where employees are challenged to find ways to improve efficiency that would free up time. We should also think about whether what we want to achieve is achievable in one, or several, steps. Do we have to solve this issue in one go?

What is stopping us moving away from the traditional working week?

For some organizations the change to the working week is a natural consequence of making the change to more effective remote and hybrid working. Having taken those steps to embed a better work–life balance and to personalize the employee experience, and at the same time resetting where and when work takes place, an altered working week seems logical. There will be specific reasons within each business too, and in our case studies in this chapter we will explore some different perspectives on this. However, the experiences many had during the Covid-19 pandemic proved that organizations could cope with rapid, large-scale change, make it work and make it stick.

This doesn't mean letting everyone set their own working week, even if that may sound like a nice idea. Working hours autonomy is perhaps not possible for many jobs, but working with employees to explore changes, rather than imposing them or ruling them out without discussion, is advisable.

There remain a lot of fears about moving away from a traditional five-day working week. There is of course the fear that fewer hours/days equals less work; however, the move to greater remote and hybrid working has already shifted measurement of work away from input and hours worked, and more towards outputs and outcomes. If remote and hybrid working is being done effectively, the mindset may already have changed to one where employees are required to deliver their outputs and outcomes in ways that suit them and the organization without obsessing about when work is done and how long that took. Equally, issues around trust may already have been overcome if implementing remote and hybrid working successfully – employees will have demonstrated that they can and should be trusted to deliver their outputs and outcomes in ways that suit them and the organization. They may already have adjusted workflows and processes in ways that now make a move away from a five-day working week easier.

Status quo bias, which was explored in a previous chapter, is likely to be one of the main barriers to overcome. There will be views that 'we have always worked this way' and worries about what stakeholders and customers may think. However, if done correctly and in conjunction with more effective remote and hybrid working, a revised working week would deliver the same outcomes to stakeholders and customers and open new and innovative ways of doing so.

What are the benefits of alternative working weeks?

My business moved to a four-day working week in April 2022. I had experimented with a reduced working week across each of the previous four summers – mostly to cope with childcare demands during the summer holidays, and partly in recognition of it being a relatively quiet time business-wise. Those experiments had shown me some pros and cons of a reduced working week and had led me to believe that it could work. What I wasn't clear on though was what model to adopt.

Through my experiments I'd tried a four-day week, which worked well but more so when my children were off school, as it gave me a day to spend with them that I wouldn't ordinarily have, and the volume of incoming work was reduced likely because my clients also had children off school.

I'd also tried reduced hours, working 30–32 hours across five days. This model worked well when my children were in school, as it meant I could do far more school runs than if I worked longer days. But when they were off school, this wasn't a sustainable model for me as I still missed out on time with them.

Throughout all these experiments my wife (who is the other employee of our business) remained steady on her three-day working week pattern. And my own experiments tended to run from late June to early September. In between times I'd revert to a traditional five-day working week and resented that each time it happened. My response was to increase my holidays, and I found myself taking at least one day off each fortnight (of course I run my own business and can do these things).

In 2022 I realized that I was already working a nine-day fortnight and that it wouldn't be a big step to fully implement a four-day week. That became the reality in April 2022, and my wife also moved to a four-day week at that point largely so that we could synchronize work and life more easily.

The benefits are great. I have a spare day each week (mostly, but not always, Fridays) where I get a lot of life admin done and where my focus is about doing things for me and spending time with my wife when she takes the same day off. As the children are mostly in school, it means they have fewer demands on my time. I get to work on my fitness. I get to take long walks, and long baths. I read more. And I have written a lot of the book you're now reading on those days.

I have had to battle against my own and others' prejudices though, in having this extra, spare, day. This is also commented on in an article in *The Guardian* (Ribeiro, 2023) – whether we feel conditioned to try to fill our time or simply rest without guilt? Is it selfish to spend time focusing on oneself?

The downsides though are notable. Although I still take the same salary from the business, overall revenue has decreased – as one of the two employees in the business, output has reduced – I'm working less, so there is less opportunity for the business to earn revenue. In a larger business that may not be an issue. And there seems reduced flexibility somehow. This is because a lot of what I do revolves around fixed-time appointments, and there are now only four days to fit these in. That makes each day busier and means I'm less able to respond to short-notice changes in work or life demands. I've also found that taking the odd one-day holiday has become harder to do. Holidays now are usually full-week blocks, though that does have pluses too.

But I've been working in a hybrid way now for over two decades and it is because of that that I've been able to look at efficient ways of working, change when, where and how work is done, and ultimately reduce the working week. To me, to all those who matter to me, and my business and its wider stakeholders – the benefits of a reduced working week far outweigh any drawbacks. I'm happier, and there have been no adverse effects on my clients or family. Much like many in the UK pilot of four-day working, it would take a life-changing amount of money to make me consider returning to a traditional five-day working week.

The benefits seem simple enough. Improved work–life balance, improved productivity and efficiency, and a big plus for talent attraction and retention. When there were several bank holidays in quick succession in the UK in April and May 2023, this gave many people a practical demonstration of what a reduced working week would look like. Liverpool Business School conducted research into what happened during that period.

They found that 51 per cent of employees felt they were more productive during the shorter working weeks, as well as feeling more rested and relaxed because of the additional days off. However, they also found that 67 per cent of employees felt their workload increased due to work being compressed – they had the same amount of work to do, but less time to do it in (Dale, 2023). This research and the experiences it captured neatly summarize the advantages and disadvantages of a reduced working week. It can work, but again – as with hybrid working – only if conscious, deliberate decisions are made about how to make it work, and not if it is left to chance.

Of course, those weren't experiences of a controlled, organized four-day working week, but give some insight into how to make it work and what the benefits could be. The recent UK pilot, and some other pilots globally, worked on the 100:80:100 model – expecting employees to do 100 per cent of their job in 80 per cent of the time, in return for retaining 100 per cent of the pay for it. To do this, productivity must be examined and probably improved.

In making a change to a nine-day fortnight, HR consultancy CharlieHR reported that there was a corresponding 24 per cent decrease in work-related stress, and a 14 per cent increase in people's ability to disengage from work during free time. They also reported an 11 per cent increase in employees' ability to focus and a 30 per cent increase in ability to do deep work (on Wednesdays there are no meetings for the day, to allow deep work to take place). Eighty-six per cent of CharlieHR's managers felt that they could hit all their performance indicators despite the reduced working time, and the nine-day fortnight has been cited as one of the top three reasons to join the company by new starters (Lord-Pottinger, nd).

South Cambridgeshire District Council began trialling a four-day working week in 2023, in what has become a politically charged experiment. The trial is reported to have saved £333,000 through being more able to fill vacancies that had been unfilled for some time. Researchers tracked sixteen different performance indicators, all of which have been at least maintained. Services to residents have remained unaltered – more staff have needed to be recruited to maintain the five-day week operation, but this is a neutral overall cost offset by savings elsewhere (Olsson and Rigby, 2023).

There are lots of other benefits. In 2019 Microsoft implemented a four-day working week across Japan and found a 40 per cent improvement in productivity. In the UK pilot concluded in 2023, time spent by male workers with their children increased by 27 per cent. Globally, companies involved in various pilots averaged an 8 per cent increase in revenues, improved ability to fill vacancies, reduced absence and improved retention (Broom, 2023). If work volumes and inability to balance work and life are a major cause of mental ill-health and stress, then a reduced working week combined with hybrid working is likely to combat that.

And unlike previous reductions in the working week explained earlier in the chapter, the drive for this change is not being led primarily by employees and their representatives. It is as much led by employers, and governments – with political parties in Spain and Scotland winning elections with promises to reduce the working week, and government backing being given to large-scale trials in Australia (Veal, 2023).

So, is it inevitable?

What may be the drawbacks?

The South Cambridgeshire District Council trial has become politically charged, as indeed has some of the debate around remote and hybrid working. The Minister for Local Government asked that the Council cease its four-day working week trial, citing concerns for value for money for residents (Cave, 2023).

Pressure from numerous sources could also affect this. A change in the financial health of the business could lead to pressure to revert to a more traditional five-day working week in the hope that more time leads to more money – and in some jobs where revenue is intrinsically linked to time worked, this could be a real risk.

The UK trials have focused on maintaining productivity while reducing time worked. There is a danger, as was seen with Liverpool Business School's research, that this would lead to work intensification and stress, as employees find themselves delivering the same volume and output of work but in less time.

The difficulties of making a reduced working week work while maintaining the same level of service delivery to customers and clients could be problematic. There are solutions – hiring more staff, splitting shifts and even reducing operational service hours – but the context for each business needs examining first.

There is a challenge in how to deal with those who already work a reduced working week. For example, if someone works 20 hours where the full-time contracted hours are 40, they work 50 per cent of the working week. If the working week reduces to 32 hours, but the rate of pay for working 32 hours remains the same as it was for 40 hours, what happens to the 50 per cent contract? Do they remain on 50 per cent by decreasing their hours from 20 to 16, and keep the same pay? Or do they remain on 20 hours, and possibly increase their pay as they would then work 62 per cent of the working week?

Other people whose jobs are paid hourly may need to work more in a shorter period to maintain pay, and there is a risk of a two-tier workforce as a result (Thompson and Czechowski, 2022). Similarly, other workers may be tempted to skip lunch breaks or intensify their working hours simply to maintain the promised productivity – and those aren't good outcomes.

It must also be noted that many of the organizations engaged in the trials worldwide have focused mostly on office-based employees, and different types of work will have different challenges – meaning the benefits will also be different and potentially harder to realize. Like issues with remote and hybrid work, this could be a divisive issue in some organizations.

There are other possible barriers around adjusting holiday entitlements, pension contributions and anything else that may be calculated based on hours worked. For some organizations, a combination of these factors may be enough to put them off the idea of reducing the working week.

How do we do it?

Much like with making hybrid working work, the answer is in being intentional about what you want to achieve, but also about being contextual to your situation. There is, as with hybrid working, no one size fits all approach. For some organizations a four-day working week is appropriate. For others, a nine-day fortnight, or split shifts, or reduced hours over the same number of days – and more permutations. You must work out what is best for your organization and not be tempted to follow the crowd. And no one has said that all employees in your organization must have the same working arrangements either.

It is important to build in flexibility. The gains resulting from effective hybrid working are premised often on flexibility. If we reduce the working week, we should not reduce flexibility but perhaps increase it further. For example, if an organization implements a four-day working week or nine-day fortnight, it may not suit everyone, and we should allow people to request to remain on their current working arrangements if justifiable. A useful approach would be to talk to each individual employee to offer them options for how to spread their hours over a reduced pattern – perhaps utilizing some of the options mentioned earlier in this chapter. Combining this with a part of the week that every employee *must* work may help with multiple cultural and internal communication issues too – like anchor days for hybrid workers.

Improving productivity and coming up with new ways of working – process redesign – is likely critical to making a reduced working week work – again, like with making hybrid working work. Some of the suggestions about changing work processes that are covered in the next chapters will likely help here too, such as examining what could be automated, what could be removed altogether and what could be done by different people or teams. You could plan for this, with groups of employees looking collaboratively at what efficiencies can be made and how to make processes (and jobs and the required outputs) workable within the available time.

Finally, you should look to phase this in over time. While there are attractions of a 'big bang' style approach with everyone changing on the same day, phasing it may be more attractive. Citizens Advice Gateshead, part of the 2022–2023 UK trial, implemented the change in three waves spread over three months to help smooth the transition. It reported that 'each wave benefitted from the learning and experiences of those who had gone earlier' (Bernard, 2023). Even the five-day working week took time to trial and implement, with Henry Ford's motor company spending three years introducing it before making it a permanent arrangement (4 Day Week Global, nd). Don't expect to solve a major challenge like this overnight, or in one go.

How does a reduced working week affect remote and hybrid working?

It may not, but it could. There is a risk that in giving employees something as significant and possibly life changing as a reduced working week, employers may feel that that is enough and not want to continue with hybrid working arrangements. Or vice versa. Research by Unispace suggested that 46 per cent of employees felt that if they could achieve a four-day working week then this would make them happy enough to come on site every day (Unispace, 2023). We must guard against this.

Hybrid working, when done effectively, involves personalizing the employee experience and recrafting roles so that there is more autonomy and more appropriate decisions are made about where and when work is done – and how it is done. The types of discussions that lead to this would also be suitable to have if discussing reducing the working week, with the same inputs and possible outputs from the discussion. Therefore, my suggestion is that they go together.

The bigger and wider debates around a reduced working week

So far in this chapter we've focused on why and how a reduced working week could benefit individual employees and by extension their organizations. The various worldwide pilots are at too early a stage to say for certain, but the initial results are promising – the benefits can be realized. This brings up several other interesting points to consider though.

Research from the Bennett Institute for Public Policy suggests that a reduced working week leads to increased community well-being and volunteering due to the increased leisure time available, which strengthens community cohesion and ties (Jörden, 2023). This could open more opportunities for different categories of people to return to, or stay for longer, in the workforce. Combined with hybrid working, which we talk about in a later chapter as having the potential to redefine how we use local communities, there is significant potential here.

There is naturally an environmental impact from less commuting that comes with both a reduced working week and more effective hybrid working. Research by the University of Massachusetts found that a 10 per cent reduction in working hours reduced individual carbon footprint by 8.6 per cent (Broom, 2023). Research in New Zealand found that a decrease in congestion on roads in Auckland would boost that city's gross domestic product by

1.4 per cent (Barnes, 2020). Research by the University of Reading found that workers across the UK would collectively drive 557 million miles fewer per week if they worked fewer days (Barnes, 2020). Changing the working week and going fully hybrid at the same time could make a huge and positive impact on climate change.

It is possible to see how our traditional working week, with largely fixed hours and locations have historical origins – as we explored at the start of this chapter. Those things no longer apply in the modern world.

When speaking to Perry Timms, Founder of PTHR, as part of the research for this chapter, I discussed with him the wider, societal implications of a move away from a traditional five-day working week. Timms can see pros and cons from an economic perspective – some parts will benefit, others may not. We both feel that one of the biggest challenges is that the compulsory education system, at least in the UK, is not compatible yet with a move away from a traditional five-day working week (although he feels in his experience that those with caring responsibilities have improved social time with those they care for when not working five days a week).

We also spoke about how some countries already have different working arrangements, with both of us thinking about the popularity of siestas in Mediterranean countries. Work flows around that, and society also copes. Timms and I also recalled a time when, in the UK, hardly anything opened or anyone worked on a Sunday, and now society and the economy is vastly more open on Sundays. Further back, our ancestors worked six days a week and would have thought moving to five a step too far. If we can cope with those changes, we can cope with a reduced working week now.

Ultimately though we increasingly live in a 24/7 economy and society. Fixing working weeks to 40 hours or thereabouts seems arbitrary. So might 30 or 32, but we don't know until we explore it. Reducing the working week will inevitably prompt bigger debates about how we use the extra time released by this, and how this might reshape society in ways not yet fully explored.

CASE STUDY ONE

Henry Stewart is the Chief Happiness Officer at Happy, an award-winning personal development and IT software training company employing around 22

people, with another 50 associates, and based in London. Happy have operated a four-day working week since 2022, having first trialled this as early as 2019. I spoke to Henry to find out more about why they did this, and what they have learnt.

Back in 2019, Stewart was conscious that there was a recurring theme in their engagement survey feedback that suggested Happy's long-standing reputation as a leader in innovative workplace practices and engagement was no longer keeping them ahead of their competition, as staff sometimes mentioned that other companies were catching up to Happy. As a result, Stewart found a renewed reason to innovate. He also felt that there were ways in which Happy could be innovative as well as significantly more productive and began to look at a four-day working week as a way of achieving both goals.

Happy began a one-month trial of working four days a week in August 2019. Stewart found that while many staff liked it, a decent number did not, and concluded that Happy weren't ready for the change. Stewart explained that they hadn't begun to quantify what gains there could be from this and had not had the specific experiences in the Covid-19 pandemic that solidified some of their thinking and employee views on the concept.

During that pandemic the idea resurfaced, caused at first by reduced volumes of work that meant many staff were partially furloughed and therefore not working their normal five-day working weeks. Stewart asked staff if they wanted to do a new pilot of a four-day working week and found overwhelming support for this – and the new pilot started in 2022 for six months when the company became part of the wider UK trial mentioned earlier in this chapter. To help address fears of not being ready for this, as happened in 2019, an action group was created to thoroughly plan how the change would work well before it went live.

The 2022 pilot worked on the 100:80:100 ratio so no staff saw salaries reduced when reducing their hours. Early on Happy were faced with how to deal with staff who were already working less than five days. Happy responded by giving each person a choice. They could keep to the same proportion of a full-time working week as before, reducing their hours and pay accordingly, or could keep working the same hours – thus increasing their proportion of the full-time working week they were working and therefore increasing their pay accordingly.

Happy was to remain a five-day operation from a customer perspective, and this was never in question. This meant that staff needed to work only four days out of the five that Happy were open for business. Teams were allowed to create and agree their own rotas for doing this, factoring in individual circumstances. Stewart has not needed to get involved in this as each team has come up with their own working arrangements easily.

Hybrid working has continued during this pilot, despite evidence in some other organizations that moving to a four-day working week in some ways reduces the availability of flexible, remote and hybrid working – some organizations adopting a 'one or the other' type approach. Happy have always been a largely remote organization and this hasn't been changed by the onset of the four-day working week. They did attempt to mandate one day per week in the office but found this didn't work, and cut across their ethos as an employer, so abandoned the idea and now, as before, let staff work out for themselves where and when they need to work. When they are delivering on-site courses, staff are, naturally, on site but otherwise default to remote working.

Happy don't have managers. They have coaches, and departmental 'leads', but nothing as formal as management arrangements, and therefore there hasn't been a need for leadership or management development to support the four-day working week. Staff are accountable to each other and there is a strong sense of responsibility in making things work.

I asked Stewart how he was judging the impact of the change. He said that clients were very happy as they were largely unaffected. If ever a client needs a five-day service, then the work is shared across multiple staff members. Shared email addresses for client work also helps continuity of service delivery across different staff.

Happy measure the success of their organization through customer satisfaction and revenue. Both have improved significantly during 2022 and 2023. Their net promoter score is now at 76 per cent and revenue grew by 15 per cent in 2022 and 10 per cent in 2023, with no increase in staffing overheads, which has previously been linked to such increases. Their employee engagement scores are the highest in their 30-year existence.

Stewart was conscious that unless productivity and efficiency gains were realized, then the effort involved in making this change could be wasted. Happy's staff reduced the number and duration of their meetings. Using techniques such as 'Pomodoro' (work in 25-minute bursts followed by 5-minute breaks) and Stewart's 'Eat Four Frogs' (the four most important things you must do each day), Happy found productivity gains easy to come by, reinforcing the success of the four-day working week.

Stewart was also aware that without reducing the amount of work via these productivity gains, staff could be tempted to just work longer hours across their four days. This has not happened. Before the change Happy saw staff who were contracted to work 37.5 hours often work 40 or more hours a week. After the change 72 per cent of staff report that they only work their contracted 32 hours, and even the 28 per cent of staff who don't do that report only working one to two hours a week more. Staff can spread their 32 contractual hours over five days instead of four, but none have chosen to do this. Staff report significant improvements in their well-being, work–life balance, levels of energy and more. The freedom and empowerment they are given is a key part of this.

Stewart's closing advice was that this kind of change can only work when staff are fully involved at each stage, and where there are accompanying and (at least) proportionate productivity gains. He sees society soon reaching a tipping point – the reduced working week is a significant plus in talent attraction and as more organizations do it, the momentum behind it will increase.

CASE STUDY TWO

Perry Timms is the Chief Energy Officer at PTHR, a small but growing and award-winning business consultancy. They have 12 staff based in different locations across Europe and have always been a remote company. They implemented a four-day working week in 2020 as the Covid-19 pandemic was at its height. I asked Timms why they did this, and what they have learnt from the experience.

Timms confessed that he had been thinking about the concept of a four-day working week for some years before the Covid-19 pandemic forced him into doing something about it. His previous thinking had been around addressing real or perceived barriers to career development for those working part-time hours, and how a reduced working week might mitigate those.

That pandemic forced the shift and change. Initially a reduced volume of work meant that the organization wasn't fully productive, but even as the restrictions were eased Timms noticed a general lack of energy in the organization – people were naturally focused on different things in their lives and struggling to regularly give 100 per cent to PTHR for five days a week. He decided to trial taking Wednesdays off for one month, speculating that splitting the working week into two two-day blocks would give the greatest energy boost to staff. Like Happy did, PTHR gave staff who were already working part-time hours a choice to further reduce their hours and pay or keep to the same hours for increased pay.

Timms' admittedly very crude analysis during the one-month pilot showed that productivity had increased, and efficiency was up by 20 per cent through more focused use of time. Based on this, the organization chose to make the four-day working week a permanent arrangement.

I asked Timms how the work of the organization and the lives of their employees are affected by the change. He said that occasionally a client will ask for work to be done on a Wednesday, and days off in lieu are given if that is the case. He equates that to if anyone is asked to work on a Saturday or Sunday and treats it in the same way. Similarly, if any work is only able to take place on a Wednesday, then the equivalent time is given back on a different day. To avoid the temptation of doing any work on Wednesdays, the company turn off emails and Slack channels on Wednesdays and encourage staff who are about to send an email late on a Tuesday to delay the send until Thursday morning. An app called Clockify helps people to categorize and track their working hours, so that they know when to stop and can see what has been taking up their time. This also allows Timms to see if staff are working beyond their contracted hours – and he says they are not.

As a company that has always been fully remote, Timms doesn't see that the four-day week affects remote or hybrid working at all. During the Covid-19 pandemic PTHR experimented with a virtual reality office to provide the ad hoc interactions that may have taken place if they were all co-located with each other. After a while they realized that this wasn't adding anything and abandoned it. They now use improved functionality on apps like Slack to manage these types of informal interactions.

Interestingly, PTHR implemented an unlimited annual leave policy like some other companies have done but needed some boundaries to enable this to make practical sense. Anything up to three weeks leave in a block is not questioned, but anything above that requires a discussion about how this affects work and others in the company.

Timms' advice echoes that of Stewart from Happy in the earlier case study – this kind of change can only be successful if you talk to each person about how to make it work. Some people are likely to feel threatened by this change – if they feel defined by going to work five days a week, then suddenly having a 'spare' day can feel unsettling. Timms would encourage different options to be considered – he says working patterns are not a binary 'four versus five' choice – and that individual circumstances and natural rhythms need to be factored in too.

Case study reflections

In our first case study, Happy, the following points stand out for consideration:

- Trials and pilots are important to get a feel for whether a four-day week would work, but even those need careful planning and cannot be left to chance.

- Making early and transparent decisions about what happens to full-time and part-time salaries is important. Giving those already working part time some choice in the matter is also helpful.

- Reducing individual contracted hours doesn't mean reducing business operational hours. It can, but it doesn't have to.

- Encouraging teams to work out their own rostering arrangements can be helpful, but only if the team is sufficiently mature to be able to do this effectively.

- Remote and hybrid working need not be affected by the implementation of a four-day working week, nor vice versa.

- Considering workflow across individuals and teams is a key part of making the change work – how will clients, customers and wider stakeholders' communications and requests, and work, be affected?

- Productivity gains must be realized if the change is to work. There are multiple ways this can be achieved but achieved it must be.

- Keeping a close eye on healthy working practices is important to avoid drift back into older working patterns and avoid simply introducing a compressed hours pattern by accident.

- Talking to staff throughout will enable their views to be heard and considered.

In the second case study, PTHR, some similar and some different points stand out for consideration:

- We can often be pushing at an open door when talking about moving away from a traditional five-day working week. Sometimes that can be to do with external factors, individual circumstances, business situations and more – but there may be sufficient momentum already to make it work.

- If you make the decision to close the business on one day, consult widely about which day this is and give clarity about how work will flow around that day.

- Be clear on what circumstances may lead to a temporary alteration to working patterns and what happens in those situations.

- Improved functionality available on many apps can open lots of potential to explore productivity, working time, working practices and organizational culture in different ways.

- Be mindful that some people will feel threatened by such a significant change. Allow them to explore their emotions and individual circumstances with support.

The action plan

If you are exploring moving away from a traditional five-day working week, the following questions could be answered:

- How compatible is the traditional eight-hour, five-day working week for the circumstances of any individual in your organization?

- What percentage of your organization already do not work a five-day week and what lessons can be learnt from their experiences?

- How could the work being done around hybrid working and redesigning tasks help you to look at reducing the working week?

- Why does your organization need to retain a five-day working week? What are the views of key stakeholders here?

- What alternatives to the five-day working week seem appealing, and why?

- How would a trial of an alternative work?

- Where do decision makers stand on this issue, and what is the process by which they would decide?

- What assumptions about the working week do you need to challenge in your organization, and how will you do that?

- Where there are public holidays that reduce the working week for your organization, how does work flow around those? What lessons can be learnt from that?
- How will you encourage employees to examine processes, workflows and productivity to enable a reduction in the working week?
- How will you treat those who already work a reduced week?
- What will be the measures that you track to see the impact?
- Does your organization need to maintain five days (or more) for service delivery? If so, what would need to happen to keep that going while reducing the working week for individuals?
- How would you avoid intensifying work and creating a negative impact on levels of stress?

References and further reading

4 Day Week Global (nd) Frequently asked questions, www.4dayweek.com/faqs (archived at https://perma.cc/4YAE-YSHL)

Baker, S and Hunt, T (2022) Legal pitfalls of the four-day working week, *HR Magazine*, 28 October, www.hrmagazine.co.uk/content/comment/legal-pitfalls-of-the-four-day-working-week/ (archived at https://perma.cc/968H-YAJP)

Barnes, A. (2020) I pioneered the four-day week – now policymakers must adopt it to fight the climate crisis, *The Guardian*, 29 January, www.theguardian.com/commentisfree/2020/jan/30/i-pioneered-the-4-day-week-now-it-must-be-used-to-fight-the-climate-crisis (archived at https://perma.cc/YZF5-ZSAR)

Bernard, D (2023) Four-day week trial hailed a success for businesses and workers, *HR Magazine*, 21 February, www.hrmagazine.co.uk/content/news/four-day-week-trial-hailed-a-success-for-businesses-and-workers/ (archived at https://perma.cc/PB5M-PZAK)

Broom, D (2023) Four-day work week trial in Spain leads to healthier workers, less pollution, World Economic Forum, 25 October, www.weforum.org/agenda/2023/03/surprising-benefits-four-day-week/ (archived at https://perma.cc/5RJ7-55ZR)

Campbell, C (2023) The six questions everyone is asking us about the four-day week, Timewise, June, www.timewise.co.uk/article/the-six-questions-everyone-is-asking-us-about-the-four-day-week/ (archived at https://perma.cc/DHU8-9S4H)

Carers UK (2019) Juggling Work and Unpaid Care: A growing issue, January, www.carersuk.org/media/no2lwyxl/juggling-work-and-unpaid-care-report-final-web.pdf (archived at https://perma.cc/F864-F7PY)

Cave, D (2023) Four-day week: Exploring the conundrums and change-reticence, *People Management*, 5 July, www.peoplemanagement.co.uk/article/1828954/four-day-week-exploring-conundrums-change-reticence (archived at https://perma.cc/7YJP-4AM8)

Crush, P (2022) Does a four-day week undermine true flexibility? *HR Magazine*, 25 January, www.hrmagazine.co.uk/content/news/does-a-four-day-week-undermine-true-flexibility (archived at https://perma.cc/WTM8-G27C)

Dale, G. (2023) The four day week – new research on the benefits and challenges, LinkedIn, 3 July, www.linkedin.com/pulse/four-day-week-new-research-benefits-challenges-gemma-dale/ (archived at https://perma.cc/3HN6-Q6JS)

Economist (2021) Could a four-day working week become the norm? *The Economist*, 8 June, www.economist.com/the-economist-explains/2021/07/08/could-a-four-day-working-week-become-the-norm (archived at https://perma.cc/CC8S-V8MZ)

Fontinelle, A (2022) The impact of working a 4-day week, Investopedia, 13 November, www.investopedia.com/the-impact-of-working-a-4-day-week-5203640 (archived at https://perma.cc/G2VD-KBGQ)

Giattino, C, Ortiz-Ospina, E and Roser, M (2020) Working Hours, Our World in Data, https://ourworldindata.org/working-hours (archived at https://perma.cc/3WE9-2BQ8)

Glover, E (2021) How a four-day week could transform society, *Huck*, 9 September, www.huckmag.com/article/how-a-four-day-week-could-transform-society (archived at https://perma.cc/8YXE-4YE3)

Grund, C and Tilkes, K R (2023) Working time mismatch and job satisfaction – the role of employees' time autonomy and gender, *The International Journal of Human Resource Management*, 34 (20), pp 4003–25

Hall, R (2024) Four-day week made permanent for most UK firms in world's biggest trial, *The Guardian*, 21 February, www.theguardian.com/money/2024/feb/21/four-day-week-made-permanent-for-most-uk-firms-in-worlds-biggest-trial (archived at https://perma.cc/E8V7-ECTD)

Hoyle, G (nd) How we successfully moved to a four-day working week, Marketing Signals, www.marketingsignals.com/how-we-successfully-moved-to-a-four-day-working-week/ (archived at https://perma.cc/U4TP-9BWM)

Ingram, H (2023) 11 four-day working week alternatives, Talk Staff, 17 May, www.talkstaff.co.uk/four-day-working-week-alternatives/ (archived at https://perma.cc/2CAS-YX26)

Jörden, N (2023) Will a four-day work week boost the economy and workforce? Bennett Institute for Public Policy, 15 May, www.bennettinstitute.cam.ac.uk/blog/four-day-work-week/ (archived at https://perma.cc/PU5D-FBGB)

Lord-Pottinger, Y (nd) Rolling out a 9-day fortnight: How it works in real life, CharlieHR Blog, www.charliehr.com/blog/nine-day-fortnight-results/ (archived at https://perma.cc/A7P3-KR4S)

Machell, M (2023) Bank holidays in May intensified workload for 67% of employees, *HR Magazine*, 6 June, www.hrmagazine.co.uk/content/news/bank-holidays-in-may-intensified-workload-for-67-of-employees (archived at https://perma.cc/M6UJ-RYTG)

Olsson, H and Rigby, N (2023) Council four-day week trial may have saved £333,000, BBC News, 18 June, www.bbc.co.uk/news/uk-england-cambridgeshire-65856527.amp (archived at https://perma.cc/Z63L-8P4W)

Otte, J (2023) 'It's just not worth it': Why full-time work no longer pays in the UK, *The Guardian*, 13 February, www.theguardian.com/business/2023/feb/13/full-time-part-time-work-no-longer-pays-uk-economy (archived at https://perma.cc/Z7N9-S5PG)

Ribeiro, C (2023) 'Can I just ... rest?': guilt, the four-day working week and what to do with the fifth day, *The Guardian*, 21 May, www.theguardian.com/money/2023/may/22/can-i-just-rest-guilt-the-four-day-working-week-and-what-to-do-with-the-fifth-day (archived at https://perma.cc/79FT-A7XA)

Thompson, S and Czechowski, A (2022) Why the four-day week won't work, *HR Magazine,* 6 September, www.hrmagazine.co.uk/content/comment/why-the-four-day-week-wont-work/ (archived at https://perma.cc/VX6W-KHZA)

Tichborne, J (2022) I just moved to a four-day week, without losing any pay. It's changed everything, *The Guardian*, 4 July, www.theguardian.com/commentisfree/2022/jul/04/four-day-week-pay-family-volunteering-produc-tivity (archived at https://perma.cc/TTD7-P4FB)

Unispace (2023) Returning for Good, www.unispace.com/returning-for-good (archived at https://perma.cc/KJZ2-545F)

Veal, A (2020) A life of long weekends is alluring, but the shorter working day may be more practical, *The Conversation*, 12 January, www.theconversation.com/a-life-of-long-weekends-is-alluring-but-the-shorter-working-day-may-be-more-practical-127817 (archived at https://perma.cc/3VKY-L8H3)

Veal, A (2021) The success of Iceland's 'four-day week' trial has been greatly overstated, *The Conversation*, 13 July, www.theconversation.com/the-success-of-icelands-four-day-week-trial-has-been-greatly-overstated-164083 (archived at https://perma.cc/U76U-JVDA)

Veal, A (2023) 4-day work week trials have been labelled a 'resounding success'. But 4 big questions need answers, *The Conversation*, 23 March, www.theconversation.com/4-day-work-week-trials-have-been-labelled-a-resounding-success-but-4-big-questions-need-answers-201476 (archived at https://perma.cc/7DXQ-R5MN)

Sketchnote Summary For Part One

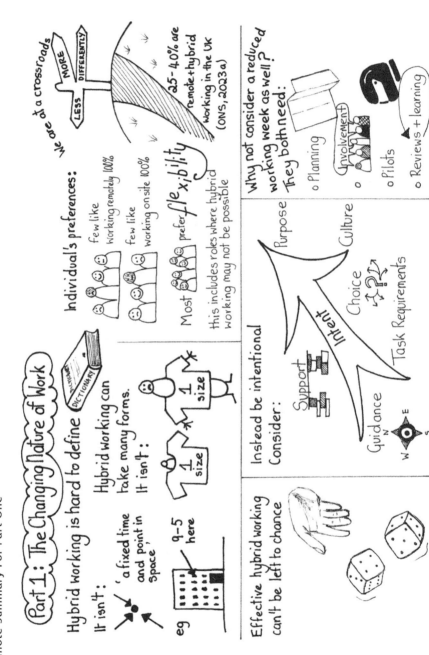

Part 1: The Changing Nature of Work

Hybrid working is hard to define

It isn't:

eg 9-5 here → 'a fixed time and point in Space'

Hybrid working can take many forms. It isn't:

1 size → 1 size

We are at a crossroads

MORE / LESS / DIFFERENTLY

Individual's preferences:

- few like working remotely 100%
- few like working on site 100%

Most prefer flexibility

This includes roles where hybrid working may not be possible

25 - 40% are remote + hybrid working in the UK (ONS, 2023a)

Effective hybrid working can't be left to chance

Instead be intentional Consider:

Purpose

Intent

Choice

Culture

Task Requirements

Support

Guidance
N W E S

Why not consider a reduced working week as well? They both need:

- o Planning
- o Involvement
- o Pilots
- o Reviews + learning

Making hybrid working work

4

No one size fits all

The shorter read

True hybrid working is more than simply allowing people to work part of their working time at home. There are different options to consider, and rarely is there a one size fits all approach for an entire organization.

What many organizations have adopted as their hybrid working approach is what can be called a fixed hybrid model, but this is often based on an arbitrary days-of-the-week split. While this could work, it is likely only to work more through luck than judgement. It can ride roughshod over the nature of the work being done, as well as individual circumstances and preferences. It can deprive employees of the autonomy they need to make hybrid working work.

There is no magic number of days an employee should spend on site versus remote working, other than a consensus that too much of either extreme can lead to significant downsides. But employers who mandate a fixed hybrid approach suffer in other ways too, as do the employees forced to work in such models. Yet there *are* other models that could be adopted, though each has their pros and cons. Your context matters, both in terms of you as an individual employee (and parent, partner, carer, etc.) and your organization. This means that individuals or teams must create their own hybrid working approach – and it is OK if that is different to what other individuals or teams do.

Clearly not all tasks can – without changing them – work in a hybrid way, but other forms of flexibility and job crafting can enable more of a hybrid approach than many would first think. The rise of artificial intelligence and greater automation supplies a wonderful opportunity to rethink how many jobs are done, including some that many would think could never be done remotely.

We know from earlier chapters that we struggle to define hybrid working. There's also no agreed definition of what working is either. There never has been a one size fits all approach to it. Each hybrid worker already has a personalized employee experience, but our organizational practices haven't always caught up to that. In the remote part of a hybrid working model, the employee has usually already personalized their space, their tasks, their equipment and much more – but rarely has that been followed through in a comparable way for the on-site part of the hybrid model. But it should.

We must carefully redesign the on-site experience, based on individual preferences, task requirements and more. There are lots of organizations that have already done this. They aren't leaving things to chance. And there is the key to making hybrid working work – don't leave it to chance. Be intentional, conscious, deliberate about each part of the whole employee experience.

Work should be designed around what the task requirements are, followed by individual preferences. Work that was previously done exclusively on site will need changes to make it work in a hybrid setting. Teams will need to coordinate workflows and communication and more. Cross-team coordination will also be needed. Managers and employees will need guidance on how to do all of this.

There are lots of hints here about the organization design implications of hybrid working. Again, this cannot be left to chance. There are cultural issues to address, and a big move away from defining work by location – or teams by location. This means changes to team structures and organizational structures, as well as the way work is done and flows across the organization. Process redesign, building in more flexibility, is necessary.

If we had a blank canvas and could build our organizations again from scratch as truly hybrid organizations, what decisions would we need to make then? It is those decisions we need to make now.

The longer read

The forced hybrid approach – arbitrary days-of-the-week splits

True hybrid working is more than just saying that people can spend some of their working time in the physical workplace and some of it working remotely. It is of course more complex than that – somehow, we must take the best bits of both experiences and blend them together into something different, something better. But what?

There will always be work that needs to be conducted face to face, and there will always be individual preferences around ways of working. However, it is not necessarily a binary choice – there are lots of different options to consider, and an individualized or team-based approach may prove a more workable solution for many.

There is no one size fits all definition of hybrid working and we need to consider multiple versions of it all happening simultaneously in our organizations. This has implications for not just where and when people do their work, but how they do it. Furthermore, the design of the places and spaces where they do it, as well as the redesigning of some of the tasks themselves.

What we see in many organizations though is a fixed hybrid model, where there is an often arbitrary days-of-the-week split – something like insisting employees are on site two days a week and work remotely for the rest, though any other similar arrangement would also be classed as fixed hybrid. There are dangers in that approach, though.

Person X was a senior leader at Company X until the middle of 2023. Person X has requested anonymity, but Company X is a healthcare charity employing around 450 people working across France, but with one office in Paris. Since the Covid-19 pandemic Company X employees had been expected to come on site around one day per month, though more senior roles had an expectation of two days per month. Many staff lived a long way from the Paris office, with Person X living on the Atlantic coast and other staff even further away. Most staff, including Person X, were happy with the loose hybrid approach – managers did not enforce the expectations and the entire company worked on the basis that they should come on site 'when the work needed you to'.

In late 2022 this approach changed. New starters were now needed to work on site two days a week. Existing staff were allowed to keep their arrangements if they lived a long way away or had particular needs, but only if they remained in the same jobs – any new job they moved to in Company X would now be a fixed hybrid one. There had been no consultation or engagement before this was announced, and no evidence was provided with the announcement to explain why this change was needed. Most staff were thus very unhappy and gave strong feedback to Company X about this approach. The views expressed by staff were not taken on board, though the implementation of the new approach was delayed until spring 2023.

Person X's own circumstances meant that they would find it impossible to achieve the fixed hybrid approach, but they were allowed to keep their existing arrangements if they stayed in the same job. This put a ceiling on Person X's career ambitions within Company X, and the same was true for all staff. Person X told me about a highly valued and top-performing member of their team who worked fully remote as they lived near the Spanish border but were prevented from reaching any more senior roles (which they wanted and would have succeeded in) because of the fixed hybrid model now in place. Again, a ceiling was put in place for this person.

Person X was a member of the senior team and reported that many of that team were unhappy about the new approach but were overruled by the chief executive. Staff turnover began to increase dramatically at Company X as people left for jobs that better suited the way they worked and their own personal circumstances. Person X hired new members of their team into fixed hybrid positions and felt guilty that these people were forced to be on site two days a week, but as a manager Person X's pre-existing arrangement was allowed to continue, and they could be on site much less as a result.

As turnover increased, Person X decided to leave also. Person X had two exit interviews and cited the fixed hybrid approach as the reason for their leaving but was told that this feedback was not going to be shared with the senior team but collated alongside other pieces of exit interview feedback, anonymized and sanitized. Person X felt the exit interview was a tick-box exercise and that Company X were not interested in listening to feedback about the fixed hybrid approach, having made up their mind that that was their preferred way of working.

Person X also shared that fellow directors who are unhappy with the fixed hybrid approach will often not enforce it and ignore those who work outside it, with no attempts to measure if people are following it. Person X wonders, if the fixed hybrid policy can be ignored, whether that raises questions about the enforceability of other organizational policies and practices.

Finally, Person X reported that Company X are keen that every member of staff has their own desk, and therefore keep a far larger office location than they need, with occupancy levels on any given day well below 30 per cent – the fixed hybrid approach is now costing the organization money.

In the example we see some of the risks in a fixed hybrid model that is arbitrary, and which therefore runs roughshod over the nature of the tasks being undertaken and individual circumstances. While in theory a fixed hybrid model sounds sensible and even attractive – striking a compromise between fully remote and fully on site – it can deprive employees of the autonomy that they often need. If we give people a fixed amount of time that they must be on site, we are dictating where and often when they should work – this isn't hybrid working in its true form, as it lacks the flexibility that is implied within it. And yet fixed hybrid models are among the most common hybrid models in place.

The downsides of fixed hybrid models

A fixed hybrid model can have downsides. The lack of flexibility can affect those whose personal lives require them to have more flexible approaches to where and when work is done. Examples may be parents or those with caring responsibilities, but also anyone who has a particular advantage when working in their own home with the set-up how they like and need it – indeed research suggests that 15–18 per cent of workers self-select as having an impairment that impacts them at work (Christian, 2023).

In a general sense, people tend to react well to situations where they feel some control over it and have some choice about what to do. A fixed hybrid model can remove those things, and therefore threatens much of the conditions under which many people feel they can thrive.

Research by the University of Leeds suggested that there is no 'sweet spot' for a specific number of fixed days on site, as too many factors influence what works best, and too much time on site is detrimental. The same research also suggests that if a fixed hybrid approach is to be put in place, it needs to factor in job tasks, business requirements and employee preferences, giving choice and control (within reason) to the individual (Davis et al, 2022).

Research by Unispace suggested that 29 per cent of employers who implemented a fixed hybrid approach (or fully on site) are finding it harder to recruit, that 42 per cent are struggling with retention and 21 per cent have lost key members of staff (Unispace, 2023).

Fixed hybrid models have also been found to be mentally and emotionally exhausting. In research done for the BBC, examples are seen of employees who initially were grateful for a fixed hybrid model but began to resent the permanency and lack of flexibility it brought (Christian, 2022). This research shows that physically keeping two identical set-ups (home and on site) and switching between the two, with all the planning that this takes in a fixed hybrid model, is exhausting for 80 per cent of managers, and 72 per cent of employees (Christian, 2022). The disruption to normal daily routines is the chief cause of this, followed by the physical carrying of work and equipment back and forth.

All these downsides assume that the fixed hybrid model has no science underpinning it – that it has been implemented arbitrarily and applies to all teams equally (which may not be what each team would want or need). And we know that this is difficult to do when work, and life, are so different for each person.

Are fixed hybrid models all bad?

Not necessarily. A fixed hybrid model can be beneficial. Research suggests that for a sizeable minority of employees, the structure and certainty that a fixed hybrid model brings can be helpful (Davis et al, 2022). And where increased flexibility can be accommodated by talking to employees and factoring in their circumstances, individual approaches to a fixed hybrid model could provide a better solution for many – for example, changing start and finish times, providing different equipment or allowing work to take place at different parts of the on-site location.

I spoke to a paralegal at a law firm based in Atlanta, Georgia. The organization has offices around the US and internationally too.

The paralegal had not worked remotely until the Covid-19 pandemic began, though their husband had, and their home had the right equipment, environment and set-up to facilitate multiple remote workers in the household. Up until 2020, they had worked on site for the organization but on reduced hours to enable them to manage childcare responsibilities. They had found working on site difficult for that reason but found that working remotely enabled them to balance those responsibilities more easily.

NO ONE SIZE FITS ALL   95

Most of the law firm's employees are on site three times a week. The paralegal goes on site once a week, which coincides with the weekly team meeting. They believe that their own arrangements are slightly different because of their greater level of experience but also to reflect their reduced hours and variable childcare commitments. They maintain good working relationships with their colleagues via Microsoft Teams channels in between the on-site days.

The increase in hybrid working by its employees has led to the law firm halving the size of their Atlanta office, meaning that most people share a workspace and access it when their sharer is working remotely. The paralegal consciously saves certain tasks for their on-site day which require them to do more physical work such as preparing hard-copy bundles (though they note that across the organization there is much less hard-copy paperwork than there was pre-pandemic).

New starters at the law firm are required to be on site 100 per cent of their time for their first six months and, assuming good performance levels, can begin hybrid working after that. The paralegal believes that this system works well and that, overall, the company is reasonably content with its hybrid working approach. They explained that some managers may want their staff on site more often simply for increased human connection, but that performance at the law firm has not suffered because of the implementation of hybrid working. The paralegal is very happy with their own arrangement, and believes most employees are too.

At the law firm in the example, we see how a fixed hybrid approach has some built-in flexibility to account for individual circumstances, and how the on-site experience is tailored to fit the work being done.

There will, of course, be potential benefits of a fixed hybrid approach in terms of bringing teams together on site at the same time, making scheduling of training, meetings and socializing opportunities easier. This may also make planning on-site spaces (desks, meeting rooms, car parking and more) an easier task too. All of this requires careful, intentional thought and action – it cannot be left to chance.

Unfortunately, in my experience many organizations with a fixed hybrid approach are indeed leaving it to chance and have not analysed whether the approach is the most beneficial one for them.

But what else is there?

If a fixed hybrid model, with an often-arbitrary days-of-the-week split, is not the most appropriate for your organization, what could be?

Table 4.1 gives some alternatives you could consider.

TABLE 4.1 Some other types of hybrid models

Weekly splits	This would see employees working on site for complete weeks, and then remotely for complete weeks. It can allow much better use of on-site locations and bring whole teams together for longer periods but can have the same downsides as a fixed hybrid model.
Team-driven fixed hybrid	This model sees each team able to decide its own fixed hybrid approach. Some teams will opt for more on-site time, and others more remote time. Teams can therefore work in ways that suit them and the tasks they do better. There would also be advantages in knowing how much on-site space would be needed, and it minimizes the risks associated with organization-wide fixed hybrid approaches. However, cross-functional working can become more difficult in this arrangement unless there is some coordination between teams.
Core hours on site	This model would see employees on site for specific timeslots on specific days (for example 10 am to 2 pm) but outside of those hours they can choose where they work. The big advantage of this is that there will be definite portions of the day where collaborative work could and should be scheduled and should lead to employees making more right choices about what work to do outside of the core hours. It can also help those employees for whom school runs are important to be able to do. For those living a good distance away from the on-site location it can be inefficient, however, leading to people almost being forced to remain on site, or wasting time commuting.
Flexible hybrid	This allows employees to choose when and where they work. It can lead to some choosing to be fully remote and others fully on site. While empowering, it can make managing on-site space difficult to plan, but does allow for people to make a choice each day about the best place to do the work they have planned that day. It also makes planning team get-togethers more complicated.

It would be possible for each team within your organization to adopt a model from the table, or a fixed hybrid approach, for itself – but for other teams to make different choices. This means that there could never be a one size fits all approach to hybrid in an organization – but that's OK.

Can any or every job be hybrid?

A controversial statement, but there is no such thing as a job that can't be hybrid. What there are though are tasks that cannot be hybrid. Where we have issues is where jobs are made up entirely of such tasks. That is the result of a conscious decision to design a job and write a job description that way. It also means it could be designed in a different way for some of the tasks.

But there will be tasks that have no chance of being done in a hybrid way. But that may also be OK. We explored in Chapter 1 some of the flexibility that may be explored for front-line roles. However, if a role could be hybrid, then my view is that it should be. There should be no return to the situation in some organizations where types of flexible working, particularly working from home, was the preserve of senior employees only. If a role cannot be worked in a hybrid way, then it should be the responsibility of the manager of that role to have a conversation about what flexibility there could be and help the jobholder(s) understand the reasons why their role cannot be a hybrid one.

Roles that need a degree of physical interaction with equipment or other humans are often accompanied by a requirement to be on site and synchronous with whatever is being interacted with (Nurski, 2021). The types of tasks that a job includes are relatively easy to analyse in terms of what can be done without a fixed time, fixed location approach. We will examine a model to help with this analysis in the next chapter, but research has shown that almost every job task has an element of it that can be done without a fixed time, fixed location requirement (Nurski, 2021). Even those tasks that currently have zero potential for remote work (such as operating machinery and moving objects) have, with automation and artificial intelligence, greater potential to move away from a fixed time, fixed location requirement.

Therefore, when answering the question 'can any or every job be hybrid?' we should not just consider jobs in their entirety but whether each task in those jobs could be hybrid. We should also consider what potential there will be in the future to make those tasks hybrid.

No one size fits all – and that's OK

We realized in our first chapter that we cannot really define what hybrid working is, only what it isn't. This means there isn't a one size fits all approach. You cannot compare apples to apples, because your definition and understanding of what hybrid working is different to how others see it. Hybrid working isn't, never has been and can never be, the same for everyone.

But has there ever been uniformity about what work is? There hasn't. We all live and work differently, and we always have. There's no one size fits all approach to working, especially hybrid working – and yet many organizations seem to think that we have to create one for hybrid working despite never doing so for working. The Covid-19 pandemic and our early experiments with hybrid working have shown that we have all had remarkably diverse experiences. Those who work hybrid may do the same job as another employee, but because they do part of it in their own home, or another space of their choosing, means that they already have an individualized employee experience. It means they already have a personalized hybrid working arrangement. We cannot treat everyone the same by applying a one size fits all approach to hybrid working when they already have their own hybrid working arrangements.

As we explored earlier in this chapter, a fixed hybrid model does have some advantages but if we impose this type of arrangement without proper consultation, we will ignore individual preferences about how, when and where people want to work. A fixed hybrid model may well work for some employees and some teams but won't work for everyone. Research suggests that organizations that mandate a fixed hybrid approach where the tasks themselves lend themselves to flexibility can see decreased engagement, reduced retention rates, lost productivity and more (Tilo, 2023). A lack of control over when, where and how work is done reduces what we get back from employees.

Instead, where tasks allow for flexibility on when, where and how work is done, we could consider personal preferences and circumstances. We may also be able to redistribute tasks across the team to enable greater matches between individual preferences and task flexibility (Nurski, 2021).

What kinds of individual preferences could there be about when, where and how work is done? Research suggests that personality influences these types of decisions – more extraverted employees choose to work more on site (Davis et al, 2022). As personality traits are long established, mandating a fixed hybrid approach that ignores such preferences is unlikely to result in personality change. It is more likely to result in resentment. Giving everyone the same hybrid working experience by mandating a set time on site is not guaranteed to improve anything – in-person experiences can be extremely helpful and positive, but they must be designed carefully to achieve the benefits we want them to have.

This means that if we do mandate fixed hybrid approaches, we must be clear what employees are to do when coming on site. So, if we implement hybrid working, we must gather information on individual preferences and circumstances but most of all how the tasks are done. We must look at what technology and equipment are needed to support each task and build something that is unique to each employee.

There cannot be a one size fits all approach unless each employee does the same tasks, in the same way, at the same time and in the same location.

This is supported by two CIPD-supplied case studies on personalizing hybrid working. In one covering Scottish Water, the organization has been led by the definition that hybrid working is about working out where the work is best done. This involves a collaborative approach to decide the right work environment for each task, and consideration of what one's team may need from the person completing the task, as well as individual circumstances. It has resulted in a wide range of working patterns and arrangements being adopted, with vast amounts of flexibility from both employer and employees (CIPD, nd).

In the CIPD's second case study, from the Principality Building Society, employees are given the autonomy to make their own decisions about how work is done. They are given the choice every day to shape how, when and where they work so that the needs of the organization, their team and own circumstances are balanced. They support this with comprehensive training for managers and employees on how to work best in this arrangement. Open and transparent conversations take place where each person shares their own arrangements and preferences about how they work, and each team then develops a way of working that incorporates these individual arrangements. Each team has a different hybrid working approach from other teams (CIPD, 2023).

Don't leave it to chance

Throughout this book I have stressed how to make hybrid working work; we must be intentional about it – making conscious, deliberate decisions about how to do it best. This means we cannot leave things to chance. If we do, we risk an aimless experience, frustrating for many or all, and not achieving anything, mostly because we do not know what we want it to achieve.

One of the more common criticisms of remote and hybrid working is that we can lose the 'water-cooler conversations' – the ad hoc, spontaneous conversations that collective memory tells us used to happen regularly when co-located on site. As I explored in *HR for Hybrid Working*, these were not chance occurrences. They were the result of conscious organization design that ensured that people doing certain tasks were co-located in a specific environment and met each other while doing those tasks. But because few or maybe none of us were around when those things were consciously designed, we think that they weren't consciously designed. We are faced with an opportunity to consciously design something different – something better – and get hung up on how impossible it might be. We have forgotten that our predecessors already did this.

What on-site working did give to some people was sight of what other people were doing. This led to whole cultures springing up around presenteeism, visibility and performance being about inputs (for example hours worked). It also led to work being viewed as being about location, and this viewpoint often dominates how many people view hybrid working – as being about location only. The model explored in Chapter 11 of *HR for Hybrid Working* and expanded upon in Chapter 5 of this book could help to examine this differently.

Work should be designed around the task, and the individual(s) performing that task. This means we must fully understand what the requirements are of each task, and what the needs of the individual performing the task are. Where a task would benefit from collaborative (or synchronous) working, we can design ways in which that will happen. Gartner calls this intentional collaboration (Gartner, 2023). We can go further and ensure all are clear on when, where and how collaboration will happen – giving guidance on how often employees should check in with each other and their managers. We should devote time to finding out how employees are working, how they are feeling, and whether the environment in which they do each task is the most conducive to that task and their unique ways of working.

The CIPD's case study from Principality Building Society shows how that organization has been intentional about hybrid working by creating a policy that:

- Sets out the reasons for introducing hybrid working and what it means.
- Clarifies the difference between hybrid working and 100 per cent home-based roles (which may be available by request).
- Outlines 10 key principles of hybrid working, including what employees can expect.

- Includes guidelines for working hours and keeping in touch, balancing the needs of the individual, team and business.

- Includes recommendations to support well-being, including taking regular breaks, not working when ill, maintaining connections, and ensuring a break of at least 11 hours between one workday and the next.

- Covers equipment entitlement, health and safety procedures, data protection requirements for remote working, and reimbursement for costs and expenses (CIPD, 2023).

This is supported with regular engagement and communication activities to find out how employees are feeling and working. Consistently evaluating what is working and what is not is critical to finding the most right working arrangements for everyone.

In the example we see Principality not leaving things to chance, and nor should we. We should ask employees how they would like to work and explore any gaps between that and the reality. Where there are gaps, we could rebalance activities and tasks across the team to ensure that we get closer to the ideal scenario. In our next chapter we will look at ways to do this and other ways of reimagining work. We should also encourage people to explore the impact that their preferred way of working has on others in their team, and on their manager – and vice versa. This may enable employees to view their work in a much broader context and see other perspectives of hybrid working.

When there are hybrid working arrangements across entire teams, someone needs to work out how the work schedule and various other aspects of team operations will work on a practical level. This does not need to be the manager. In Chapter 10 we will look at ways to do this. Expectations must be set and agreed between all team members, and with their manager, about how and when work is done, how communication is managed and more.

Nivedita Deshpande is HR Director at Visible Alpha, a fintech organization with locations worldwide. Deshpande is based in their office in Mumbai, India.

Visible Alpha have a hybrid working model which sees all employees at all their locations worldwide spend two days a week on site. These two days are fixed as Wednesday and Thursday but, for the remainder of the working week, employees can choose where they work. The two on-site days are called 'core days'. They are particularly valued by new starters for helping them understand more about the culture and ways of working (with even those employees who are full-time remote workers coming on site for two days each quarter for this reason), but Visible Alpha ensure that various other things happen on those days to make them more worthwhile for employees. Leadership meetings, team meetings, one to ones and training are all scheduled for Wednesdays and Thursdays, whereas the non-core days are best for global calls. This way they maximize the time spent together in the office.

In and around those times, the nature of Visible Alpha's global business means that digital forms of communication have always taken priority and are second nature to all employees. Deshpande commented that many businesses in India operate more on a relationship basis than a strict hierarchy, and so the on-site days are designed to promote building those relationships, as well as creativity and brainstorming. Their work could easily be done 100 per cent remotely, but a conscious decision was made to adopt a hybrid approach as they feel a 100 per cent remote organization may lack something around relationships. They also feel it can speed up the learning curve, especially when learning new skills.

I asked Deshpande what advantages she sees in their hybrid model. Like other examples, she commented that the flexibility and autonomy given to employees is crucial, with engagement, attraction and retention all seeing positive shifts and outweighing any frustrations. Company overheads have reduced, and diversity and inclusion has been impacted positively. She states that Visible Alpha have a relatively young, and gender-balanced, employee demographic. Many of those employees have a range of outside work interests and/or young families, and the hybrid approach enables them to manage those things.

As with many organizations though, there are some frustrations about hybrid working at Visible Alpha. Deshpande notes that culture can become fragmented. This is because it is often created within teams by individual managers. Organizational culture may thus become slightly watered-down by the inconsistencies present in individual managerial skill sets and mindsets. However, Visible Alpha are taking steps to tackle these things by solidifying expectations about what should take place on the collaboration days and encouraging teams to work out their own ways of working and behaving derived from the corporate culture and guidance.

Deshpande concluded by speculating that demographic changes may be the eventual champion of hybrid working and the death of fully on-site organizations (at least for those organizations where tasks *could* be remote/hybrid). As other examples have mentioned, many entering the workforce now and in years to come will have grown up with virtual collaboration and relationship building, asynchronous communication and in-person relationships that are not defined by where they work. As greater remote work enables greater talent mobility, she feels that these workers will consciously seek to build remote and hybrid careers that enable them to move around more easily.

In the Visible Alpha example we see how many elements of the fixed hybrid approach have been consciously designed to allow for recognition of individual circumstances, the benefits of planned on-site working and the nature of the work being done. And it works, for Visible Alpha. But it may not work everywhere.

To enable greater cross-functional collaboration and mitigate against cultural deterioration, which we talked about in Chapter 2, each team's hybrid working schedule needs comparing to and aligning with those of teams it works closely with, and the managers of such teams should work together to ensure that their teams are communicating and working together effectively (Robin, 2023). This will need careful coordination across the organization to examine the flow of work and information and ensure hybrid working patterns for teams are aligned to those things.

Technology and equipment cannot be left to chance either. While we will explore more in Chapter 6 about what technology we need to make the most of, we must make it easy for employees to book spaces they need on site, and to access the equipment they need to perform their tasks. Analysing hybrid working patterns and the needs of each person for each task will inform decisions about physical location design, and potentially strategic decisions about real estate.

All these things require employees and managers to be comfortable with and confident in working in these ways. For most, if not all, there is a training requirement so that they learn and evolve the skills and behaviours they need to make hybrid working work.

Don't leave that to chance. Imagine what would happen if you did.

Organization design implications

Throughout this chapter I have been strongly hinting that we must consciously design hybrid working and not leave it to chance. This has implications for organization design and development, which I will summarize in this section. It is important that we consider how the organization is set up and works to optimize it for hybrid working.

Danny Seals, Founder of Venndorly and KNOT, talks about the challenges people face coming into organizations that are hybrid working. He says that before the Covid-19 pandemic, organizations that were co-located on site had unwritten but almost tangible elements of bonding, trust, interdependency and community – where collective hive knowledge was easy to tap into, and it was easy to observe 'how we do things round here' (Seals, 2022). He goes on to contrast that with how things can be in many organizations now, where new starters can feel isolated, something I also talked about in *HR for Hybrid Working*. It doesn't have to be that way, but left alone, that is very much how it will be. To combat this, we must look at what makes things work in organizations – and notice the effect of remote and hybrid working on these. We must then help to set expectations and guidelines about how we make things work in a remote and hybrid working environment and ensure that people understand these things. Seals talks about designing better employee experiences at macro, micro and nano levels to create shared languages and shared patterns – things like how we do meetings, how we deliver feedback, how we celebrate wins and share failure, and whose role it is to uphold these things or be the glue that holds these things together (Seals, 2022).

When thinking about organization design for a hybrid working organization, we must move beyond the assumption that workers will be co-located on site and interacting in person. That will happen, but it won't be the default situation for everyone. Organizational support functions, such as HR, L&D, IT, finance and others, need to work in ways that centralize their services rather than distribute them geographically – there is no sense in locating them physically close to those they support. Equally, grouping employees together in teams based on them doing the same tasks is a familiar way of designing organizations, but we could organize based on outcomes – for example by product or customer type. *HR Executive* suggests a couple of examples of how this could be done for front-line customer-facing roles (Lane and Karr, 2021) and we know from the All Saints example in Chapter 1 that this can easily be done.

Organizational workflows and processes should be examined to see how they work across remote, hybrid and on-site working arrangements. If all three are present in your organization, then these processes will need to have more flexibility built into them – processes that are too rigid or formalized could slow down decision making and create bottlenecks around team leaders. Processes need to be optimized for employees to make quicker, easier decisions if they cannot access their manager at any given time. They also need to be as agile and flexible as possible, focusing on the outcomes each process or workflow delivers, instead of procedural steps. While processes are being examined, this could also give opportunity to ensure workloads are more balanced and achievable in a hybrid working environment. We could perhaps increase the diversity (but not amount) of tasks that any individual employee must do, to encourage more collaboration with others outside of their immediate team (addressing issues discussed in Chapter 2).

We should also examine the structure of the organization, namely the number of layers and the spans of control. While the current structure is likely to have a suitable amount of both, it is based on the co-location premise again and in creating more rigid and bureaucratic ways of making decisions. A more agile, hybrid working organization will need a different number of layers and spans of control. Where employees are given more autonomy, it may free up management time and allow for wider spans of control – but just because we can, doesn't mean we should do that as it could lead to other issues. We will look in a later chapter at how to support managers of hybrid teams, but managers will increasingly take on roles as 'connectors' (Knight, 2021) – ensuring that remote and hybrid employees are connected to the right people, the right networks of support and the right information to be able to do their jobs effectively.

In Chapter 2 we looked at the ways to ensure organizational culture is promoted and does not deteriorate, but organization design is wider than that, as this section shows. It challenges and requires new thinking about established routines and communication channels, and ways of thinking, along with changes to the way places and spaces are used, and the technology adopted to support this.

Why would you leave such important things to chance?

Imagine if we waved a magic wand and could design our organizations entirely from scratch, blank canvas style. Imagine the types of decisions we would need to make to ensure our organizations were truly hybrid in their approach.

Let's make those decisions now.

CASE STUDY ONE

Sarah Fern was, when I interviewed her, the Chief People Officer of Velocity Global, a technology company specializing in global employment, with just under 1,000 employees based across 60 countries and six continents. As a technology company, Fern says they found the transition to enforced remote working in the Covid-19 pandemic relatively easy, but from a cultural perspective the transition was more challenging. This is partly because, being based in 60 countries, they have a vast range of national cultures present, which impacts how work is done. Because Velocity Global grew both organically and through acquisitions in various parts of the world, this presented a few unique challenges. They bought companies that ranged from fully remote to never remote and each had vastly distinct cultures, again affecting how work was done.

In some of the countries where Velocity Global are based there are historic offices, but in other countries Velocity Global have no office base. In those countries employees are encouraged to use co-working spaces or lease individual offices if they are needed. Fern says they often are, and explained that many employees either didn't have the ability to work from home due to the environment there, or simply didn't know how to work from home effectively. As an example, Fern said they had 100,000 applicants for 120 roles last year based on the roles being advertised as work-from-anywhere (for example digital nomads), but that there was some higher turnover in those roles. Fern believes that this is because although work-from-anywhere sounds attractive, people often are not set up physically, mentally or in any other way to do that and need more help to be able to do so. People were burning out, with little structure to help them, in a culture where the 24/7 nature of the service meant that many felt they needed to work those hours to be visible within the company.

All this meant that Velocity Global needed to focus on everyone to work out what each person needed to be successful in their role. For some people, that was remote work. For others, it was regular travel. For some, it was the physical closeness to others that comes from on-site work.

Essentially, there was no one size fits all approach that could be adopted with hybrid working across the whole company, but this was leading to some challenges.

Fern began by focusing on Velocity Global's leaders and what they were role modelling. Consciously avoiding the remote monitoring of people's activity, Fern collaborated with leaders to help them to manage on outputs and outcomes, and to get leaders to share other things they were doing during their days to encourage others to take time away from their desks. Velocity Global's Chief Executive began openly talking about the exercise regime they follow during the working day and how this helps, and Fern herself shared her regular walks and what those helped her with.

Fern also realized that the geographical spread of Velocity Global's locations sometimes made it difficult for people to collaborate effectively across time zones. She put in place a rule where managers had to be within five hours' time difference of each person they managed and created virtual time zone hubs to help more synchronous working. This latter aspect helped overcome team silo working by creating more naturally occurring opportunities to meet with and get to work alongside others in various parts of the organization. Fern believes, as we have explored in earlier chapters, that culture can be consciously designed with the right effort.

Believing that there is no one size fits all approach to work let alone hybrid working, Fern developed a set of principles that she feels Velocity Global employees understood and could work around. She encouraged each individual employee to share their own working arrangements and talk about what works for them and what doesn't, so that others – particularly new staff – could learn from this. She encouraged open discussion about what people were sharing so that a more collaborative approach to hybrid working was developed through conversation and open dialogue. This embedded a positive employee experience for those at Velocity Global, personalized around their needs but meeting the needs of Velocity Global.

Moving into job design, Fern looked at the nature of each job, recognizing that each was different. Each job required a different level of collaboration and communication, and therefore could have a different level of flexibility. Fern was led by the demands of the task, something we will explore further in our next chapter. This helped employees see what was possible and what was not for each individual task, job and employee.

What Velocity Global built was an arrangement based on team needs, locations and specific requirements for specific roles. One size could never fit all for them – and that's OK.

CASE STUDY TWO

Sasha Deepwell and Samantha Young are, respectively, the Chief Executive, and People, Technology and Innovation Director at Irwell Valley Homes, a social housing organization employing around 280 people based in the north-west of the UK. When Deepwell joined the organization in 2017 they were based across three main office locations, which often lay part-empty, and she wanted to ensure that Irwell Valley's employees were given the right equipment and the right information to work regardless of where or when that might have been. Many of their staff were mobile, only coming to an office location temporarily and infrequently. This led to a great many inefficiencies, such as getting caught in traffic while travelling to and from the office base. The amount of travelling was not helpful from an environmental perspective, either.

Deepwell was also conscious that modern lifestyles, particularly family ones, were often incompatible with the traditional working week. During her first year she encouraged people to experiment with and pilot alternative ways of working. She assessed different scenarios with them, for example, what if you always worked at home? What equipment would you need? What things would make you come into the office? What would you miss if you didn't?

At the same time, as with almost all housing organizations, Irwell Valley didn't want to move away from the communities they served, and Deepwell's plan did meet with a fair amount of resistance. Deepwell says this was mostly at middle manager level (for reasons we have explored in other chapters about trust) and from some specific teams. The objections were largely process based. Some teams had developed many complicated processes that required people to double-check another person's work, and had evolved those processes so that those people sat next to each other to make that double-checking more efficient. Often, they were unable to visualize new ways of achieving their outcomes. In general, many staff 'liked' the offices but only because of the relationships they had with the people they saw there – not because of any task that needed to happen there.

Deepwell moved Irwell Valley from three office locations to one (intentionally not allowing enough room for all employees) and collaborated with an interior designer to design and build the right environment for the right type of work. This project involved challenging people and processes. For example, how many meetings people *really* needed, and how long they needed to be. And challenging the status quo bias existing in some teams' views of their processes. The new office has areas that are intended to be for quiet, focused working, and areas that are intended to be for more noisy, collaborative working. Large spaces within it are configurable with easily moveable tables and chairs, so that groups can work out what they need based on the requirements of the task they are performing and who is there.

Deepwell and Young considered this the start of their agile working approach, allowing employees to work wherever and whenever they choose. The systems and processes to support this had just been put in place as the Covid-19 pandemic hit and accelerated some of their plans. They needed to help their colleagues understand the difference between their traditional ways of working and becoming agile, with each day planned according to what needed to be done, where and when. This lack of an obvious structure was a challenge to many, but the Covid-19 pandemic was already forcing Irwell Valley to examine ways of working so this came naturally.

The agile working approach at Irwell Valley is based on trust and treating people like adults. Deepwell feels that 99 per cent of their employees are fine with this approach and don't want to risk losing it by abusing that trust. The agile approach takes the view that customer appointments must come first when planning where and when work takes place, and that partnership working with other organizations that are less agile must come next, but that everything else can be flexed according to individual needs and preferences.

With some roles having a great volume of fixed-time customer appointments, those roles do have less autonomy but can start and finish their days at different locations, including home, and can request that their customer appointments are at specific times such as evenings or weekends if they want to have time not working during the week. There is, naturally, some feeling about there being a two-tier workforce, but most employees understand the common-sense approach being taken. Some staff in customer-facing roles have taken lateral moves within the organization to more flexible roles.

For the rest, there is considerable autonomy. Some staff choose to work on site because of problems in their home environment meaning it is difficult to work there. Some staff choose never to work when there are school runs to do but perform their hours at different times of the day or week instead. This type of approach has needed Irwell Valley to manage by outcomes and what they call 'successful conversations' – rounded conversations between two human beings. The trust needed to make this work is underpinned by strong organizational values and behaviours, standardized procedures, and thorough manager and employee guides during induction and afterwards on how to work best within this approach. Again, one size fits all as an approach to working doesn't matter here.

Deepwell and Young have worked hard to ensure that the organizational culture does not suffer because of individualized approaches to work. As well as ensuring each team develops its own charter for working together (which we explore as a concept in Chapter 10), they host regular short all-company virtual get-togethers and a quarterly in-person get-together. Their advice is to focus on communication and engagement while developing the no size fits all approach to agile (and therefore hybrid) working.

They are rightly proud of their approach. In efficiency savings alone this has saved Irwell Valley Homes a lot of money. It has helped with talent attraction and retention, and has helped them to develop a multichannel, more responsive and expansive service to their customers. All by recognizing that there really is no one size fits all approach to work.

Case study reflections

In our first case study for this chapter, Velocity Global, the following points are worthy of consideration:

- Organizations that are based across multiple time zones may already have well-developed ways of working asynchronously and accommodating diverse ways of getting work done. Perhaps there is someone you could talk to in your network or organization who has that experience.

- We should not underestimate the preparation people need for working at home, or indeed working in a co-working space.

- The behaviours of organizational leaders are critical in role modelling the culture and behaviours the organization wants to see from everyone, and can normalize conversations about integrating life with work – and healthy working practices.

- Consciously designing opportunities for people to work across the organization can be helpful in many ways.

- Sharing individual working arrangements and openly discussing them is an effective way to engage the whole organization in examining what hybrid working means for each person.
- Being led by the demands of the task is a good starting point. We will cover this in greater detail in our next chapter.

In the second case study, Irwell Valley Homes, the following points stand out for consideration:

- Traditional ways of working may have developed a great deal of inefficiencies and are often ripe for challenge.
- The traditional working week is often quite incompatible with modern family life, and this should be addressed.
- Status quo bias around process change is often the source of resistance to implementing a more agile approach to work.
- Deliberately challenging the way people work is an effective way to get them to be more creative about that.
- Developing a culture based on trust, shared values and behaviours, and standardized guidance is a helpful way to go if everyone cannot be treated the same.
- It is OK not to treat everyone the same!
- Giving people autonomy to design the way they work, as well as where and when, can improve the customer experience as well as the employee experience.
- Deliberately creating culture is necessary to avoid the risk of fragmentation of culture.

The action plan

If you want to tackle the issues discussed in this chapter, the following questions could help you do that:

- What are the risks of a fixed hybrid model? How could you mitigate them?

- If you implemented a fixed hybrid model, what would you need to do to avoid the mental and emotional exhaustion that employees could be experiencing?
- What decisions need to be taken at an organizational level to better coordinate teams across a fixed hybrid model?
- What would be the advantages of other hybrid working models for your organization?
- How can you encourage flexibility in roles that might not currently be suitable for hybrid working?
- How can you encourage experimentation with new ways of working in roles that might not currently be suitable for hybrid working?
- What are your employees saying about hybrid working?
- What flexibility do you need to build into processes and workflows, and how will you do that?
- What equipment and technology needs does each task have? How well has this been mapped?
- If you gave every employee autonomy about when and where work can be done, what would happen?
- What kinds of intentional collaboration opportunities could you create for remote and hybrid workers?
- What types of rebalancing of workload, workflow and tasks would need to happen in your team to make hybrid working work more effectively?
- How much do you know about the working preferences of your team members? How much do they know about yours?
- What training do employees, teams and managers need to make hybrid working work?
- How can you make cultural expectations of hybrid working more explicit?
- From a structural perspective, what changes to organizational layers, spans of control and team groupings would enhance hybrid working?
- How will you enable teams to work on process improvements that could enhance hybrid working?
- If you were building your organization from scratch as a truly hybrid one, what decisions would you need to make? And what is stopping you making them now?

References and further reading

Akhter, M (2022) 4 hybrid work schedules and how to roll them out? Envoy, 1 December, www.envoy.com/blog/the-4-office-schedules-that-power-hybrid-work/ (archived at https://perma.cc/MNK7-RGUY)

Christian, A (2022) Why hybrid work is emotionally exhausting, BBC Worklife, 21 January, www.bbc.com/worklife/article/20220120-why-hybrid-work-is-emotionally-exhausting (archived at https://perma.cc/BPW7-3BXP)

Christian, A (2023) Why hybrid return-to-office mandates aren't as flexible as they seem, BBC Worklife, 13 June, www.bbc.com/worklife/article/20230613-why-hybrid-return-to-office-mandates-arent-as-flexible-as-they-seem (archived at https://perma.cc/P3FL-RRNN)

CIPD (2023) Flexible and hybrid working: Principality Building Society, 25 May, www.cipd.org/en/knowledge/case-studies/flexible-hybrid-working-principality/ (archived at https://perma.cc/673T-HSMV)

CIPD (nd) Flexible and hybrid working: Scottish water, CIPD, www.cipd.org/en/knowledge/case-studies/flexible-hybrid-working-scottish-water/ (archived at https://perma.cc/SL73-AD5Y)

Davis, M C et al (2022) Where is your office today? New insights on employee behaviour and social networks, University of Leeds, October, https://futureworkplace.leeds.ac.uk/wp-content/uploads/sites/86/2022/10/Where-is-your-office-today-Oct-2022-2.pdf (archived at https://perma.cc/N6B8-ZGWA)

Devlin, R (2022) How to create a hybrid & remote teams policy template, Servcorp Blog, 1 July, www.servcorp.com.au/en/blog/business-networking/how-to-create-a-hybrid-remote-teams-policy-template/ (archived at https://perma.cc/J2HE-2Z3Q)

DiRomualdo, T (2023) One-size-fits-all hybrid work policies are a bad idea, Unleash, 6 March, www.unleash.ai/future-of-work/one-size-fits-all-hybrid-work-policies-are-a-bad-idea/ (archived at https://perma.cc/V4JE-67XU)

Gartner (2023) The secrets to implementing a successful hybrid work model, 10 January, www.gartner.com/en/podcasts/thinkcast/the-secrets-to-implementing-a-successful-hybrid-work-model (archived at https://perma.cc/F7S4-J6AH)

Hi Bob (nd) The advantages of the hybrid work model, www.hibob.com/guides/hybrid-working-model-advantages/ (archived at https://perma.cc/9DQN-N38C)

Knight, J (2021) Rethink organisational design to maximise benefits of hybrid work, *HR Magazine*, 16 March, www.hrmagazine.co.uk/content/comment/rethink-organisational-design-to-maximise-benefits-of-hybrid-work/ (archived at https://perma.cc/356J-QM3D)

Lane, R and Karr, A (2021) 4 ways organization design can enable the hybrid workplace, *HR Executive*, 28 January, www.hrexecutive.com/4-ways-organization-design-can-enable-the-hybrid-workplace/ (archived at https://perma.cc/7CRU-U2F6)

McCartney, C (nd) Flexible working in front line roles: What is possible? CIPD, https://community.cipd.co.uk/cipd-blogs/b/cipd_voice_on/posts/flexible-working-in-front-line-roles-what-is-possible (archived at https://perma.cc/XP42-LZUQ)

Morgan, J (2022) Why hybrid work doesn't work, LinkedIn, 20 September, www.linkedin.com/pulse/why-hybrid-work-doesnt-jacob-morgan/ (archived at https://perma.cc/TP7H-DX4E)

Nurski, L (2021) Designing a hybrid work organization, Bruegel Blog, 5 July, www.bruegel.org/blog-post/designing-hybrid-work-organisation (archived at https://perma.cc/M7K2-6PLS)

Robin (2023) Hybrid work models and schedules: Examples, benefits and challenges, 27 March, www.robinpowered.com/blog/hybrid-work-models-and-schedules (archived at https://perma.cc/4398-643C)

Sarin, B (2020) Organizational design for a hybrid future of work, *People Matters*, 30 November, www.peoplemattersglobal.com/article/strategic-hr/organizational-design-for-a-hybrid-future-of-work-27737 (archived at https://perma.cc/KL64-DF4P)

Seals, D (2022) Two cultures of hybrid work – a few years of reflection, Unleash, 24 October, www.unleash.ai/organizational-design/there-are-two-cultures-of-hybrid-work/ (archived at https://perma.cc/7R89-6EKN)

Sen, P, Deb, P and Kumar, N (2021) The challenges of work from home for organizational design, *California Management Review*, 31 July, https://cmr.berkeley.edu/2021/07/the-challenges-of-work-from-home-for-organizational-design/ (archived at https://perma.cc/4DF7-JCYX)

Thompsons Solicitors (2022) Avoid 'one size fits all' hybrid working, *Employment Law Review*, 776, 16 June, www.thompsonstradeunion.law/news/employment-law-review/weekly-issue-776/avoid-one-size-fits-all-hybrid-working (archived at https://perma.cc/39U4-LLX2)

Tilo, D (2023) One-size-fits-all approach not recommended for hybrid work, *HRD America*, 27 April, www.hcamag.com/us/specialization/employee-engagement/one-size-fits-all-approach-not-recommended-for-hybrid-work/444138 (archived at https://perma.cc/SWQ9-U8GF)

Unispace (2023) Returning for Good, www.unispace.com/returning-for-good (archived at https://perma.cc/E7RY-S7VE)

5

Personalizing work

The shorter read

The personalized employee experience is already upon us. The psychological contract has been shaped by experiences people have had of remote and hybrid working. Parts of that are done in places away from other people and which are unique to each person, meaning each experience has been unique too. In the world of employment, we haven't necessarily caught up to that yet. But we need to.

We are already used to personalization as consumers, but not so much in the workplace – and yet the data is already there if we know what to look for. We can use it to shape approaches to the on-site and remote environment, rewards, well-being, work–life balance and much more. Treating people the same by asking them to work as others do is an outdated idea.

For most remote and hybrid workers, each day can be different and should be led by the tasks they are performing throughout the day. For that to really work, they need to be able to move around their workspaces according to what they are doing and rarely should remain in one place, even in their own home.

Work can be personalized too and the four-box model from *HR for Hybrid Working* needs an update. We can use it to analyse each task, job, team process and ultimately the organization. From this we will see the right hybrid working approach and working pattern for each person and can tailor that to both the requirements of the task and the preferences of the individual.

Where work isn't flexible enough, we can ask lots of questions about how it could change to engage people in redesigning their work and build in flexibility for the future to achieve a closer match to what they need. But even that should not be set in stone once agreed, as flexibility still is the key – we can agree default approaches but also the circumstances under which these need to change.

There are consequences for communication methods and processes if we personalize work, and we are likely to see a need for more asynchronous communication. There is technology available to help with this, but it is as much a mindset shift as anything else. We must fight against what we are used to doing to create new ways of working that work.

We could examine network maps and sociograms of our teams and organizations to see how people connect with each other and how this is affected by hybrid working. Once we know who the more influential people are we can design work to use this influence and spread it. We can also then consciously design ways to overcome the bottlenecks in networks and ensure that each employee has the right number of social connections.

But these social connections exist outside of the on-site workplace too, and if a hybrid worker lives in a multi-hybrid worker household (or uses co-working spaces) there will be added considerations. As employers we should examine the arrangements in place in the household and guide individual hybrid workers on how to make the most of a personalized remote workspace where there are other hybrid workers from different employers in the same location. That may not be possible for some, and we should be prepared to create on-site spaces that replicate the ideal remote workspace.

The longer read

Is the personalization of work inevitable?

In the last chapter we explored how there is no one size fits all approach to hybrid working. This means that each employee will experience it in diverse ways. The personalized employee experience is perhaps an inevitable consequence of this. Consequently, we must move away from policies and practices for the many, and towards those tailored for the individual.

The CIPD's Responsible Business report comments that 'A greater sense of individualism and unwillingness to compromise on working habits that have become personal preference' is what is facing many organizations now and goes on to conclude that 'The employer–employee relationship needs to be reset to what one HRD described as "a system of mutual accountability", with obligations on both sides' (Hope Hailey and Jacobs, 2022). Again, if we follow through on that, we must create individualized, personalized employee experiences.

We may already have a personalized psychological contract. Many people have got so used to working when, where and how they choose, that they are reluctant to go back to a more collective contract and experience – they prefer to do things how they want to. The labour market is currently a tight one and could be described as a 'sellers' market' – this means we must appeal to individuals to give them a personalized experience.

The CIPD points out that being trusted to get on with your job where and when you want is a key part of a good psychological contract (Hope Hailey and Jacobs, 2022). If we therefore try to force people to work in a specific location at a specific time, we destroy some of the hard work done already and can ride roughshod over individual preferences too. The pandemic and early attempts at hybrid working have shown we have had remarkably diverse experiences. It has already individualized the psychological contract. We just haven't caught up enough.

What could we personalize?

The digital era we live in has already acclimatized us to personalization as consumers. It is everywhere. Look at the way services such as Facebook and Amazon tailor your experience. Almost all our online experience is based on our preferences, past experiences and choices, behaviours and interactions. Sometimes I can just be discussing something with my wife and then it appears on Facebook or Amazon – like witchcraft.

We rarely do that in the workplace, even though the data (whether captured or not) is there and the technology is there too. A hybrid worker, with an element of remote working, probably generates more data than someone who is in the office all the time. We just don't go looking for it, or don't use it. We must personalize the employee experience – using the data points, captured by systems that will bring it all together – to check what people need, how they prefer to work, how engaged they are and how they are performing. In the next chapter we will look more at data and use of technology, but if we harnessed this available information it could lead to personalized approaches to reward, technology, working patterns, contracts, the remote and on-site environment, and more.

We must ask questions. At an individual level – everyone's experience of remote and hybrid working is different. It is done in different homes, with different people in them; with different equipment and distractions – and with different impacts on the demands and needs of their families and leisure pursuits.

Over time, a remote worker figures out, through trial and error maybe, the environment and set-up, and approach to work–life balance that works best for them. This affects their values and perception of work, and so we need to reflect that in the organizational values and policies. We shouldn't ignore the experiences people have had and continue to have as remote and hybrid workers – in fact it is critical that we don't.

Once we design the personalized employee experience, a hybrid working approach suited to that individual's job, working preferences and life just falls into place, as we have data and evidence to support what we are doing.

Each person is motivated by different things, and this evolves throughout their life. This means there is no one size fits all approach to motivation, or the rewards that could incentivize motivation. In *HR for Hybrid Working* I explored what rewards may need to change for remote and hybrid workers, but as time has progressed and the personalized nature of the employee experience has become more pronounced, an individualized reward package is also likely to be beneficial. Have you asked your employees what each of them would really like work to provide for them? Have you considered how each person's responses to that are tailored to their unique situation in their remote workspace?

The same is true of well-being and the achievement of work–life balance. Both concepts evolve throughout a person's life. We need to offer choices to enable people to get more of what matters for them. And the people around them – all their stakeholders.

Why do we think that a mandated fixed hybrid approach for everyone is going to achieve that for anyone? It might, but more through luck than judgement. We are well past the point at which we can treat everyone the same.

We must do better.

We must also help employees to personalize their workspaces, both the remote and on-site versions. Later in this chapter I will give some examples of how I move around my own home, working in different spaces according to the task I'm doing. I know for some this may not be possible, but the point is that it is task-driven, and that's the principle we must follow here. Each task any person does requires different equipment, different technology, different furniture and fittings, connections, acoustics and more. If a person can't achieve that (even with our help) in their home, we must provide similar spaces suited to the tasks within the on-site location. Again, the data helps us with this – we can work out how much time employees spend on certain tasks and craft a proportionate range of workspaces based on this.

Work is not just definable by where it takes place but by the type of work being done. This could be synchronous, alongside other people in real time, or asynchronous, working alone and at a time when others may not be. In Chapter 6 we will examine the changes needed to the physical locations in more detail. People care about how work is done, alongside where and when. Research shows that when employees can personalize their approach to work it delivers greater job satisfaction and performance – and giving autonomy about the how can offset any restrictions about where and when in jobs that cannot have the same amount of hybrid working as others (Davis et al, 2022a).

If we treat everyone the same by applying rules to everyone and creating policies that work for the majority, we risk alienating some people and missing out excellent opportunities to craft something different, something better.

How can we personalize work?

In Chapter 11 of *HR for Hybrid Working* I introduced a four-box model for recrafting work, and this is developed further in this book due to the popularity of the concept. The model is about breaking roles down into their component parts – tasks – and working out whether the individual tasks have a fixed location or can be done anywhere, and whether they must be done synchronously at the same time as other people, or at any time. The advantage of the model is that it allows jobs to be examined in detail to see what proportion of their tasks lend themselves to hybrid working, and which require on-site presence in the traditional working day. When entire teams adopt this model, they can see what hybrid approach is possible for them, and the same is true for organizations. Organizations can then make more informed decisions about real estate and technology since each task may need a different type of space and equipment/technology. This allows the organization to ensure that form follows function as it designs work and its hybrid approach.

The updated four-box model is shown in Figure 5.1.

FIGURE 5.1 Updated four-box model

	When must the task be done?	
Where must the task be done?	Synchronously with other people On-site in a fixed location	Asynchronously at any suitable time On-site in a fixed location
	Synchronously with other people Any suitable location	Asynchronously at any suitable time Any suitable location

Let's look at some examples of common tasks and how they map onto the model:

- **Replying to an email or message.** In almost all jobs, this task can be done at any time, and at any location. Therefore, this would go into the bottom right box of the model. Of course, these could be done in a synchronous manner if the organization dictates that, but the task itself has no such fixed approach.

- **Attending a live webinar.** This has a fixed time – it is only taking place at a specific time. While the host is virtual and the attendees likewise, each attendee has some choice about where to attend from. This could be a remote workspace, or on site. Again, organizations could specify one or the other but the task itself has no fixed location where it must be done from. This task would go into the bottom left of the model. Listening to a recording of a live session would change its location though, as at that point it would have no synchronous nature and the task could move to the bottom right of the model.

- **Supporting at a meeting that is taking place on site.** While we could debate whether the meeting must be on site, in this example it does. The meeting has a fixed time as it is a synchronous activity with others present, and the location is also fixed at an on-site location. Clearly this task is going into the top left of the model.

- **Cleaning an office.** This obviously has a fixed location – on site. However, the task could be done asynchronously. Organizations could specify a time, and there could be benefits of doing so, but the task has no fixed time approach and so it would go into the top right box.

We could go on, but you see how this works, I hope. What you should also see is that there is a natural place on the model for each task, but that organizations (or teams, or individuals) can make choices about where and when they want tasks to be done, which could change the location of the task within the four-box model. There could be advantages to doing so, and you should explore these. Doing so could enable you to ensure that work is done in a particular way that suits the organization, though of course there could also be disadvantages to this.

Once all major (and possibly minor too) tasks have been analysed in this way based on how they are currently – and not ideally – done, you can see what percentage of tasks fit into each box of the model. You can then work out how much of a job's available time is spent in each box of the model, and you can then work out the right hybrid working approach for that job based on how things are done now.

TABLE 5.1   Applying the analysis from the four-box model

Job has most tasks/time in...	A good approach would be...
Top left box (e.g. fixed time, fixed location)	On-site working with little remote working, and no choice of working pattern and hours
Top right box (e.g. any time, fixed location)	On-site working with choice of working pattern and hours
Bottom left box (e.g. fixed time, any location)	Fixed hybrid working with specified times and locations for each day
Bottom right box (e.g. any time, any location)	Flexible hybrid working with choice of working pattern and hours as well as location

It could be that once you have done the analysis you realize that the way that tasks are done and placed in the four-box model is not where you'd ideally like them to be. That's quite likely. In such situations we need to start re-examining each task, asking questions about it to see what flexibility there could be. Currently there may be little or none, but we need to consider the potential future ways tasks could be done too.

Questions like these:

- Can we change where it needs to be done?
- Can we change when it needs to be done?
- Can we change how it needs to be done?
- Can we change who it needs to be done by?
- Can we outsource it?
- Can we move it to another team?
- Can we use technology to change the nature of the task?
- Can we automate it?
- Can we automate it in the future?
- Can we stop doing it?

Of course, there are more questions that we could ask, but these are a good starting point. Involving people – especially the jobholder themselves – in answering these questions is likely to raise their engagement with the hybrid working debate and help them to gain some ownership of what work looks and feels like.

A useful example of how technology could change a role is that of a receptionist position. The tasks themselves involve supplying services to visitors to a fixed physical location, on site. They take place when the on-site location is open, so the tasks naturally sit in the top left of our model. However, using video calling technology and the right type of interactive kiosk the receptionist could be found anywhere, even if the people they are talking to are in the on-site location. If this is done, then the tasks move to the bottom left of our model instead.

Individual circumstances may lead us to consider more changes to enable people to work in a way that suits them. For example, someone with childcare responsibilities who needs to do school runs may benefit from the technology switch in the previous paragraph, or from swapping tasks with a different job so that they have more time flexibility, for example to do school runs at set times and perform the tasks at different times instead.

The concept of Workstyle covers how to restructure work in detail and is built to design out bias around inclusion in work (Hirst and Penny, 2022). Examples include people with disabilities where it is easier for them to perform tasks in a remote workspace than it would be on site, though the same is true for anyone with caring responsibilities or who just wants a more flexible approach to work. Workstyle involves taking the tasks to the people who are doing them, not requiring the people to go where the tasks need to be done.

How to keep it flexible

The nature of hybrid working means that flexibility is key. Once work has been personalized using the four-box model, that does not mean that's how it remains. Sometimes fitting things into boxes is too neat and may not account for the day-to-day changes that work – or life – may bring. However, we must be mindful that although having control of how, when and where work is done does seem to be beneficial, giving too much or complete control could be chaotic and may be too stressful for some employees. We must keep it flexible, without creating chaos. But how?

Employee preferences will evolve over time just as the nature of the tasks will evolve. The organization will evolve too. While personalization is helpful, we cannot assume that, once the personalized hybrid approach is agreed, it is set and will never change. It will, can and must.

We could develop personas for our employees, to look at how such personas may typically work and the situations that they may face, which might cause their arrangements and preferences to change (Froud, 2021). Examples could be moving house, a long-term health issue, a relationship change or new family member, a new starter in the team or the onset of school holidays. This reinforces how important it is to talk to employees and be transparent about working preferences and arrangements.

The CIPD supplied a case study on how Pearson, an education company based in the UK, had implemented their personalized hybrid working approach. Employees were able to have conversations with managers about how, when and where work is best done and the percentage of time they were intending to spend on site versus remote. Priority was given to those with personal and family commitments to be able to deliver on these around work commitments. Pearson supplied the right equipment, software and support, based on the way work was then agreed to be done.

Pearson report that the flexibility allows people to consider when and where they are most productive, and work in those ways. This often means people choose to work virtually more than not, but when they come on site it is for purposeful collaboration in an attractive workspace. Trust is at the heart of this personalized approach – treating people like adults and letting them make choices that suit them and the business (CIPD, nd).

As we design the hybrid working approach and consider flexibility within it, I would recommend that each personalized arrangement gives thought to what is non-negotiable within that arrangement, and where the limits of autonomy and empowerment might lie.

There are consequences to almost every decision made around hybrid working. A decision to adopt a fixed hybrid model where all employees must be on site for a set amount of time may subconsciously create or reinforce a culture of presenteeism and reduce the ability of employees to work in a way that is best suited for them and the tasks they are doing. There will be groups within an organization that would be delighted if all employees did come on site for a minimum amount of time, just as there are those who would be horrified by the mere thought of doing so. This point reinforces how there can not be a one size fits all approach, and personalizing the approach may be the most effective way forward.

There are ways to encourage more flexibility even within fixed hybrid models. Increasing the reference period or using percentages instead of days – for example X days per year, or X per cent of time across a quarter – may prove more workable and flexible enough to accommodate peaks and troughs in work volume, changes in personal and work circumstances, and more. In addition, giving purpose to the on-site experience – team development, co-creation and collaboration activities, and more – will avoid creating resentment.

The implications of personalization

There are implications to consider when designing personalized work, which affect the individual and how they could work within their team, as well as how the team works within the organizational system. When we redesign tasks, we are rebuilding parts or perhaps all of the organizational system. Perry Timms, Founder of PTHR, likens this to building a piece of flat-pack furniture from IKEA – piece by piece, assembling the finished product (HR Happy Hour, 2022), and I hope you can see why.

What we are faced with is more than just deciding when and where work is done. We have what the University of Leeds calls a socio-technical problem, where the choices around hybrid, individual circumstances, technology, workspace, culture and ways of working are entangled and contingent on each other (Davis et al, 2022a).

Communications

Changing how, when and where work is done to enable a hybrid approach will have an impact on how people need to communicate with each other. Previously, this may have been via a virtual or on-site meeting, and it still could be. But it doesn't have to be. Using software or apps such as Slack, Teams and Zoom, with multiple channels available for different topics and discussions, enables asynchronous communication to take place that can be logical and easy to understand for new and existing staff alike. In Chapter 3 we examined how the organization PTHR has re-organized itself for a four-day working week – and a key part of that is encouraging asynchronous communication. In PTHR, meetings are still only when co-creation or co-decision making is needed. In between those occasions, PTHR employees collaborate on virtual whiteboards and on Slack or Teams channels. This allows people to contribute at times that suit them, but also allows Timms to check whether communication is prompt and effective (HR Happy Hour, 2022).

We must consciously re-engineer processes and ways of working so that they match the way people will work. This will require new skill sets around organization design, systems thinking and agile working for managers, people professionals, and likely staff involved in the decision making too. Applying some of the things discussed in this chapter is likely to be a good start, but more professional support could be needed for larger and more complex organizations.

Social connections

Organizations are networks, and within them exist an often complicated web of social connections. Have you tried to map this out to show how well-connected certain people may be and how this supports information flow and collaboration between them and others they work with? Have you thought about how remote and hybrid working could change that? It will – it must. But we can do something about that. You could start by thoroughly mapping this out for any given job and/or team – perhaps your own. Network maps help to show who is connected to who, and why/what for.

Research by the University of Leeds showed that time spent on site alongside other people improved social connections and a strengthened bond to the organization itself, made greater as the number of social connections increased (Davis et al, 2022b). Where a hybrid team communicates mostly within its own boundaries and is rarely on site with other teams, all team members will see a deterioration in their social connections, their bond to the organization. Such people will be a flight risk to the organization, and if they are knowledge workers then they could take their specialized knowledge out of the organization if they do leave. Therefore, if we encourage teams to consciously co-locate with other teams when on site, to socialize with them or to take part in cross-organizational initiatives, we reduce the risk of them leaving and increase the bond they have to the organization through increasing their social connections.

A sociogram researched by the University of Leeds shows that those who spend least time on site have the fewest number of social connections. However, it qualifies this finding by saying that those who spend more time on site will have a higher number of social connections if they consciously co-locate themselves near other highly connected people, but not if they spend time on site but working in relative isolation (Davies et al, 2022b). This shows that the way we design the on-site workspace, and where we encourage hybrid workers to work from when on site, will have a direct bearing on how connected they are, and the strength of their bond to the organization.

Again, we cannot leave that to chance. We must consciously think about who is on site, why they are there, and who they are likely to need to connect and communicate with. We must also design spaces where this will happen, either informally (what are often popularized as water cooler conversations) or formally (planned, structured discussions). As we examine the tasks themselves this could become clearer, but without that analysis and use of the four-box model it is guesswork.

We could use sociograms and network maps to show those employees who are the least connected – whether that is because of how little time they spend on site or not. Such people may need greater synchronous virtual collaboration, for example a greater number of tasks that are in the bottom right of the four-box model – so the network map or sociogram could lead to further job design changes. The network map should show where bottlenecks – what Leeds refers to as brokers (of information, data, resources and connections to other people) may reside, as well as inefficiencies in how information flows around the organization and where some employees may be overloaded (Davis et al, 2022b). The Leeds research provides further guidance on how to overcome issues that can be discerned from a network map analysis, such as deliberately co-locating people together to build connections and relationships, moving people around when on site regularly, cross-organizational initiatives both virtually and on site, and simply bringing other people into meetings and collaborative discussions (Davis et al, 2022b).

The network map should also reveal who are the more 'powerful' people for ensuring work gets done, who are the ones who are great at passing on information, and who are the ones who are great for social and emotional support. We could have multiple network maps for different purposes, which again would illustrate whether certain types of hybrid working would be better for certain people and tasks. It would also show the potential impact of changing working arrangements and working patterns.

Social connections obviously don't exist only in the workplace. They will be present if we work at a co-working space, or if we have a multi-hybrid worker household – something that may raise some issues to address.

Multi-hybrid worker households

When we consider what a workplace is, we can no longer consider the on-site location we own or lease, or even look to other similar locations. We must now consider co-working spaces and the remote workspace each employee and their family have created.

As hybrid working grows in popularity and coverage, the likelihood of many households containing multiple hybrid workers is also growing. This will be attractive to many households but comes with implications for their respective employers. These households will become like co-working spaces, and could be treated as such, but with distinct differences that again speak to how hybrid working is personalized.

Neil Goodrich was, when I interviewed him, the Corporate Performance and Planning Manager at Orbit Group, based in the Midlands in the UK. He and his wife Georgina are both hybrid workers, but for different employers (Georgina worked first for an elite sports equipment manufacturer as a hybrid worker, but now runs her own business). Until the Covid-19 pandemic, they had not worked in the same location at all despite both having the ability to do so. Since that pandemic, working in the same location has become the norm for them.

Initially, both struggled to co-work in the same location. While Neil's employer supplied a good range of equipment to enable him to set up a remote workspace (donating office equipment no longer used in the offices), Georgina's employer supplied little, and the difference in their working experience was stark. Even though the equipment provided for him was suitable, his remote environment was not. The Goodriches worked in the kitchen and living room. This had an impact on particularly Neil's mental health as he often took breaks in the same location as he worked. He did not really benefit from such breaks, and without the physical impact of a commute, neither had the break between work and life that most people need.

Over time, the Goodriches have – mostly through trial and error – worked out their preferred working spaces in their property. Neil has equipped a spare bedroom with a larger laptop and two large screens, and Georgina works in a separate space. This avoids the awkward situations they faced when both working in the same space, around taking video and telephone calls, and inadvertently seeing sensitive information on each other's screens. Their experiences of working in the same household have led to them establishing ways of working and living together while working – such as how and when to organize household chores in between work, and how to communicate any restrictions around working time or availability to the other so that the impact is minimized.

Having both adults in the household as hybrid workers has benefited not just their household but the local community in which they live. The Goodriches report that they have more time as a couple and more time for their personal interests and hobbies. Both are putting back into the local community via voluntary roles with local sports teams, which they could not do if they worked on site. They also believe they have benefited financially from having multiple hybrid workers in the household. Although energy and food costs have risen for the household, the reduction in fuel costs due to fewer commutes have offset this, as have reductions in car insurance costs through reduced mileage on their vehicles. They have also saved money on dog walkers. Dog walking has become a way to take breaks and have rest from work. Neil believes his own job performance has improved and is pleased that he has been able to craft a personalized hybrid experience alongside his wife. The Goodriches value their muti-hybrid worker household to the extent that neither would consider a fully on-site role and if either of their employers asked them to work fully on site, both would leave.

In this example we see how a multi-hybrid worker household can work effectively. The Goodriches have made sensible and considered decisions about how to work and live together, and it could be that the ways in which they have set up their household could add value to their property also. However, the Goodriches have no children, which would otherwise complicate their decision making about how to manage a multi-hybrid worker household, and again we must say that there is no one size fits all approach to hybrid, whether the location being considered is the remote or the on-site one. The Goodriches have needed to implement a system of communication and working together because they are co-located, even though they work for different employers. That isn't written down, as few marriages need that (and I speak as someone who has been married twice), but helps them both to make sense of things and to give their best to their respective employers as well as to each other. There are multiple stakeholders in a hybrid working arrangement, and in a multi-hybrid worker household even more so.

Having the right spaces within a multi-hybrid worker household is important and some households simply will not have space for more than one hybrid worker to work effectively. This can be further complicated if there are children, particularly older ones, doing school or college work remotely too. I am reminded here of the situation in my household. Both my wife and I are hybrid workers, and work in the house for around 90 per cent of our time. During the Covid-19 pandemic we also had four children occupying the same spaces during the working day, competing not just for internet bandwidth but for the devices on which we each needed to do our work. Again, setting up ways of working and living among all of us was the only way we could make sense of our situation.

So how did we get around this?

Since that pandemic it is increasingly just my wife and I at home, but even then, there is a greater need for communication between us. If either one of us is varying our normal remote working routines, we must inform the other in suitable time to minimize any potential impact. If either of us is having a client meeting, whether virtual or occasionally in our home offices, we must ensure the other is aware and can cope with any disruption. The other person also needs to be aware of any spaces that are reserved for clients coming into the house, or need to be used as backgrounds for video calls (which will mean no accidentally wandering into the same space to make a drink or similar).

We each have a dedicated space where we prefer to work for most of the time, but even here there is no one size fits all approach. We work where the task requirements are best suited. For example, if I am delivering a virtual training session, I use an upstairs bedroom where I have personalized the equipment and environment to best suit the task. If I am doing admin tasks or replying to emails and messages, I will do that while watching television in the lounge, sat next to my wife. If I am doing focused work where I need no distractions I will remain in the upstairs bedroom and inform my wife not to disturb me. If I am doing work where it is helpful to talk to someone and bounce ideas off another person, then I'll co-locate myself at a table with my wife. She makes similar decisions for similar reasons. We both work in the same business but servicing different clients in diverse ways, and we move around our household based on what the specific requirements of our tasks are. We have no one fixed working location, much like we should not expect one fixed working location in an on-site working experience either.

When there are three or more of us all working or studying in the same building it becomes extremely tricky to manage everything, and it could be that our house and other similar locations with three or more hybrid workers become akin to a co-working space. This may bring with it a need for more structure to how the location works and the expectations for everyone – but there's little fun in that if these are family members, as that is rarely how family dynamics work. However, if the same three people were in a professional co-working space that's exactly how it would work, along with guidance from the respective employers on confidentiality and more.

In such situations it may be easier to avoid multi-hybrid worker households where the dynamics of the close relationships between such people, and the limitations of the physical location, become too problematic. In such cases, one or more of the hybrid workers could base themselves on site at their employer, which would then require the employer's physical location to have suitable spaces that replicate the remote working space the individual has left. More on that in our next chapter.

CASE STUDY ONE

Prodromos Mavridis is the HR Policy and Reward Lead at the London Borough of Barnet, a local authority in the UK in the Greater London area employing around

2,000 staff. Mavridis's views here reflect his own personal views on the organizational approach. Like many local authorities Barnet had made significant cuts during the period of austerity in the UK in the early 2010s, with lots of services being outsourced or ceased entirely. As the Covid-19 pandemic hit they had begun to look afresh at the effectiveness of service delivery, and the impact of that pandemic was to accelerate this review.

The authority adopted a remote-first approach, recognizing the benefits in terms of efficiencies that remote working offered. They were aware that being too draconian about how this could be done may be counterproductive and wanted to give their staff choice and autonomy about where, when and how they work. This considered the type of work being done but also individual circumstances (as some staff did not have a suitable remote working space available to them). Consequently, each service and job role would have noticeably different requirements within the approach taken by the authority.

Service managers could request staff work a set amount of time on site but were asked to justify such requirements, and in general the authority did not adopt an arbitrary days of the week fixed hybrid approach. Theirs was entirely situational based on job requirements. There was some flexibility built in by service managers. For example, when a new person joins a team, and particularly if that person is less experienced in the world of work, there is an expectation that their line manager, and possibly the rest of the team, will have a greater on-site presence for a period while the new starter learns about their job and the team.

The authority allows their staff to work from outside the UK, subject to the appropriate tax implications being addressed, for up to six months per year. Staff who do this are encouraged to be flexible about their working hours to overcome time zone barriers to collaboration and communication. Mavridis himself worked in Brazil for a period and adopted a 5 am to 1 pm working day so that he could align with colleagues still in the UK. Occasionally he would vary this and do 5 am to 10 am, then break for several hours, before resuming work later in the Brazilian day. He also spends a portion of his working time in Greece each year to visit family, working from their homes, and has worked in multiple countries within the same week on more than one occasion.

Barnet attracted some negative publicity in a national newspaper about staff who worked abroad, but recognized the diversity and inclusion benefits that the remote approach was bringing to its culture and services. The negative publicity did not change the approach.

Mavridis reports that most staff are very happy with this arrangement, and that the authority itself is very happy too. One of the main indicators that the authority is tracking in all their work is their progress towards a target to achieve 'net zero' in its operations by 2032 – and their hybrid working approach moves them much closer to that goal. It has also enabled them to attract a wider pool of job applicants. Jobs at Barnet are benchmarked against pay levels in outer London boroughs despite many staff living nowhere near London. This is a significant increase for those people and has helped Barnet avoid the use of market supplements and find a neat way around otherwise troublesome restraints on pay. Mavridis doesn't want to work anywhere else, even for a much higher salary. He values the flexibility of the hybrid approach and says others feel the same – it is thus a big aid to retention as well as talent attraction.

Some Barnet staff have moved to other parts of the country. Mavridis cited an example of a social worker who moved to a different part of the country. The social worker's client base remained in Barnet and the nature of the work meant that it had to be done in Barnet, face to face. There were elements of the social worker's role that could be done as remote or hybrid, but large parts of it could not. This led to some employee relations issues at first, which were eventually resolved through the employee agreeing to be seconded to a role that did not require regular on-site attendance. In Mavridis's own case, he has moved to Birmingham as most of his own work can be done remotely.

Mavridis explained subcultures within teams often set the tone for the hybrid working approach. He explained there is one team whose culture is that they feel they should be near their client base, and that this is then represented in how that team works and behaves. Another team have a very traditional Monday to Friday, 9 am to 5 pm culture, which also tends to create an expectation of staff being physically present in the office. Mavridis commented that the department-based nature of culture has often been dominant over organizational culture within local authorities in the UK, where the regular cycles of outsourcing, insourcing and transferring of services has led to team cultures being almost detachable from the main organizational culture. Hybrid working hasn't made that better or worse, but in ways has solidified it. However, the authority has begun to consciously provide more opportunities for staff to get involved in other parts of the organization – more cross-organizational networks and working groups, greater cross-organizational learning and development opportunities, and continuous improvement groups. Mavridis believes such initiatives are easier to implement across a remote and hybrid organization than they ever were if staff were on site.

Some managers have struggled with making hybrid working work. There have been debates within Barnet about whether remote and hybrid workers are productive or not. For some managers, the solution is therefore to restrict remote and hybrid working, rather than addressing the nature of any performance issues. Within Barnet these managers have been given help and support, and it has prompted the authority to look at managerial capability at a corporate level and to provide additional coaching on an individual basis.

Like other organizational case studies in this book, Barnet have begun leasing out parts of their buildings. This generates revenue, and careful choice of tenants has led to significant boosts to community-based initiatives. The authority have also redesigned the remaining parts of their building to make better use of different ways of working, again being led by the nature of each task and job role.

There are, naturally, many jobs in the authority where there is currently no possibility of hybrid working, and this is occasionally commented on by the relevant trades unions (usually about the increased cost that comes from having a regular commute to an on-site location). In general, though, Mavridis believes that all staff and unions understand that the nature of each service must take priority, and that work is arranged based on that, the tasks undertaken and the individual job-holder's circumstances.

CASE STUDY TWO

Alys Martin is the Head of People at what3words, a technology company employing 150 people, around three-quarters of whom are in the UK. Martin joined the organization in early 2023 after they had begun their hybrid working approach in the middle of 2022. That hybrid approach had been a fixed hybrid model, with London-based non-business development staff on site two days a week, and everyone else internationally and the business development team on site three days a week. There were different views on the management team as to the best number of days on site, with some preferring staff on site for all their time, feeling this would help the internal community, but Martin explained that they were realistic enough to accept the prevailing views within the organization.

Based on feedback from staff, the organization softened their stance, reducing the on-site requirement to two days a week for all UK-based staff, although staff based overseas do still have a three days a week on-site requirement. The rationale for this difference was that the smaller the site, the more on-site collaborative working would be needed – and sites outside of the UK were much smaller than the UK sites. Even then, though, Martin reports that some leaders within what3words felt that creativity and spontaneity was being lost because of the fixed hybrid approach, and she has helped the organization to adapt the approach based on this feedback. While the fixed hybrid approach is still in place, each team can decide its own two days on site based on the requirements of the work being performed and with sensible crossover with teams working on similar projects.

Martin recognized that there needed to be room for manoeuvre within the fixed hybrid approach. Complicated absence policies had been created to cover any member of staff who could not come on site on their required days, as the first approach had been to treat the two on-site days as rigid and inflexible, even though the remote days were treated in the opposite way.

In addition, what3words have brought in a six-week work-from-anywhere policy. This is worked out as two days per week for six weeks, equalling twelve days in total. In practice this allows staff to request remote working on days when they should be on site. This is extremely popular, and Martin reports that most staff use the full 12-day/6-week entitlement to remain remote for that time. Added to this the organization have two well-being days available for any member of staff to use to be able to spend time looking after their own mental health, and many choose to use these to avoid coming on site on their given days. Staff are also able to avoid coming on site on their required days due to travel and/or weather disruption days that are also available to claim.

All of this sounds as if the organizational commitment to a fixed hybrid approach is more flexible than first thought. Martin acknowledges this and feels that these compromises allow for the organization to achieve a personalized hybrid approach based on individual circumstances.

Their on-site base has reduced in size, with what3words giving up one floor of their office. They have remodelled the rest to encourage collaborative and cross-functional working, and actively encourage staff and teams to plan to do such things on their on-site days. All meeting rooms are equipped with state-of-the-art technology to factor in those who may not be on site – whether through working remotely or being based internationally.

what3words have given guidance to staff on their remote working set-up and have provided them with a budget to help get the right equipment and environment. They have encouraged staff to obtain very portable equipment for their hybrid approach to avoid having to carry bulky equipment back and forth across the country.

I asked Martin how what3words are measuring the impact of their hybrid working approach. She reports no discernible impact on organizational performance indicators, and no trouble recruiting to any vacancies. She also reported positive employee engagement and that this is one very tangible measure they are tracking – it is what matters to the organization.

Given the organization's geographical spread they have been used to working asynchronously across time zones for some time and make effective use of technology that enables such things – Slack primarily. They are still conscious about organizational culture though and include whole-organization brunches, town hall meetings and other things to consciously embed organizational culture that cut across time zones.

Teams within what3words have a social budget, and this is enhanced if they socialize with another team. This is intended to encourage cross-organizational communication and most teams do something quarterly with at least one other team.

In the future, Martin wants to streamline many of the organization's policies and to promote managerial discretion, feeling that this will further the personalized approach that is beginning to take root in the organization. She reports that some leaders still have trust issues and may default to wanting people to be on site due to a feeling that on-site work is more productive. As a response to that, she feels what3words will supply more support to leaders on how to address poor performance and why it is important to do that instead of fixating on where people work.

what3words are part way through their journey to personalizing the hybrid approach. They have moved away from rigid fixed hybrid approaches and found ways around most of this, to encourage the individualization of employment arrangements. They still have a way to go, but the direction of travel is positive according to Martin.

Case study reflections

In our first case study, the London Borough of Barnet, the following points are worthy of consideration:

- Where an organization is already looking at, or wanting to look at, how to improve efficiencies in service delivery, a hybrid working approach can supply a useful reason to do so.

- Considering the nature of each job role, the tasks it undertakes, and then individual job-holder circumstances, will lead to a personalized approach to hybrid working.

- If you choose to allow staff to work outside the UK, expecting greater flexibility on working hours may help with collaboration and communication.

- If being a net-zero organization is an important thing to achieve, hybrid working will move you closer to that.

- Allowing staff to live in areas nowhere near the on-site location may allow them to reduce their cost of living as well as saving on their commuting costs – and both combined could be a considerable boost to recruitment and retention.

- However, be mindful that many jobs will require some on-site presence – this will mean there is a need to redesign the job so that hybrid working can work for it.

- Where teams can create their own hybrid working approaches, be watchful of team cultures beginning to override organizational culture, as we covered in Chapter 2, and take steps to address this.

- Providing managers with corporate-level guidance and encouragement, and individual coaching, is likely to overcome many difficulties and objections.

- Reducing on-site space can lead to revenue-generating opportunities and the chance to create community-based spaces that may help organizational reputation.

- Personalizing the working experience can be an incredibly powerful tool to make hybrid working work.

In our second case study, what3words, the following points are also worthy of consideration:

- Adopting a fixed hybrid approach is an easy decision to make but has downsides if there is no obvious reason for it.

- Listening to staff feedback is important – every employee will have different preferences and needs and will perform tasks with different requirements – asking them about these things is critical to making hybrid working work.

- Rigid organizational policies have a place, but where they prevent people getting what they need from the employment relationship there may be a need to work around these.

- Building in added flexibility to create room for manoeuvre may be worth investigating.

- Consciously remodelling the on-site experience to encourage the right kinds of on-site working is helpful, as is giving guidance on how to optimize the remote working set-up.

- Working across time zones creates lots of helpful experiences about how to work asynchronously, and harnessing this along with the right technology is advisable.

- Incentivizing teams to socialize with other teams is interesting but could be extremely positive.

The action plan

If you want to personalize the hybrid working experience, answering the following questions will be helpful:

- What data exists about the way hybrid workers work (either in your systems or elsewhere)? How do you need to use this?

- What are the motivations of your hybrid workers and how can you best leverage these?

- What personas, needs and preferences do your hybrid employees have?
- What would the four-box model reveal about your work?
- How will you help others in your team and organization to analyse their work using the four-box model?
- What will you do to redesign work if the initial four-box model analysis is not the outcome you or the organization want?
- What are the non-negotiables of hybrid work from an organizational perspective? And yours?
- What kind of flexibility will you build into hybrid work arrangements?
- How will you encourage asynchronous communication among employees?
- What kinds of process redesign will you do to optimize them for hybrid working?
- What does your network map or sociogram reveal about connections at work?
- What are the strengths and weaknesses of how individual hybrid workers, and their teams, are connected in the organization?
- How will you ensure that working patterns and workspaces connect the right people in the right ways?
- What guidance must you give to individual hybrid workers about their remote workspace, particularly if this is in a multi-hybrid worker household or co-working space?

References and further reading

CIPD (nd) Flexible and hybrid working: Pearson, www.cipd.org/en/knowledge/case-studies/flexible-hybrid-working-pearson/ (archived at https://perma.cc/7VX9-3P93)

Davis, M C et al (2022a) Report: Where is Your Office Today? Part ONE, University of Leeds, 26 May, https://futureworkplace.leeds.ac.uk/ao_report_052022/ (archived at https://perma.cc/Y2D3-NATY)

Davis, M C et al (2022b) Where is your office today? New insights on employee behaviour and social networks, University of Leeds, October, https://futureworkplace. leeds.ac.uk/wp-content/uploads/sites/86/2022/10/Where-is-your-office-today-Oct-2022-2.pdf (archived at https://perma.cc/JUD6-2PCY)

Froud, B (2021) The hyper-personalisation of work and hybrid personas, LinkedIn, 4 May, www.linkedin.com/pulse/hyper-personalisation-work-hybrid-personas-bryan-froud (archived at https://perma.cc/XD3Q-TEKX)

Garner, M (2022) 'No one size fits all for hybrid working', workingmums, 31 May, www.workingmums.co.uk/no-one-size-fits-all-for-hybrid-working/ (archived at https://perma.cc/E74V-E65H)

Hirst, A and Penny, L (2022) *Workstyle: A revolution for wellbeing, productivity and society*, Nicholas Brealey Publishing, London

Hope Hailey, V and Jacobs, K (2022) Responsible Business Through Crisis: Has COVID-19 changed leadership forever? Executive Summary, CIPD, November, www.cipd.org/uk/knowledge/reports/responsible-business-through-crisis/ (archived at https://perma.cc/PP5U-BVQG)

HR Happy Hour (2022) HR means business 2 – rethinking our approach to work with a new model for HR, 19 December, www.hrhappyhour.net/episodes/ hr-means-business-2-rethinking-our-approach-to-work-with-a-new-model-for-hr/ (archived at https://perma.cc/2NWM-PEZ8)

INC Group (nd) 5 ways to personalize a hybrid work environment, www. inc-solutions.com/5-ways-to-personalize-a-hybrid-work-environment/ (archived at https://perma.cc/XXX2-K96K)

Jameson, L (2021) Seven ways to personalize hybrid work environments, *Work Design Magazine*, 10 March, www.workdesign.com/2021/03/seven-ways-to-personalize-hybrid-work-environments/ (archived at https://perma.cc/7VJT-L4GJ)

Manning, C (2021) The future of personalisation in the workplace, *The HR Director*, 26 December, www.thehrdirector.com/features/future-of-work/ the-future-of-personalisation-in-the-workplace/ (archived at https://perma.cc/ LP3D-X8RZ)

6

Technology and spaces

The shorter read

Organizations that want to make hybrid working work need to invest in using technology to make this easier. However, there are barriers – organizational culture and the adoption of mobile technology in the workplace, among others. The workplace and its use of mobile technology often lags behind what we are used to in our personal lives. Therefore, it isn't a skill or will issue with employees, it is organizational choices that hold us back.

Many of the pieces of technology available will blend seamlessly into a modern and well-designed workplace, offering more of what individuals and teams need to be able to work effectively as remote and hybrid workers. But adding more technology into an employee's daily life could lead to digital overload. We must make careful choices to get this right.

The right technology will enable greater flexibility about when and where work can take place, which may accelerate moves away from the traditional working week, as we discussed in Chapter 3. The technology could speed up workflows, reducing bottlenecks and improving decision making. Organizations must decide what they want to achieve, and how technology will address the pain points that employees experience. It may be that work is needed on a cultural level before innovative technology is implemented. Organizations also need to ensure the closest match between the digital customer experience they provide, and the digital employee experience.

Automation and particularly artificial intelligence (AI) give us lots of ways to improve the hybrid employee experience. Taking out manual stages from a process will again improve the flexibility of that process, which will aid hybrid workers. Letting AI take the strain out of synchronous tasks may allow for more asynchronous working to be possible. But again, organizations must be clear on what they want AI to achieve for them, and much of this will be a cultural decision.

We must also ready the physical workplace for the growth in hybrid working. The balance of functions that the physical on-site workplace provides needs to be different, and the remote workspace also needs to be different, with multiple spaces, each suitable for diverse types of work. This requires employees to move around the different spaces through the day, which will bring them into contact with different people and keep them performing at an optimum level.

Redesigning the on-site experience is necessary if we are to overcome some of the challenges that remote and hybrid working creates for organizations. We cannot leave that to chance.

The longer read

Throughout this book we have noted that there is no one size fits all approach to hybrid working, and that personalizing the employee experience is likely to work more effectively being led by the task requirements and individual preferences. Allied to this we must ensure that the right technology and equipment is provided to employees, and that they are in the right environment for the task.

Technology and hybrid working

Many organizations have invested heavily in fully equipping their workplaces and employees with technology and equipment, so that they can feel connected and productive regardless of how they work. But how do we know what the right technology is? Unified communications solutions make switching between working locations easier, and mobile-enabled software or apps allow for work to be done on different devices, but which ones?

I teach on CIPD qualifications occasionally, and in one lesson I asked students roughly how much of their personal admin they could complete using only a smartphone. The average answer was 90 per cent. I then asked them roughly how many of their work tasks they could complete using only a smartphone. The average answer was around 25 per cent. This perhaps underlines the scale of the challenge we face. We must make the adoption and use of technology for and by hybrid workers easy.

Nicky Hoyland is the CEO of Huler, a technology provider based in the UK but with clients globally. She sees a divide between organizations who want to go back to the pre-pandemic world of work, and those who are moving forward and embracing technology. In the former types of organizations, she feels that the people teams (HR, L&D) are not working closely enough with the IT and legal teams to fully understand the people implications of technology developments, and that often the contractual side of things prevents some organizations and their employees from keeping pace with what technology can now offer them. Hoyland believes that technology has advanced sufficiently that many knowledge workers could now become gig workers, but that many organizations cannot or do not want to take that step.

Conversely, Hoyland sees many forward-thinking organizations addressing the mismatch that exists between the digital customer experience and the digital employee experience. She counsels that we must be mindful of asking employees to continuously learn new technology, which will add to their cognitive load – we must make it easy, and intuitive.

Based on this I asked Hoyland how Huler as an employer themselves were coping. While they have supplied no specific hardware or equipment beyond a smartphone and a laptop, they have realized they need far more software licences (for collaborative software where multiple people will use it synchronously). They make effective use of Slack and Asana to encourage collaboration and manage workflows and communication. Hoyland says that it can be difficult to know what communications go on what media and channels, and that Huler has worked hard to become more intentional and conscious about what they do. The Huler Hub, one of their main products to clients and customers, is also used internally and provides lots of inbuilt recognition and sharing of praise/feedback in case things are missed on the main channels.

Huler, like many other organizations, have redesigned their workplace and now only have hot desks and flexible meeting spaces. They aren't big enough to need to use hotelling software (which automates the management of spaces) to manage this, but their product does offer integrations with such software, which would give greater visibility over who is going to be where, sometimes weeks in advance. This would allow for better forward planning of meetings and collaboration. To make such things work more effectively, Huler have created Team SLAs (what we will examine as Team Charters in a later chapter) and Team Statuses (to alert others about changes to working arrangements on any given day).

The Huler example shows how a tech-savvy company can make the most of blending changes to the work environment with the right technology. There are other platforms that can offer more of what hybrid workers and teams may need. One example is Mo, which offers automation of engagement and recognition, the ability to create group social posts, to link and gamify behaviours to company values, to allow sharing of 'Moments' (similar to Stories found on other social media platforms), build employee profiles and link to Slack/Teams discussions It also allows for crowdsourcing ideas on company platforms.

This sounds like organizations have many options – and they do – at least around technology, potentially less so around the real estate issues that they must also face up to. However, it can be challenging for organizations to work out what they need to use technology for and to find the right solution.

Often the inertia around decision making is driven by fear of the unknown or a fear of overloading people. Microsoft comment on the concept of 'digital debt', where the inflow of data outpaces our ability as humans to process it all (Microsoft, 2022). We must do something about this. Hybrid working inevitably needs employees to use more technology than on-site working might. Microsoft's research points out the scale of the issue we face in how people work, with the average employee spending 57 per cent of their time in meetings or sending emails/messages – and the number of meetings having increased by 192 per cent since the Covid-19 pandemic (Microsoft, 2022). This shows that there are considerable inefficiencies in the way we currently work. But we should also consider if changing the mindset about the way we work could help – why do things have to be synchronous, when technology could enable more asynchronous working?

As hybrid working has grown in popularity, we have noted how the traditional working week has declined in popularity. Cloud-based solutions and collaborative tools now enable hybrid working and individual preferences about working patterns to be achieved. Many tasks *can* allow people to work when and where they want, as the technology eases that (although whether they should do so is up for debate in some organizations).

Technology can improve how work is done and can also improve the efficiency of how it is done, but only if the decision is made to do so. This is as much a cultural matter as anything else.

As we will examine later in this chapter, automation of tasks can speed up workflows, but it is the human decision making that can slow it down. We must therefore give the right guidance to managers, teams and organizations about how to do this better.

Alan Price is CEO of BrightHR, a software provider to 90,000 predominantly small businesses mostly in the UK. Price believes that many organizations still have trust issues, which mean they struggle to adopt and fully use what the technology gives them. Like Hoyland in our earlier example, Price sees different behaviour. He sees some employers using technology to track what employees are doing, and when they are working. He also sees some employers using technology to force disconnect from work tasks and prevent burnout. BrightHR can be used for either purpose.

BrightHR have seen a rapid and consistent move to mobile use of their product, reinforcing some of our earlier points about how mobile-enabled and mobile-facilitated our lives – at least at home, but increasingly at work – have become. Price has noted that technology that isn't fully mobile-enabled is being superseded by technology that is, with organizations clamping down on use of non-standard technology to focus on what works for most of their workforce.

BrightHR themselves have evolved to supply more of what hybrid workers need. In their early days they supplied a service based on rota and absence management, but now offer far more on document management, rewards and gamifying of values, as well as offering a wider range of rewards and discounts that are not tied to a specific location. Many of the rewards now offered apply to whole households or families rather than individual employees, recognizing that hybrid workers have a wider range of stakeholders than on-site workers may. On document management, Price continues to see a move away from paper-based processes that he says may sound obvious, but he feels that technology doesn't always support this move given that the related processes are bespoke to a given company. He believes there need to be improvements in connectors between systems to minimize rework (such as APIs, no-code tools and similar).

He has seen an increase in the need for technology to create spaces for company noticeboards and social interactions and recognition. Whereas these spaces would have been on site in previous years, for hybrid working they must be digital, and Price commented that while there may be big tools in this space, they are not easy to adapt and apply to work that isn't naturally desk-based – he sees opportunities for improvement here .

Price's example shows how organizations face choices. We must ensure we get it right. What kind of help do organizations need?

Giving the right advice about selecting the right technology

Without establishing how to choose the right technology, organizations can feel baffled. Here are some points to consider when guiding your organization:

- Be clear on what you want technology to be used for and how you will know if it is being used effectively. Take time to establish the drivers for bringing in technology and be clear on the potential barriers – a force field analysis may be helpful here.

- Don't expect to solve all your problems straight away – technology implementation should be seen as an iterative approach, with regular points to review what is working and what needs to change. This means not wasting time looking for a 'perfect' technology solution.

- Work out employee pain points across the organization and gather data to illustrate these. Talk to technology providers about how they can help with these – rarely will their standard offerings be bespoke enough for any specific organization, but if you can find a technology provider who can work with you on the pain points and make something bespoke for you, that will be very helpful.

- Consider what the culture is around communication and use of technology now. Are teams maturing enough to cope with modern technology and platforms? If they are not, perhaps there is work to be done on what you already have before anything new is brought in.

- While platforms such as Microsoft Teams, and Zoom, are very useful – they are successful because of the way they are packaged to the market (particularly Teams). Such platforms are designed to appeal to a majority of, but not all, users. In many organizations there will be pockets of resistance against using such platforms because they don't offer what specific teams and users need. Consider the pros and cons of going away from the more popular platforms.

- Ensure there is a match between the digital employee experience and the digital customer experience – there could be clashes between the way employees communicate with each other and the way they are expected to communicate with customers. This could lead to confusion, so there could be cultural actions to take before new technology is brought in.

Organizations also need to work out whether artificial intelligence and automation of processes can supply a more effective solution than individual employees using new technology. In many cases this will be true, but what decisions do they face?

Automation, artificial intelligence and hybrid working

To make hybrid working work more effectively, we must allow technology to take some of the strain out of previously manual processes. Hybrid work needs efficient and effective technology to be able to thrive. In *HR for Hybrid Working*, I posed a question about what we could automate and suggested that we adopt an 80:20 rule – look at the 20 per cent of the processes that take up 80 per cent of your time and automate these. Since that was published though, the world has seen significant and fast-paced developments in AI and its role in automating and digitizing processes. Nonetheless the point remains – search for the pain points and the major processes that employees are experiencing and using.

Throughout my career I've had a fondness for process mapping as a way of identifying where efficiencies can be made and in ensuring that processes are optimized. Doing process mapping for all major tasks would enable you to see where bottlenecks occur. It would enable you to see what impact automating or using AI could have, and how steps in tasks can be used to consciously build in-person collaboration or to allow greater flexibility in when/where/how they are done.

Microsoft suggest that there is great optimism about the potential for AI in changing the way we work. They suggest that 76 per cent of employees say they would be confident using AI for admin tasks, and a similar percentage report confidence in using AI for analytical or creative work. They also report that 86 per cent are looking to use AI to find information and answers, and that 80 per cent will use AI to summarize meetings and action points. Leaders also want to use AI to improve productivity – but not to reduce headcount (Microsoft, 2023).

There are already multiple products on the market that will do these things. Transcription services from Otter.ai and SmartyMeet (among others) remove the requirement for note- or minute-takers, but index meeting content so that quick searches can be done across many meeting notes. Platforms like Personio allow the centralization of initial employee queries (usually to an HR team but can be adapted for other purposes) to track and distribute work more easily across a hybrid team, offering integrations with Teams and Slack channels via chatbots, and allowing customized automated workflows for less simple employee-driven processes. The metaverse also provides digital immersive spaces for meetings and team collaboration, with employees represented by avatars.

Put simply, if there isn't a piece of technology that can do what you would like it to do, there soon will be. That's also without really examining what the next generation of AI could do.

Part of the problem is that many organizations have not yet decided what they want to use AI for and have not defined the problem it could solve. Again, an iterative approach may help here, much like it would with hybrid working in general – experiment, learn, repeat. The CIPD suggest that organizations should establish principles about how they will use AI responsibly, how they will engage and develop their people in AI skills, and how they will use AI to achieve organizational strategy (CIPD, nd). In earlier chapters I have made similar points about hybrid working – be clear how it will help, how you will develop and engage employees, how it will be regulated, and more. The future of hybrid working will increasingly be linked to the future development and successful deployment of AI, given how that may change when/where/how work is done.

AI could help by changing the nature of tasks to allow more scope for hybrid working – it could remove the anchor that ties a particular task to one box of the four-box model. For that to work, hybrid workers will need training on how to use AI but also how to use the new processes once AI has changed those. Managers will also need training on how to coach their teams on effective AI use.

Forbes comments on some of what AI can offer hybrid workers:

- Better coordination of data and information, enabling more efficient access and sharing of knowledge, and more intelligent recommendations for meetings and resources.
- Platforms that can match skill sets and interests to optimize team formation, and create peer-to-peer learning and mentoring.
- Analysis of patterns in employee behaviour and performance to show areas for improvement in time management and prioritization of tasks.
- Finding and getting quicker access to subject matter experts, and curating content and resources from these.
- Monitoring data generated by hybrid workers to make observations about well-being and give recommendations for improvements in mental and physical health (Tsipursky, 2023).

And that isn't an exhaustive list either – but even if AI can achieve only a few from that list, it will go some way towards addressing some of the support that individuals, teams and their leaders need around hybrid working. It may make coming on site much easier to do as the experiences would be less random or unplanned, and more focused on in-person collaboration. It would make the remote experience a more productive one given its ability to improve information sharing, enhance communication and provide access to required knowledge.

And could this go further? Some commentators have guessed that the shift to remote and hybrid work has readied us for working with virtual AIs rather than physical humans (Samuel, 2023).

Automation, different use of technology and the growth and implementation of AI can have a significant impact on remote and hybrid working. However, we must ensure that the physical spaces in which work is done are conducive to the tasks being performed. Currently few organizations have given this much thought, but if we just implement new technologies without addressing the physical environment, we have only gone halfway towards solving hybrid working.

On-site working design and hybrid working

All of this means that the physical workplace and the on-site experience needs to be quite different. No longer can we have offices made up entirely of rows of desks and the odd meeting room. The balance of these needs to change to account for diverse types of working. In *HR for Hybrid Working*, I talked about five types of spaces that a modern workplace needs to have:

1   Touchdown spaces for people to work for short bursts of time before moving on to another space.

2   Flexible spaces with easily moveable chairs, tables and other furnishings and equipment to enable those using the space to tailor it to their needs, with plug and play technology that enables quick access to whatever people need to work together. I've since renamed this the village hall approach. If you consider a typical village hall, with a hireable space, it has a large open space that is used for a wide variety of different purposes by separate groups. It is set up for each group as and when they need to use the space, and tidied up afterwards.

3   Areas that replicate the atmosphere one may find in a library – quiet, focused and largely interruption-free spaces that enable people to work individually on asynchronous work.

4 Hot-desking facilities, bookable in advance and enabling people to work with others who have booked such spaces for their entire working day.

5 The more traditional fixed settings we may be more used to.

Since *HR for Hybrid Working* was published, I've been pleased to find lots of examples of organizations remodelling their workplaces along these lines, but some of these report that the spaces are not used as intended, or effectively. Some of this is old behaviours not being addressed, such as individuals wanting their 'own' space. This is understandable but we must be task-led here. Employees themselves need to be ultra flexible and be prepared to move around different spaces as they do different tasks. This, however, relies on employees knowing what environment is best suited for each task they undertake, and being able to make the right decisions each time. It also requires some forward planning and coordination of tasks so that the movement is seamless and relatively easy.

In Chapter 5 I updated the four-box model for hybrid working and we looked at how this helps us understand the way that work can be done differently. I've updated it further in Figure 6.1 to map the spaces in the list above onto the four-box model.

FIGURE 6.1 The four-box model with addition of spaces

	When must the task be done?	
Where must the task be done?	Synchronously with other people On-site in a fixed location • Flexible spaces • Fixed settings	Asynchronously at any suitable time On-site in a fixed location • Touchdown spaces • Hot-desking spaces • Flexible spaces • Library-type spaces
	Synchronously with other people Any suitable location • Fixed settings (on site or remote) • Flexible spaces (on site or remote)	Asynchronously at any suitable time Any suitable location • Flexible spaces (on site or remote) • Library-type spaces (on site or remote)

This relies not just on the creation of these types of spaces but a raising of awareness of the purpose of the spaces, and general agreement about how, when and why to access them. The CIPD's case study from Principality talks about how that organization achieved that, incorporating employee feed-back during the design phase so that all the spaces I have mentioned are provided. They also let employees book the spaces via an app, which also allows them to see who else is on site on any given day, and to create their own hubs with whomever they wish (CIPD, 2023a).

In 2012 the organization I worked in decided to combine nine offices, all based in one town, into one. I led on the people and culture side of the project. The building itself was a new-build property, and along with the rest of the senior team I wanted to make this a clean break with our past, a once-in-a-generation opportunity to influence or perhaps even reset our culture, implement new ways of working and to better engage employees. I was conscious that the physical workplace does not set culture alone, and this project was tied into many other wider changes in the organizational system also.

Employee consultation was embedded throughout this process. One of the first decisions was about the siting of the new building. Politically it needed to be within the town centre environment, but I also received strong feedback from employees that they wished it to be close to public transport links and local amenities, which meant that a town centre location was also their preference. Another point for discussion was car parking. We had been in a situation where every employee at their various existing offices had a designated car park space, and yet we had been moving to increasingly agile and mobile ways of working, which meant that many car parking spaces weren't occupied throughout the day. We had been having a big push on remote working or at least using third spaces like co-working spaces in between customer appointments if going home wasn't feasible, and therefore many desks weren't fully occupied throughout the day either. I consulted employees about creating the new office so that it could never accommodate all employees, and even fewer cars (considering our push to be a more socially and environmentally responsible employer and the proximity to public transport links). Initial reactions were strongly negative but through gentle challenging of assumptions and showing how new ways of working could be adapted to cope with this environment, this ended up being exactly how the new office was designed.

When it came to the interior design, I involved employees in every decision I could, from the number and names of the meeting rooms to colour schemes for carpets and walls, to how many shared spaces and private offices we had –

everything. We discussed how the new ways of working being implemented required particular environments (see Figure 6.1) and looked at the balance of how much of each type of work was taking place. This was then reflected in the balance of how the different spaces were built into the end design.

As move-in day approached I realized that I needed to do more, and that it was individual behaviour that could make or break whether these new spaces worked effectively. I then facilitated sessions with employees that looked at expectations of behaviour in each space, among teams, in other shared spaces such as kitchen areas, and drafting etiquette and area charters that were placed on walls. We also looked at how ways of working and communication needed to be adapted for those who were working remotely on any given day so that processes involving people working remotely and those in the office were not affected by a location change.

The new on-site experience needs to be flexible enough to make it easy for those who are moving between a remote workspace and the on-site workplace. Both require several types of spaces within them to allow for diverse types of work being done. In Chapter 5 I give examples of how I move around different spaces in my remote workspace, but others may not have that freedom. This means we must provide the widest possible range of spaces on site too, for those who either cannot access the requisite spaces in their remote workspace or, because of the demands of their day, need to be on site for most of their tasks to collaborate with other people and may only be doing tasks that are suitable for remote work for short bursts of time.

This leaves the on-site workplace as a hugely diverse one. It will have each of the spaces that we have examined in Figure 6.1, striking the right balance between the types of tasks that need to be done when employees work there. What it will do, which the remote workspace cannot fully, is supply in-person connection – and therefore the way that people are encouraged to use the on-site workplace when they are planning to be there is to be based around in-person connection. There will be few spaces that are personalized to the individual in the way that their remote workspace can and will be, but there should be a sense of the on-site workplace being a temporarily configurable experience and somewhere that feels like 'our space' instead of 'my space' (INC Group, nd). Teams may congregate around certain spaces but should have easy and frequent access to areas where they will meet other teams – and where possible this should be coordinated in advance.

Coordinating in advance is made easier using the four-box model examined in several chapters in this book. When you know the types of work that you need to do, and how frequently you'll be doing it, you may be able to plan those tasks so that they are actually or nearly adjacent to each other, enabling use of on-site workplaces to be for tasks in the top-left of the box that require collaboration and talking to other people, and for use of remote workspaces to be largely for tasks in the bottom two boxes, requiring quiet, focused time where other people are not as important. Much of the reason that hybrid working may not be working in some organizations is because not enough thought is going into this, or there isn't enough flexibility on task allocation or task forward planning to make good enough use of either individual time or workplace spaces. What could happen then?

> My wife is a director of our business and runs the bookkeeping and accountancy services that EPIC provides. She works with a range of her own clients and is a subcontractor to various local accounting firms. One of the latter is keen for her to go into their offices to perform her tasks, despite the tasks not requiring either synchronous work or a fixed on-site location. She is reluctant, primarily because she feels that the noise levels and distractions in the (unmodified) office would prove too much for her and severely reduce her productivity.
>
> In the years leading up to the pandemic my wife did not like remote working, as she felt she needed people around her to talk to. Since the pandemic she has come to enjoy remote working, and now feels that the increased sound levels of an office and distractions from other people would affect her ability to concentrate and decrease the quality of her work.

My wife is probably not alone in having found a perfect environment for the tasks she undertakes – a remote one. *HR Review* comments that employees who are used to performing asynchronous tasks away from other people, mostly remotely, find office banter, nearby videoconferencing and eating at desks the most irritating things, along with humming, singing and other bodily sounds such as breathing and scratching (Brand, 2023).

Therefore, if we are asking employees to come on site, we must supply the widest range of suitable environments, and this includes providing areas on site which replicate the environment they will find at home. This works on the assumption that employees know which space supplies the right environment for the task they are working on – and they may not. Once we have examined the task requirements, we must give guidance on the environment requirements.

But we must also make sure that the environment is comfortable as much as it is productive. Research from the University of Leeds shows that:

- Employees working from private workspaces report the highest level of performance and the greatest comfort.

- Employees working from social workspaces (e.g. on-site collaborative spaces) report the greatest access to task-related information and feedback from colleagues, but the lowest level of comfort (Davis et al, 2022).

Clearly employees cannot do their work with just the right technology and the right space alone. A comfortable as well as productive environment is needed for all types of employees and all types of tasks to ensure that they can remain productive for as long as they are working in the specific space. Brilliant design is one thing – a comfortable workspace is another.

CASE STUDY ONE

Alex Holly is the Head of People and Assets at the West of England Combined Authority, which employs just over 300 people based primarily in the southwest of the UK, providing a range of services to nearby local authorities. As Holly's job title suggests, he combines responsibility for people with responsibility for IT and property/accommodation. This is a useful combination because of the need to coordinate people, spaces and technology to enable effective hybrid working.

Holly reports that the organization had a traditional approach to working until 2019, and that the default approach to technology was to provide employees with desktop computers, landline phone connections and fixed desk settings. The chief executive was reluctant to provide employees with laptops and mobile devices, but Holly was able to persuade them to roll these out and had completed the implementation of a peripatetic working approach just before the Covid-19 pandemic hit. That pandemic moved the organization 'forward decades', says Holly, in terms of attitudes to work, use of technology, and leadership behaviours and mindsets.

As that pandemic receded, Holly began thinking about the spaces needed for the type of work that people were doing. This coincided with the expiry of the lease on their office, which was due to happen in December 2022 – so they had a burning platform, which focused decision making. Holly decided that the best way was to find a brand-new location, and design that around what hybrid workers needed. He undertook consultation and generated lots of engagement by asking employees what type of work they were doing and what space would help them to do that. Employees were also asked what they would like to see and be able to do on the occasions they came on site.

The organization's new building is purposely designed for hybrid workers. It has quiet areas with specially designed acoustics to reduce noise, allowing for quiet and focused individual work to take place. It also has project areas, collaboration spaces, and lots of moveable and configurable furniture and fittings. Some of this cost little, with existing desks repurposed into project tables. The whole idea, says Holly, was to recognize that the world of work is different, that the on-site experience needs to be different to make it attractive and effective, and that employees need to want to come on site rather than it being mandated.

The design of the new building considered not just the type of work but the styles of the individuals undertaking it and the prevailing culture in each team as well as in the wider organization.

To make it work, the organization needed new technology, and invested in hotelling apps so that employees could view available spaces and book them quickly and easily. Employee laptops and mobile devices were upgraded so that they could more easily cope with the varying demands of different apps requiring synchronous collaboration or multiple video calls. The Wi-Fi in the building was also upgraded to full capacity, and security protocols around using public Wi-Fi in external shared spaces were reduced to make it easy to use third spaces such as co-working spaces and coffee shops to undertake work. Meeting rooms are now hybrid-enabled with omnidirectional cameras and microphones, though Holly has had to do some training on how to best use and behave in such spaces.

The organization asks employees to be on site two days a week, but this is not enforced, and each employee is able to decide how best to achieve this. Holly reports that teams coordinate this well among themselves. He also notes that the building itself is not fully utilized, especially on Mondays and Fridays, and that even on midweek days occupancy may only reach 50 per cent. To help, they rent out meeting space to other organizations. Within the building, the new areas such as project tables, social spaces and quiet pods tend to be very well utilized, and it is the fixed settings that are more underutilized. Holly reported some teething trouble with hot-desking, as some employees were still thinking about themselves as desk-based workers and were underutilizing some of the new spaces where their work would be better suited, but notes that these issues have resolved themselves over time.

Holly states that the new building costs more than their old one, but that the organization is happier with it and feel that it suits their culture and employees much better. His advice is to base on-site design around what people are doing and be led by that. In line with other case study advice in other chapters, talking to employees is a great start point, but Holly recommends going further and challenging employees' assumptions about what space they really need. He does not recommend mandating on-site attendance. From a technology perspective he recommends making things easy – things like booking rooms and other spaces must be as close to one click as possible, and intuitive to complete.

CASE STUDY TWO

Jacqui Summons is Chief HR Officer at EMIS Health, a software provider to the UK healthcare industry, with 1,400 employees (1,100 in the UK and 300 in India). Like many organizations, remote and hybrid working was not commonplace in EMIS until the Covid-19 pandemic, but during 2020 and 2021 almost the entire organization worked remotely. As that pandemic receded, EMIS consciously didn't use the word hybrid to describe the way they now wanted to work. Instead, they describe themselves as a 'mainly working from home company' and, except for a couple of teams, all employees are almost entirely remote with limited on-site time.

Consequently, EMIS have closed several major on-site locations in the UK and may yet reduce even further. They have converted what remains into collaborative hubs, with touchdown and hot-desking spaces, but are finding that employees do not choose to use even these. On-site working, and the interactions that flow from this, remain sporadic and unplanned. Summons reports some challenges in getting teams to forward plan their collaborations and interactions. She also notes some problems around the way people choose to work – there are lots of back-to-back meetings, with some employees not leaving their (remote) desks even for short periods and working through lunch breaks, etc.

Within EMIS, Summons has noticed demographic differences with regard to remote, hybrid and on-site working. She feels that it is the older generations who are wanting to work more remotely, and that the younger generations are wanting to come on site more. While she acknowledges some generalizations here, the impact is that informal mentoring and knowledge sharing is suffering. She feels that organizational culture has been weakened somewhat, and that individual benefits have been prioritized over organizational needs.

Because of this, Summons is now taking steps to address some of the cultural issues and challenges. She is bringing whole teams on site to be able to socialize with each other and other teams on site at the same time. She is also beginning to challenge how productivity is viewed. Some managers have held a consistent view that remote workers are not working, and little of this is measurable or evidence based. When challenged, some managers have stated that a reduction in email traffic is 'proof' that the employee is not working as much, and this has enabled Summons to have useful conversations around the organization about what is working and what is thinking and what the true output-based measures should be within the organizational culture. EMIS are using a network monitoring tool to show areas of high and low productivity and use this to find and evaluate potential improvements. As we will examine in a later chapter, managers who have become managers since the Covid-19 pandemic are coping better with the need to view and manage productivity and performance differently than those whose early management career was in face-to-face environments.

Summons told me about differences with their employees based in India, where they have mandated three days a month on site. This is because almost all EMIS India employees relocated during the pandemic to spend lockdown in their family areas instead of where the on-site location was and have been reluctant to voluntarily relocate again, having got used to living and working with their families. This does lead to some challenges as most households are larger than they are in the UK, and busier households pose their own issues for EMIS India employees. Summons believes that in India few companies have been able to make hybrid working work effectively, and have either mandated a full on-site return, or increased days mandated on site – a decision that faces EMIS in the future.

However, Summons does note that hybrid working has had no detrimental impact on business performance, and there have been slight positives from decreased overheads on offices and travel. She also reports that engagement and attrition have improved in the first six months, but there has still been considerable attrition, which she puts down to hybrid working being a popular concept but one that was left too much to chance in the organization's early days of trying it – and frustrated employees voted with their feet. Now, they are doing things on, and with, purpose.

Case study reflections

In our first case study, the West of England Combined Authority, the following points are worthy of further consideration:

- Having a person with oversight of people, technology and real estate can bring greater cohesion for the decisions needed on each that affect the others.

- Consciously planning for the end of any lease on buildings provides a natural break point and milestone on the journey towards effective hybrid working – but starting early with that planning is also crucial.

- Consulting employees about what type of work they are doing and the spaces they feel they need – and gently but firmly challenging assumptions around these things – is helpful.

- Designing in a range of distinct types of workspaces to account for diverse types of work will allow for more effective hybrid working to take place and need not cost too much.

- Easily accessible and usable software or apps are needed to make the different arrangements work more efficiently.

- Insisting on enhanced equipment around the building and in meeting rooms will supply added flexibility and functionality.

- Renting out unused spaces to third-party organizations has been seen in many case study organizations in this book and is a sensible move to provide more revenue and building occupancy.

In our second case study, EMIS Health, the following points are also worthy of consideration:

- Combining on-site locations can make financial sense, but careful consideration is needed to ensure that employees know what the purpose of coming on site is, and how to design their work to make best use of the spaces.
- Working habits may not be conducive to effective hybrid working and may need examining and challenging.
- Leaving on-site interactions to chance is likely to lead to a deterioration in organizational culture and give rise to frustrations that 'hybrid isn't working'.
- Some managers may need to have their views on productivity and performance challenged, and the conversation around output-based working widened to include the entire organization.
- International differences around the way people live and work could pose their own challenges and make it near-impossible for multinational companies to adopt a uniform approach to spaces, places, technology and hybrid working.
- If hybrid working isn't working, despite having the right technology and the right spaces/places, work out why this is the case. It is likely that the cultural issues have been left to chance and override the best of intentions and decisions about technology and spaces/places.

The action plan

If you are examining both the technology and right workspace for your employees, the following questions would benefit from being answered:

- How would you assess the level of digital (over)load among your employees?

- How will you challenge whether tasks should be performed synchronously or asynchronously?

- What would a force field analysis of the drivers and barriers to introducing more technology reveal in your organization?

- What will help to ensure that you take an iterative approach to using technology? What reassurances will your employees need?

- How will you decide the most appropriate pain points for your employees that new technology needs to address?

- What is the current culture around technology use – from both a customer and an employee perspective?

- How much do standard software packages such as Teams and Zoom meet the needs of your employees? What would happen if you moved away from these?

- What are the 20 per cent of processes that take up 80 per cent of employees' time that could be automated? How will you identify them and how will you automate them?

- What does your organization see AI doing for employees and customers? How can that be more clearly mapped?

- Where could automation and AI remove anchors about when and where tasks are done, enabling more flexibility for hybrid workers?

- What spaces do your employees' tasks need to be performed in? How many of these do you have?

- What can you do to repurpose the on-site workplace so that it more closely matches what the tasks require?

- How will you challenge employees' beliefs about the right workspace for the tasks they perform?

- How will you encourage employees to be more flexible about moving around different spaces on any given working day?

References and further reading

Abbasi, F (2020) AI and the hybrid workforce revolution, techUK, 9 November, www.techuk.org/resource/ai-and-the-hybrid-workforce-revolution.html (archived at https://perma.cc/HKC9-J63U)

Brand, A (2023) Bosses confirm offices are failing to adapt to hybrid working, *HR Review*, 30 January, www.hrreview.co.uk/hr-news/bosses-confirm-offices-are-failing-to-adapt-to-hybrid-working/150467 (archived at https://perma.cc/TB67-QPYR)

CIPD (2022) Using technology responsibly to manage people, 19 December, www.cipd.org/uk/knowledge/guides/responsible-technology-use/ (archived at https://perma.cc/9V57-HSK7)

CIPD (2023a) Flexible and hybrid working: Principality Building Society, 25 May, www.cipd.org/en/knowledge/case-studies/flexible-hybrid-working-principality/ (archived at https://perma.cc/J8UF-99VC)

CIPD (2023b) Preparing your organisation for AI use, 30 June, www.cipd.org/uk/knowledge/guides/preparing-organisation-ai-use/ (archived at https://perma.cc/2V6F-G3KF)

CIPD (nd) Automation, AI and technology, www.cipd.org/uk/views-and-insights/cipd-viewpoint/automation-ai-technology/ (archived at https://perma.cc/A2H6-K6Y7)

Davis, M C et al (2022) Where is your office today? New insights on employee behaviour and social networks, University of Leeds, October, https://futureworkplace.leeds.ac.uk/wp-content/uploads/sites/86/2022/10/Where-is-your-office-today-Oct-2022-2.pdf (archived at https://perma.cc/RMR2-KGJB)

Hancock, B, Schaninger, B and Yee, L (2023) Generative AI and the future of HR, McKinsey & Company, 5 June, www.mckinsey.com/capabilities/people-and-organizational-performance/our-insights/generative-ai-and-the-future-of-hr (archived at https://perma.cc/MR2D-2ZK6)

HR Magazine (2023) Skills for the future, hr.mydigitalpublication.co.uk/publication/?i=786866 (archived at https://perma.cc/URR7-LJEL)

HR Zone (nd) How do you maintain culture in a hybrid workplace? www.hrzone.com/community/blogs/terkel/how-do-you-maintain-culture-in-a-hybrid-workplace (archived at https://perma.cc/K9RE-JERV)

INC Group (nd) 5 ways to personalize a hybrid work environment, www.inc-solutions.com/5-ways-to-personalize-a-hybrid-work-environment/ (archived at https://perma.cc/BY6U-VHUG)

Jameson, L (2021) Seven ways to personalize hybrid work environments, *Work Design Magazine*, 10 March, www.workdesign.com/2021/03/seven-ways-to-personalize-hybrid-work-environments/ (archived at https://perma.cc/AJT3-QMA4)

Microsoft (2022) Great expectations: Making hybrid work work, 16 March, www.microsoft.com/en-us/worklab/work-trend-index/great-expectations-making-hybrid-work-work (archived at https://perma.cc/QK4F-B6RV)

Microsoft (2023) 2023 Work Trend Index: Annual Report: Will AI fix work? 9 May, www.microsoft.com/en-us/worklab/work-trend-index/will-ai-fix-work (archived at https://perma.cc/U49A-JKK3)

Mitel (2023) The rising mental and monetary costs of remote and hybrid work in 2023, 20 March, www.mitel.com/blog/the-rising-mental-and-monetary-costs-of-remote-and-hybrid-work (archived at https://perma.cc/Q3U3-NJ48)

Reddy, R (2023) Digital transformation: 3 ways it improves hybrid work, The Enterprisers Project, 18 April, www.enterprisersproject.com/article/2023/4/hybrid-work-digital-transformation (archived at https://perma.cc/5P8C-44UK)

Samuel, A (2023) The new 'Hybrid work' is 'AI + humans', *JSTOR Daily*, 7 July, https://daily.jstor.org/the-new-hybrid-work-is-ai-plus-humans/ (archived at https://perma.cc/MPK9-3VF5)

Tsipursky, G (2023) The AI revolution transforming hybrid and remote work and the return to office, *Forbes*, 9 May, www.forbes.com/sites/glebtsipursky/2023/05/09/the-ai-revolution-transforming-hybrid-and-remote-work-and-the-return-to-office/ (archived at https://perma.cc/V4Y3-E2QG)

Von Kries, C (2022) Optimising hybrid work models with process automation, *The HR Director*, 13 November, www.thehrdirector.com/features/hybrid-working/optimising-hybrid-work-models-process-automation/ (archived at https://perma.cc/3BRE-5XV9)

7

The hybrid employee experience

The shorter read

When we read research showing that a sizeable part of the global workforce is disengaged, we must wonder why this is. The world of work has changed – we now have a personalized employee experience, and hybrid working is a key part of that. How organizations do hybrid working shapes how people feel. People want to feel as if the working arrangements and environment suit their circumstances.

The employee experience is broadly shaped around the life cycle model taking an employee from the first awareness they have of the employer to post-termination activities. Each of the major stages of the life cycle model has data which can be captured to tell us how the experience is for a typical employee at that stage. But the hybrid model could fragment and individualize this because of the unique situation each employee is in.

We are used to hyper-personalization as consumers, but not as employees. The data is there to be used, but few know what to look for or what to do with it. Systems can bring this together for you, but even informally it can be done. If we ignore the individual experiences a hybrid employee has, we are doomed to fail in our efforts to make hybrid working work.

There are unique aspects to a hybrid employee experience that matter more than to a purely on-site employee. These include the ability to make and keep close friendships to combat isolation and loneliness, the ability to connect easier with people in and outside of one's immediate team, and more besides.

A values-based approach to designing the hybrid employee experience is a suggested way forward, avoiding rigid policies and rules and ensuring that the organizational values are fully embedded within the principles of hybrid working. The on-site experience should also be reflective of the organizational values and provide purposeful connection for all. Agile principles may be an effective way of achieving some of these important aspects.

We can learn lessons from how we create and shape our customer experiences, which is usually done in a hybrid way and with significant personalization. To do the same for our hybrid employees we need to talk to everyone – and if that is logistically difficult then we could create and assess personas based on age, career stage and type of work done by each employee.

We should be mindful of the specific needs that types of hybrid employees will have. Young workers, those with caring responsibilities, those returning to work after lengthy periods out of work, older workers, and workers from any minority group will require careful treatment and unique employee experiences based on their requirements and preferences. Left to chance, we risk alienating these groups or creating something that doesn't work for them.

Focusing on major touchpoints in the hybrid employee experience will enable us to forward plan and design the right guidance, support, connections and learning for hybrid employees at any of these touchpoints. Left to chance, we might succeed but more through luck than judgement. Individuals, teams and their leaders and managers need more from us than that.

The longer read

The Gallup Global Workplace Survey for 2023 reveals that only 23 per cent of employees feel engaged in their work or with their organization (Gallup, 2023). Why is this? Consider the experiences the world has had since 2020. Lockdowns and Covid-19 restrictions have represented a disproportionate amount of many employees' time and experiences, and particularly for those employees who are younger than others, a rude awakening into the world of work. Employees of all ages have seen work side by side with their lives in the same place, many for the first time, and have judged life to be as or more important than work. They may not want to mess around in jobs that do not engage them. Their experience at work matters to them.

Attempts to mandate employees back on site even for set days per week may completely underestimate how many people have got used to working wherever and whenever they want to. They may not want to go back to collective employee experiences. We exist in a seller's labour market – we must appeal to the individual. As we discussed in an earlier chapter, personalizing the employee experience is critical. But what is the hybrid employee experience anyway? Is it different than what we understand as employee experience in a general sense? And how do we account for any differences?

The employee experience (EX)

Consider the broad journey that each employee experiences through a typical role with a company. We can highlight shared areas and specific shared experiences that map onto a life cycle model, mirroring what many companies will do for their customer journeys. This enables powerful thinking to take place about how an employee engages with the organization at these various stages:

- **Brand awareness and attraction** – raising awareness of the employer brand and creating a good impression for potential job applicants who may be interacting with it as customers or perhaps just casually becoming aware of you as an employer.

- **Talent acquisition** – all the processes and interactions that lead to becoming an employee, from the advert to the job offer and all points in between.

- **Onboarding and induction** – the period from the job offer to the point the new employee is at optimum performance, with all the information provision, knowledge acquisition and tailored support needed to do that.

- **Growth and development** – the ways that employees will encounter opportunities to develop their skills, knowledge and behaviours, and to consider career growth and development.

- **Employee relations** – the processes that are used to manage the employee's behaviour, attendance and concerns they may have.

- **Talent retention** – the things that a company does to keep employees motivated, performing and willing to remain with the organization.

- **Exit management** – the many ways that an employee can part company with the organization, whether started by the organization or the employee. This would include the policies and procedures that underpin these aspects, and the way the employee is treated leading up to their final day and, potentially, beyond.

There will be measures available at each stage in the list above that will show you how each part is working – effectively, efficiently or some other insight. These measures will also be able to show you where and how improvements can be made, which can be linked to wider organizational goals and to improve the overall experience for employees by acting on the moments that matter most to them.

One of the issues organizations now face is that the hybrid employee experience potentially fragments these general experiences. Each hybrid employee is likely to have had different experiences, not necessarily because of the way the organization manages these aspects or touchpoints, but because they do part of their work in a unique and bespoke environment – their home. That home has different equipment, different people in it, different distractions and attractions than the on-site experience does. Combined, this makes the hybrid employee experience a personalized one (unless, of course, two or more employees who do the same job in the same team also happen to live in the same house and work in the same way).

The hybrid employee experience

The digital era we live in has already acclimatized us to personalization as consumers. It's everywhere. Look at the way Facebook and Amazon tailor your experience. In fact, almost all your online experience is based on your preferences, past experiences and choices, behaviours and interactions.

But we rarely do that in the workplace, as we discussed in Chapter 5. There are systems that will bring together this data for you – how employees prefer to work, how engaged they are and how they are performing. Qualtrics, an experience management technology provider, have some but there are others. They could connect the dots for you about the hybrid employee experience.

While everyone's experience of hybrid working is different, we must find out about that or at least make efforts to tailor the organizational part of things to that experience. Over time, a remote worker works out, through trial and error maybe, the environment, set-up and approach to work–life balance that works best for them. This affects their values and perception of work, and so we need to reflect that in the organizational values and policies. We shouldn't ignore the experiences people have had – in fact it is critical we don't.

If an organization can collect lots of data about its customers and use this in an interface/system to tailor services and products around what that customer has said, done, etc – then the same is possible, and desirable, for employees. Even with a small number of employees it ought to be possible in a more informal way.

For example, most people practice systems store a lot of data about employees but most of this data is relatively static, and although used for statistical purposes there are not many systems, or organizations, that actively use this data to segment employees and map the employee journey in the same way they would a customer group. There are not many people practice systems that have a record of every employee interaction with the organization, and that tailor services and the employee experience based on these. But we could unlock greater employee engagement by focusing on the employee experience and tailoring that to the individual employee. Some systems can supply greater visibility and data that can be used to manage productivity more effectively, particularly in a hybrid workforce. For this to happen managers need to be comfortable using data to gain insights and acting on such insights.

There is a considerable amount of research that tells us what the hybrid employee experience is like in general. The percentage of employees working in a remote or hybrid way is set to reach 56 per cent, up from just 9 per cent prior to 2020 (Rudbeck and Fisher, 2022). Seventy-five per cent of hybrid workers feel that it has had a positive impact on their work–life balance (citing an average of 73 minutes saved per day per hybrid worker), and 47 per cent feel it has improved their well-being (Wilson, 2023).

However, many employees have worked longer by carrying on working when they would have been commuting, some out of gratitude to employers to allowing hybrid work. This has led to issues around burnout and job dissatisfaction after longer periods of remote work (Wilson, 2023). Fifty-nine per cent of hybrid employees have fewer work 'friendships' since going hybrid, 50 per cent feel lonelier at work than before hybrid working and 66 per cent say doing informal coffee chats (and similar) virtually are a chore (Microsoft, 2022).

From a team relationships perspective, 58 per cent of hybrid workers feel they have thriving relationships with their team, and 48 per cent say they have the same with people outside of their immediate team. However, employees who have joined since March 2020 are likely to respond more negatively here, being less likely to feel included (60 per cent versus 64 per cent), having weaker relationships with their immediate team (51 per cent versus 58 per cent) and being at greater risk of leaving (56 per cent versus 38 per cent). And 48 per cent of hybrid workers would like to spend less time answering emails and scheduling meetings (Microsoft, 2022).

Marc Weedon is the Senior Director for HR (International) at Zuora, a global technology organization. I spoke to Weedon to find out how their employee experience had changed because of hybrid working. Zuora's direction of travel is to keep the current hybrid status quo, making it easy for employees to work from anywhere. As a technology company one would expect a high-tech approach from Zuora and indeed this is the case, making effective use of a range of communication and collaboration software to keep employees connected and working effectively.

Zuora have decided to avoid mandating any on-site attendance but do encourage it, based on what work is being done by each team (and supplemented by things that make on site attractive, such as free food and social events). As a result, each location and team have a different approach to hybrid working. All of this is underpinned by extensive consultation and showing employees that their outcomes matter far more than where or when they choose to work.

Weedon explained some barriers faced by Zuora and their employees, including reframing understanding of productivity and what constitutes 'productive work'. He feels that remote working is good for catching up on work, while on-site working is good for catching up with people – and has promoted this distinction around the organization.

Zuora are aware that each employee's remote set-up and environment is different. Some people may find remote work difficult because of isolation or their environment, and therefore they would get a better employee experience by coming on site to work. Weedon has encouraged all employees to find ways to work differently based on the varied employee experiences that a team could have, while keeping things as light-touch as possible based on Zuora's values.

The focus on values is important for Zuora. Weedon explains that culture is about how things are done, not where or when. Zuora's culture promotes change, growth and adaptability – and Weedon feels hybrid working felt a natural extension of that. Zuora also focus heavily on their employees around well-being and work–life balance, so considering the overall hybrid employee experience again felt natural to them. Sticking to such values and cultural aspects meant that hybrid working didn't change them or detract from them.

In the Zuora example we see how the hybrid employee experience is a values-based one. While we may want to adapt and evolve our approach to rewards, benefits and engagement, we should also focus on organizational values and how these create the employee experience. How employees feel about working at an organization is based on how concepts like trust, accountability, belonging, inclusion, flexibility, etc are experienced. Perhaps the hybrid employee experience could be consciously designed around such concepts and not around rigid policies. We also see how the on-site part of the hybrid employee experience is designed to give employees something they cannot access remotely – chiefly the ability to spend time catching up with other people, allowing them to be productive and social at the same time. There is also a recognition that employees need to use the on-site experience for different things, and that some employees may be on site doing work best done in quiet locations for focused activities simply because they cannot do that in their remote workplace.

As we have examined in other chapters, we need to explore choices with everyone to enable them to get more of what matters to them and their wider stakeholders. Treating everyone the same by applying rules to everyone, creating policies that work for the majority, risks alienating some people and missing out on excellent opportunities to craft something different, something better. Zuora, like some other organizations, work on guiding principles rather than set policies. This allows more room for flexibility and evolution, as well as aiding trust to be built and maintained. Consultation with employees will ensure that the key things affecting their overall experience are given priority.

An agile approach is needed

Agile is a term that can be applied to different contexts. In the context of hybrid working, I intend it to mean creating something that is fluid, flexible and not set in stone, which considers the fluctuations in types of work and in individual preferences. Agile methodologies are not covered explicitly in this book but could enable greater flexibility, autonomy and collaboration, which are things that improve the hybrid employee experience. HR Congress provides examples of different companies blending agile methodologies with hybrid working to enhance the hybrid employee experience. Examples include:

- Agile development plans that allow employees to take ownership of their development and career progression.
- Agile performance management to enable employees to receive continuous feedback and coaching from their managers and peers.
- Agile learning platforms to enable employees to co-create learning content and share knowledge with peers (Nagy, nd).

The CIPD provide a case study from Zenith that also focuses on the use of agile principles. Like many organizations covered in this book, Zenith have given guidance on which activities are best undertaken on site and which remotely. They promote that their hybrid working approach is agile – fluid from one day to the next, with each team deciding how to best meet customer needs, team needs and individual preferences. They have trained their leaders and managers in scenarios, not policies, recognizing the flexibility and ambiguity that moving away from a prescriptive one size fits all approach may need to embody (CIPD, 2023).

Mirroring the customer experience (CX)

There may be lessons to learn and adapt from how our organizations deal with customers. The customer experience (CX) is often already a hybrid one. There are often a range of high-touch customer experiences to make the hybrid model more seamless for customers, who demand a mix of digital and physical experiences (Bibb, 2022). In a hybrid CX model thought is given to culture, personalized experience and what could cause disconnect. The hybrid employee experience model requires the same, delivered with compassion and understanding rather than rigid policies or micromanagement (Bibb, 2022).

But with so many employees, how can we do this? The same as organizations do with customers when creating CXs – by asking questions, and by creating personas. Across any organization there will be different employee personas. These could be functional or based on demographics or career experience – or perhaps a blend of these. It is possible to map out the interactions that each of these personas has with the organization, bearing in mind that various organizational functions will contribute to this (such as HR, L&D, finance, IT, facilities and more). It would then be possible to find out at each stage what is happening to typical employees in each persona. Looking at the main touchpoints during this hybrid EX journey would enable an organization to determine, much like it does with a hybrid CX journey, what needs to be changed or improved at each point and whether any persona or type of employee is going to face any barrier or detriment along their journey. In the following sections I'll explain some types of employees whose hybrid experience we must be particularly mindful of.

Types of employees whose hybrid experience we must be mindful of

Younger or less experienced employees

This group encompasses those who are of a younger age, as well as those with less working experience. Both types may be in their first job, or perhaps what my dad would have called their first 'proper job'. Some research has suggested that hybrid employees aged under 20 score lower engagement compared to older age groups, lower levels of well-being and generally poorer remote working set-ups (Cholteeva, 2023). Some of the criticisms levelled at remote and hybrid working have also centred on this demographic group, suggesting that remote working is more detrimental to younger or less experienced people because they miss time on site to understand organizational culture, learn from more experienced colleagues and build the requisite connections. As we have noted in earlier chapters though, hybrid working doesn't have to come with any negative impact – all it takes is conscious effort to avoid the negative impact. But where does the negative connotation come from?

It could well be true that younger workers may find remote working more of a challenge. I remember times during Covid-19 lockdowns when both my wife and I were remote working but suddenly joined by two older children who also then needed to use internet bandwidth, the same workspaces and sometimes devices. It would be rare for households to have multiple suitable spaces, and while not impossible to overcome, it would be understandable if the junior members of a household were the ones to have least access to the most suitable spaces and devices. Even if living away from parents, it is more likely that younger workers have less disposable income to afford the best equipment and spaces.

From a networking perspective, those with less working experience would naturally not always have built up as large a network as more experienced workers. They could therefore feel more isolated by remote and hybrid working. Access to more experienced colleagues is something that those with less working experience would need to happen more often to enable them to pick up the right behaviours and skills as well as cultural knowledge and 'nous'.

Some of these things will be affected by remote and hybrid working if it is left to chance. Requesting and receiving feedback, forming friendships, and intentionally seeking information are all behaviours and actions that are important for younger or less experienced workers, but these also matter to other employees (Jörden and Alayande, 2022). The difference is the level of confidence that younger or less experienced workers may have in undertaking these actions. They need more help. They need planned interactions with key members of the organization. Spending time on site may help this, but only if those key members of the organization are on site at the same time. This may mean that there isn't a magic number of days that younger or less experienced workers need to spend on site, but the planned and intentional nature of on-site days is what is likely to matter more. We must show when on-site experience is likely to have the biggest impact and must schedule or plan these things so that they happen at the right time for these groups.

We could also find an increased level of comfort from younger workers with digital forms of communication. Those whose formative years have been dominated by easy access to social media, contributing to online communities, with relationships not constrained by physical location, and handling a significant amount of their personal transactions online too, may be much more comfortable with doing such things in the working environment than others who have had different experiences. Unless we ask them though we may never know, but we must guard against making assumptions about the way we think they may wish to work if those assumptions are based, largely, on our own and not their experiences.

Those with caring responsibilities

While there is a lot of research to examine the impact of hybrid working on men and women in general, in this section I will consider how it shapes the experience of women returning to the workplace after a break, either to care for children or another reason. I will also look at employees with caring responsibilities in a more general and less gender-specific way. Around 54 per cent of women were classed as hybrid workers compared with 48 per cent of men (Mutebi and Hobbs, 2022). Sixty-five per cent of women agree that the Covid-19 pandemic has made them rethink the place that work has in their lives, with many women spending five to seven hours a week more on caring responsibilities since that pandemic (Gartner, 2021). We must factor in these changed expectations into working arrangements. Spending more time on caring arrangements may be something that cannot be undone, and therefore mandating on-site attendance could have a disproportionate impact on those with caring responsibilities, the majority of whom are women. On the other hand, the increased flexibility that can come from hybrid working may allow more freedom to manage caring responsibilities alongside work, so it is easy to understand why many women with caring responsibilities will find this attractive.

Data shows that those with caring responsibilities are more likely to want to work remotely to allow them to better fulfil those responsibilities. Employees with children make up a greater proportion of hybrid workers than those without children (Mutebi and Hobbs, 2022). Such employees will present different EX challenges from any other groups and we must tailor the experience to their needs. Parents, for example, may want to work more remotely in the summer due to school holidays and want to work more on site in term-times – so having a rigid hybrid model is unlikely to work for such employees who may need to evolve their hybrid approach based on their individual circumstances. Given that being on site may be more of a logistical challenge for those with caring responsibilities, making sure that it is a valuable experience is even more important. They may benefit more from one day a week on site if their entire team are present, than they would from three days a week where only some people are present.

If an employee (female or not) has been absent from work for some time, perhaps because of caring responsibilities or some other reason, returning to work can be a daunting prospect. Returning to a role that is a hybrid one may be even more daunting. We know that hybrid work includes a lot of virtual meetings – if we are not careful, there is a danger this leads to cognitive overload for those who have spent lengthy periods away from work. They have been used to having no such interactions and may be plunged into a role that has lots of frequent meetings – they could find this difficult.

There are often criticisms of hybrid working that it can reduce visibility of employees and mean they are the victims of proximity bias compared to those working on site. This is a likely occurrence if nothing is done to combat it, and if a greater proportion of women than men are hybrid workers, we have the potential for indirect discrimination to occur. Training for leaders on avoiding proximity bias is a promising idea, but knowing your data about the gender split of hybrid working is the starting point. We should also consider how to equalize the provision of information and availability of knowledge within organizations. If they are only or predominantly available to those working on site, we are creating unequal and inequitable employee experiences that disadvantage remote and hybrid workers. If events where employees can socialize and network are only held on site, we should consider remote and hybrid workers' ability to access these – could they take place at different time slots to encourage easier attendance? Could they be planned further in advance to allow better forward planning around caring responsibilities?

Those with caring responsibilities, who are predominantly women, could find returning to work a strain on both their mental and physical health. Working full days after significant periods away from work and then having the (often unfair) expectation of taking on the main burden of domestic responsibilities after work will be a drain on the energy of any employee, and adding commutes to that may make the situation worse. Building in flexibility around not just where but also when work can take place may allow employees in this situation to better make work flow around their energy levels and other responsibilities. Giving greater access to benefits such as paid/unpaid parental leave, increased annual leave and health benefits would all be helpful to consider also – while reducing the reliance on benefits that are only available for on-site employees.

Older employees

While UK-focused, labour market statistics point to a rise in people aged 50–64 leaving the workforce (Wilson, 2023). The research suggests that much of the exits are voluntary, caused by being financially able to retire or simply deciding that work wasn't meeting their needs any more, as opposed to being enforced through ill health. In the UK there have been moves to entice some of these early retirees back into the workforce, and hybrid work is one way to achieve this. Again, research suggests that hybrid working is more popular among middle-aged and older employees compared to younger employees, even pre-pandemic but we must create the right experience for these demographic groups (Wilson, 2023).

Providing some form of hybrid working but tailoring it to the needs of older employees may convince those who could retire to continue working for longer. We could usefully ask older employees what they want and need from their employee experience. Like other groups, purposeful on-site experience is likely to feature highly – employees will find this better than if it is just left to chance. Employees want to be able to connect with, socialize with and share experiences with other employees when on site. When the home is such an enjoyable and pleasant place to be, bringing older employees on site to do things that they a) could and b) would much rather do at home may tip them to consider leaving the workforce altogether, so we must be intentional.

Should any early retirees be tempted back into the workforce, it is unlikely to be to work on site for all their time. We should consider some of the same points we have considered when talking about those with caring responsibilities returning to work after a period of economic inactivity – similar issues are likely to be faced and similar solutions are likely to help.

Those with disabilities

Data shows that workers with disabilities have experienced both positive and negative impacts from remote and hybrid working. The majority have seen a positive impact on things like having more energy due to less commuting, greater control over their working environment and having more personal time to look after themselves, therefore positively affecting their mental and physical health (Mutebi and Hobbs, 2022). Indeed, most workers with long-term health conditions believe that there should be a statutory right to work remotely if there is no strong reason why the job cannot be done from home (Wilson, 2023).

Your own organizational data will be crucial here to understanding the scale of the issues faced. How many employees do you have who identify as disabled? What jobs do they do? What jobs could they do if you improved the flexibility and autonomy in those jobs? It would be a simple reasonable adjustment to ensure that some or all tasks could be done remotely, and there will be few strong reasons why some work cannot be done remotely or in a hybrid way. Mandating certain on-site attendance patterns is likely to create barriers for those with disabilities, and special arrangements may need to be put in place for them – but then, isn't that what a personalized employee experience is all about?

Other minority groups

There is data to suggest that those who live alone or, at the other extreme, in busy households may find the remote part of hybrid working quite negative (Mutebi and Hobbs, 2022). This shows that we should tailor the employee experience again to their specific needs and provide such employees with added flexibility about where and when, and indeed how, work should be done.

Other research has shown that:

- Non-binary employees are 14 per cent more likely to prefer hybrid working than cisgender colleagues.
- LGBTQ+ employees are 13 per cent more likely to prefer hybrid work than heterosexual colleagues, and 24 per cent more likely to quit a job if it did not provide hybrid working.
- Black employees are 14 per cent more likely than their white colleagues to quit a job if it did not provide hybrid working.
- Employees with disabilities are 14 per cent more likely to quit a job than non-disabled employees if it did not provide hybrid working (Wilson, 2023).

In this we see that managing the stigmas often associated with such protected characteristics can be much easier with a greater element of remote working. Again, our own employee data is key to beginning to understand this, before adapting the hybrid employee experience to better suit individual needs.

Typical touchpoints in the hybrid employee experience

There are multiple touchpoints in any employee experience, and we have covered some of the main aspects of the employee life cycle already in this chapter. But from a hybrid perspective there may be some touchpoints where more thought and action are needed.

Firstly, a new starter. In *HR for Hybrid Working*, I talked about the ways in which we need to adapt onboarding and induction processes for hybrid workers. As more people change organizations to seek the right balance and hybrid working approach for them, the onboarding and induction processes need further tailoring to individual circumstances. Where there are multiple new starters, having them form a cohort is a helpful way to build friendships. Having them on site more often in their early days is likely to help embed the culture and ways of working more easily. Because of this, their teams, or at least their immediate colleagues, may need to be – temporarily – on site much more often to help build relationships and share knowledge that can then be taken to a greater remote footing. We should consider how in the early days we get across the principles of hybrid working and factor in the individual circumstances that each new employee will be keen to have considered. Open and honest conversations will be needed here between manager and employee, and between the new employee and their teammates. In this, and other touchpoints, we should also consider how to connect the new starter to existing communities of practice to enable them to access help and support when they need it. Much of this would also apply to those who move jobs within the same organization.

Secondly, when a hybrid employee is faced with changes in their role. The changes could be from new systems or processes, or from collaborating with new people because of structural changes, or even from large-scale organizational changes. At each point there will be support needs for a hybrid worker, and because of the nature of hybrid working we should be creating both on-site and virtual opportunities to connect with other people in the same situation and share ideas and thinking. We should be supplying learning content in different mediums to enable the hybrid worker to learn at their own pace and in their own space. We should be reviewing the balance of on-site versus remote working while such changes are worked through, as there could be strong reasons why more on-site working would be beneficial, at least on a temporary basis.

Thirdly, when a hybrid employee is leaving the organization. In *HR for Hybrid Working*, I talked about the unique nature of offboarding hybrid employees but again as more hybrid employees leave organizations, we must tailor this approach and learn as we go along. Leaving aside any discussions about equipment and system access, the critical thing to focus on here is the imminent loss of that hybrid worker's knowledge. That knowledge needs to be shared or at least captured somehow. Thus, in their final weeks the hybrid worker should spend time sharing and capturing their knowledge, and both tasks could be done in different ways. Sharing of knowledge may be best done on site and therefore there could be a need to temporarily increase on-site working for both the hybrid worker who is leaving and those with whom they are sharing their knowledge. The capturing of knowledge may be best done remotely to allow quiet, focused time to write down or record it in other ways, and therefore the balance of their hybrid working arrangements may change due to this.

The best way to create the hybrid employee experience

In this chapter I hope you have realized that a top-down, mandated, rigid hybrid approach is not always going to create the best hybrid employee experience for anyone. A bottom-up, empowered and adult–adult approach is likely to work better. For that though we must equip our managers with the right tools, thinking and guidance to be able to do it effectively. We must consider what support and guidance everyone may need. And we must consider how the teams themselves will need to embed new ways of working to underpin all of this. These will be covered in the third and final part of this book.

CASE STUDY ONE

Kate Bishop is the Global Head of HR at IFS, a fast-growing enterprise technology provider with over 6,000 employees based across 80 countries. Along with HR, Kate's portfolio includes sustainability and facilities, and she is the board chairperson and executive sponsor for all offshore operations in Sri Lanka and India. As we noted in an earlier case study, having someone with broader responsibilities than just HR/people is an innovative idea for a helicopter view of what hybrid working requires.

Bishop reports that IFS have always been flexible as an organization, and indeed agile is one of their values. She says that IFS have always been very empowering, with individuals given a lot of autonomy in how they choose to work. Remote and hybrid working came naturally to them and they were largely unfazed by the changes brought about by the Covid-19 pandemic. However, the executive team are keen to bring employees back on site two days a week to get them to reconnect with each other and the organization. This goal has some logic – Bishop reports some evidence of cultural deterioration across the organization – but is acknowledged to be a difficult mandate to fulfil given the culture of autonomy and empowerment. Bishop believes that the lack of on-site presence is not perhaps the only reason for the cultural deterioration, and that IFS need to focus on helping employees to make the right connections, particularly in a company that is growing fast and outpacing the market. Bishop recommends a cultural audit when reviewing hybrid working approaches – consider what it helps with, what aspects of the hybrid culture need to be kept and how that can be done, what the impact of cultural deterioration would be, and more besides.

IFS recognize that creating the right on-site employee experience makes a significant difference. They have redesigned all their physical locations, with a wide range of different spaces for diverse types of work. At the same time, they have reduced the number of physical locations they have, part of their drive to reduce their carbon footprint. Bishop acknowledges that this means that if the desire to bring people back on site is successful, they will be over capacity in these locations on some days and need managers to help balance the virtual and physical worlds. IFS are considering gamifying being on site to help further encourage employees to come together in IFS shared and redesigned locations.

Bishop reports that in many ways hybrid working has been a success for IFS. As a global organization they had been used to asynchronous working across time zones for many years, so most performance indicators were unaffected or even improved. IFS have always had elongated operational hours because of the global spread of their locations, and hybrid working helped make this much easier. With sustainability in her portfolio, Bishop has been keen to see if hybrid working has had an impact on reducing IFS's carbon footprint, and reports that it has, through reduced energy consumption and less commuting. She also cites great improvements in inclusion and diversity because of hybrid working. IFS use their employee survey, run three times a year (with 95 per cent global participation) to provide feedback. In the latest survey, employees scored IFS at 87 per cent when asked 'My physical & virtual work environment contributes positively to my ability to do my job'.

This has brought home some learning points about how to treat distinct characteristics that employees have. In Sri Lanka, IFS's employee demographic is considerably younger than anywhere else they have locations. They are now consciously focused on how to create culture for employees who have fewer work experiences than in any other country, and how to create the right learning experiences for these people too. IFS are also aware that their executive team are generally of a different demographic compared to the average employee demographic at IFS. This may feed into how senior leaders see the world of work, and how on-site working may be easier for them than for the average employee. Ultimately, Bishop's role is to ensure a balance and challenge the leadership to have different ideas and ways of thinking.

Bishop has implemented an 'ages and stages' approach to the hybrid employee experience. She has created personas to craft what hybrid working is for employees of different ages, allied to the stage they are at in their career.

To manage employees' reluctance to come on site two days a week, IFS managers have told teams to decide which two days that is, but to allow individual employees to be flexible within that. Bishop recognizes that some individuals, based on the 'ages and stages' approach, and also considering the needs of those who are neurodiverse, may be uncomfortable around lots of people, so has encouraged an individual approach to managing the two days on-site requirement by moving towards a 40 per cent of working time requirement instead of two days a week. This has allowed some employees to come on site for specific tasks but then work remotely for other parts of their day. To help with this, Bishop also clarified that only employees within a 'reasonable' commuting distance are expected to be on site two days a week.

IFS also encourage employee mobility, something that again is tailored to the 'ages and stages' approach and are generally happy for employees to relocate to another country if it doesn't cost IFS any extra and if IFS has a base in that country already.

Bishop ensures the leadership role model behaviours that are allied to hybrid working, such as giving up their fixed desks and offices and consciously moving around the on-site locations, based on the type of task they are working on. She has also been exploring technology that would help embed hybrid ways of working and improve the on-site employee experience, such as hotelling software that improves visibility of who is going to be working where, to improve planning. There has been greater focus within leadership development on managing by outcomes, reframing what IFS understand as productivity, and promoting adult–adult conversations about individual and team flexibility. The aim is to get each employee to reflect on how they want to work, based on their 'age and stage' as well as work preferences, but being clear that the needs of IFS are also met to ultimately ensure a motivated, engaged workforce where the individual, the team and IFS can grow and thrive.

CASE STUDY TWO

Heather Barlow is a People Partner at Centrica, an international energy services and solutions company. Centrica is the parent company of British Gas, a leading energy supplier in the UK employing 20,000 people across the UK. Within Centrica, guiding principles, known as FlexFirst, have been set to help create the right hybrid employee experience and to find the right balance for their customers, teams and individual employees.

FlexFirst is based on the premise that the customer comes first. What, where and when an employee needs to do is decided by customer needs. The team needs come after this – Centrica believe that on-site working for teams offers the best chance of connection and collaboration, but that each team can decide for themselves what that looks like, allowing for individual preferences to be accommodated too. FlexFirst aims to provide each employee with the right balance of on-site and remote working to stay connected to the business, do their best work as a team and manage their well-being – but acknowledges that this will look different for each person, and that each employee will have a personalized experience based on their role, what they are doing at any time, and other factors too. They recognize that diverse types of work require different approaches and that there could not be a one size fits all approach.

Employees are encouraged to plan their life around the concept of FlexFirst, and managers are given tools and development to support this on the basis that each team and person is different. Employees are expected to collaborate with their manager to decide what the right balance is for each person, and the expectations on both sides. Each employee is expected to spend some time on site each month, with the frequency predominantly determined by the role they do.

Guidance is given on the best remote working environment and set-up, and careful thought is given to the equipment needed by each employee to enable working on site, remotely or moving between the two, safely and comfortably. Where employees are expected to be on site outside of their normal arrangements, as much notice as possible is given. Where employees choose or want to work on site more (or perhaps for all their contracted hours) this is arranged by request on the understanding that the employee requesting such arrangements will be on site for at least 80 per cent of their working time. However, very few employees have taken up this offer of a permanent fixed desk on site.

Centrica have given thought to the on-site experience too and have turned their on-site locations into community hubs so that there is a similar experience on each site with people from various parts of the large business working together with 'energy, fun and community'. Previously, on-site locations were specific to functions or divisions, while now they are for anyone who happens to live or be working in the vicinity. Events, such as summer barbeques and team lunches, are planned on site to encourage collaboration and connection. Added to this, Centrica have given guidance about the types of work that they feel is better done on site, to allow employees and their managers to consciously plan such things in advance. They include:

- Complex training
- Team-building events
- Meetings that require physical interaction or equipment only available on site
- Collaborative team working where frequent interaction is needed
- Networking and learning from others
- Problem solving and complex decision making
- Where relationships need to be improved
- Where performance needs to be improved by one-to-one support
- Where remote working equipment is not working effectively
- Where being around other people would help individual well-being
- When a new starter or returnee becomes part of the team

The FlexFirst approach is a positive one, at least in theory. I asked Barlow how it had been working in practice. She commented that the expectation that employees would be on site at least once per month began as a specific requirement – one day per month, and not 'at least once per month'. The specific requirement was a barrier – some employees came on site for their specified one day per month and then would be very reluctant to be on site again until the following month. More flexibility around arrangements was needed, and the FlexFirst approach was adapted accordingly.

An in-house FlexFirst app has been developed to allow employees to book specific desks and organize the required security access to on-site locations. This is well utilized with advance booking ensuring teams can sit together and make the most of their site-based collaboration and team days. Barlow reported that a lot of work has been done to support managers about how to forward plan on-site activities. Other development work has taken place to help managers to learn how to manage remote employees, how to build trust and accountability, and how to gently (or firmly) challenge working arrangements. Incentives have also been given to encourage more on-site attendance, such as subsidized restaurant menus on specific days.

Barlow feels that corporate culture is now more difficult to embed in new starters. She sees this as a challenge, but one that the organization can respond to by being more intentional about such things. She gave an example of whole cohorts of new starters starting work in the same week so that they build an informal community of practice, and ensuring that these cohorts all work entirely on site for around eight weeks in total before any hybrid working starts. During this time, their adjacent colleagues and teams are encouraged to be on site more often, and the overall aim is to connect new employees and managers not just to each other but to the wider corporate culture and organizational community. The organization is heavily dependent on seasonal fluctuations in things like weather in the ways it serves its customers, but it also expects its employees to adapt proportionally – busier teams because of increased seasonal customer demand are expected to be on site more often in the winter months for example.

Centrica are also very aware that in some roles there can be no hybrid working and have responded by offering a range of other flexible working options.

Barlow finished by commenting on her own hybrid working arrangements, which she is happy with. At times in her own household there can be four people working remotely all at once, which shapes not just family dynamics but also working arrangements and choices/priorities around use of technology in the house. The guidance given by Centrica's FlexFirst approach considers this type of hybrid employee experience and has helped Barlow to get the most from her own arrangements.

Case study reflections

In our first case study, IFS, the following points stand out:

- Combining an HR/people focus with facilities and sustainability allows for a good perspective on what hybrid working offers.

- It is worth considering whether organizational values are in line with the hybrid working approach – for example, a mandated hybrid approach may not fit with values such as agility and empowerment.
- A cultural audit of hybrid working is a clever idea and may help your organization to fully appreciate what impact hybrid working is and can be having on organizational culture. It may also help people to feel heard and supported.
- Segmenting your employee population can reveal the different impacts that hybrid working arrangements can have on distinct characteristics and enable a differentiated hybrid working approach to be implemented.
- Comparing your average employee demographic to the demographic of the executive team may force some initially awkward but powerful realizations about perspective and viewpoints around hybrid working.
- Building personas for typical 'ages and stages' that employees have may enable you to view what hybrid working needs to be for each of these personas.
- Encouraging adult–adult conversations between employees and their managers would help to individualize the hybrid working approach and create a better employee experience for each person.
- If you have a mandated hybrid approach, allowing teams and individuals to vary arrangements while keeping the 'bottom line' is an effective way of working around reluctance.

In our second case study, Centrica, the following points stand out:

- Focusing on customer needs, followed by team and finally individual needs is a helpful way of establishing priorities for hybrid working.
- Recognizing that there is no one size fits all approach to hybrid working and being led by the needs of the task, with each job being different and each task different within that job, is a sensible approach.
- Managers will likely need some support adapting to this type of approach.
- Encouraging adult–adult conversations about what works for each job and the jobholder is an effective way to explore possibilities.
- Employees should be given help and support to craft the right remote working environment, and guidance about when that might not be the best place for them to work.

- The creation of 'community hubs' is an interesting way to break down silo thinking and encourage cross-organizational relationships to be built and supported.

- Giving explicit guidance about the types of activities that are best done on site is helpful to managers and employees to be able to forward plan accordingly.

- Technology is needed to give visibility to hybrid working arrangements and enable better forward planning.

- Encouraging new starters to be on site more often, and their teams likewise, for temporary periods, is likely to help them to settle in and adapt to the culture more effectively. However, we must be mindful of those unable to do this and find ways to connect employees that are not geographically focused.

- Where there is no choice about where work needs to be done, looking at when the work can be done may enable other types of working arrangements to come to the fore.

The action plan

If you are considering how to craft or improve the hybrid employee experience, it is worth answering the following questions:

- What percentage of your hybrid employees (as opposed to fully remote or fully on site) are engaged? What do you need to do to improve this?

- What would you learn if you mapped out and gathered data on the typical employee journey through your organization?

- How can you factor in individual hybrid worker experiences into the typical employee journey?

- What data would you like to have about the personalized hybrid employee experience, and how can you get it?

- How are your organizational values seen in your hybrid working approach?
- Would more general guiding principles work better for your organization than rigid policies and rules around hybrid working? Why is this?
- What help and support might your organization need to embrace agile principles in designing the hybrid employee experience?
- What lessons are there from your organization's hybrid customer experience that could be applied to the hybrid employee experience?
- How will you create personas for your hybrid employees and what do you think these could tell you?
- How will you create unique hybrid employee experiences for younger or less experienced workers?
- How will you ensure that those with caring responsibilities, mostly women, are catered for with your hybrid approach?
- What support will you give to those returning to the hybrid workplace after some time away from it?
- How will you create the right hybrid approach for your older workers?
- What flexibility needs to be given to those hybrid employees with disabilities?
- What guidance, support, connections and learning content will you need to create for new starters, job movers and those hybrid employees experiencing change of any sort?
- What change management support will be necessary for the plan you will implement?

References and further reading

Access Group (2023) Young people and low-income workers risk being left behind by hybrid working, new research finds, 12 January, www.theaccessgroup.com/en-gb/about/news/young-people-and-low-income-workers-risk-being-left-behind-by-hybrid-working-new-research-finds/ (archived at https://perma.cc/VC8L-9NCB)

Bibb, A (2022) Ex and CX go hand-in-hand but how do they factor into hybrid work? 22 August, annebibb.com/ex-and-cx-go-hand-in-hand-but-how-do-they-factor-into-hybrid-work/ (archived at https://perma.cc/MG9N-CUR5)

Cholteeva, Y (2023) Is hybrid work good for everyone's wellbeing? *People Management*, 15 June, www.peoplemanagement.co.uk/article/1826471/hybrid-work-good-everyones-wellbeing (archived at https://perma.cc/LHA6-7D9U)

CIPD (2023) Flexible and hybrid working: Zenith, 25 May, www.cipd.org/en/knowledge/case-studies/flexible-hybrid-working-zenith/ (archived at https://perma.cc/7U9S-2V9D)

Dalal, K (2021) Reinventing work: How your hybrid workplace can deliver on CX and EX, Reworked, 13 September, www.reworked.co/employee-experience/reinventing-work-how-your-hybrid-workplace-can-deliver-on-cx-and-ex/ (archived at https://perma.cc/69X8-73Z8)

EY Foundation (nd) Engaging young people through hybrid working, www.eyfoundation.com/uk/en/news/engaging-young-people-through-hybrid-working.html (archived at https://perma.cc/S5GX-TUZH)

Gallup (2023) State of the Global Workplace report

Gartner (2021) What women want from a hybrid work experience, 13 December, www.gartner.com/en/documents/4009451 (archived at https://perma.cc/QUT9-8U7B)

ISE (2023) Do young people like hybrid and remote work? Institute of Student Employers, 13 June, https://insights.ise.org.uk/development/blog-do-young-people-like-hybrid-and-remote-work/ (archived at https://perma.cc/ZZ9H-ASXS)

Jörden, N and Alayande, A (2022) Screens and water-coolers: Why young knowledge-workers need special attention in the world of hybrid work, Bennett Institute for Public Policy, 24 November, www.bennettinstitute.cam.ac.uk/blog/screens-and-water-coolers-why-young-knowledge-workers-need-special-attention-in-the-world-of-hybrid-work/ (archived at https://perma.cc/2QFM-LXQQ)

Judge Business School (2022) The future of work: Has the hybrid work revolution thwarted progress towards gender parity in business? University of Cambridge, 2 March, www.jbs.cam.ac.uk/2022/the-future-of-work/ (archived at https://perma.cc/5RA5-UUUQ)

McMenamin, L (2021) Why younger workers want hybrid work most, BBC, 3 August, www.bbc.com/worklife/article/20210729-why-younger-workers-want-hybrid-work-most (archived at https://perma.cc/X66G-EYVN)

Microsoft (2022) Great expectations: Making hybrid work work, 16 March, www.microsoft.com/en-us/worklab/work-trend-index/great-expectations-making-hybrid-work-work (archived at https://perma.cc/PE3K-54N2)

Morrone, M (2023) Women are returning to work, but there's more to the story, BBC Worklife, 15 September, www.bbc.com/worklife/article/20230914-women-are-returning-to-work-but-theres-more-to-the-story (archived at https://perma.cc/H7C5-9KBV)

Mutebi, N and Hobbs, A (2022) The impact of remote and hybrid working on workers and organisations, POST, UK Parliament, 17 October, https://post.parliament.uk/research-briefings/post-pb-0049/ (archived at https://perma.cc/GNT3-FJZY)

Nagy, M (nd) How agile HR is shaping a better (hybrid) employee experience, HR Congress, https://hr-congress.com/how-hr-is-shaping-a-better-hybrid-employee-experience-through-new-ways-of-working/ (archived at https://perma.cc/GCU9-ETUS)

Oktra (nd) What is hybrid working? Everything you need to know about hybrid, www.oktra.co.uk/insights/what-is-hybrid-working/ (archived at https://perma.cc/N7TJ-ZF35)

Qualtrics (nda) Increasing employee retention through employee journey mapping, www.qualtrics.com/uk/experience-management/employee/employee-journey-mapping/ (archived at https://perma.cc/VGG4-9PJT)

Qualtrics (ndb) Understanding the 7 stages of the employee lifecycle model, www.qualtrics.com/uk/experience-management/employee/employee-lifecycle-model/ (archived at https://perma.cc/W8HV-6LNS)

Rudbeck, S and Fisher, F (2022) Hybrid working and the employee experience: 10 key reflections, WTW, 1 September, www.wtwco.com/en-gb/insights/2021/07/hybrid-working-and-the-employee-experience (archived at https://perma.cc/3TLU-D2DH)

Unispace (2023) Returning for Good, www.unispace.com/returning-for-good (archived at https://perma.cc/NFQ6-Y372)

Wilson, J (2023) Hybrid work commission – new research, Public First, 13 August, www.publicfirst.co.uk/hybrid-work-commission-report.html (archived at https://perma.cc/M3MA-SDNK)

Workplace (nd) Five ways to build culture in a hybrid workplace, Meta, https://en-gb.workplace.com/blog/hybrid-workplace-culture

Part 2: Making Hybrid Work Work

There is more than one way of hybrid working

Identify which tasks can be remote?

Consider *flexibility*

+ job crafting ✂

for jobs that may not be able to be hybrid

There are alternatives to:

TASK / Job Role

+ which tasks are?

from... to...

only here

fixed location

Fixed hybrid working

fixed time

Investment in using technology is needed for hybrid working

to speed up workflows

🚫

reduce bottlenecks

speed up decision-making

Making a success of hybrid working involves

□ → ○ → □
△ ← □

back to the drawing board for organizational design and work processes

A variety of spaces will be needed on-site

Library   Touchdown   Flex-Space   Hot-desking

Help employees to know which area is best for each type of task

It is about personalizing work

This is my way

This works for me + my teams work

Different approaches will work for different types of work, different teams _and_ for specific individuals

Consider the hybrid employee experience

At different points in the employee life cycle:

For different types of employee:

Young
Caring
Older
Hybrid Worker
Returner
others with specific needs
with specific disabilities

Help and support

8

Helping managers

The shorter read

We must help managers adapt to hybrid working. They are perhaps the most critical part of the organization to get right if we are to make a success of hybrid working. Too many managers are used to face-to-face management, on site – so many of them are struggling because of this.

Yet, if we can get the support right, we can solve a lot of potential struggles that managers often have in a remote and hybrid environment. We can move them away from being the 'squeezed middle' and help them embrace their role as the enabler of employee engagement via the hybrid employee experience. Much of this is a mindset shift, away from management being a sensory experience to one that uses data, and evidence.

And there is plenty of data available to use. The problem is often that managers don't know it exists, or where to find it, let alone how to use it. A remote or hybrid worker generates multiple data points with each interaction with the organization. We don't have to implement employee monitoring systems to look at these data, but we could. There are also numerous pieces of data in communications channels, any app used by employees, HR/L&D systems and in ad hoc conversations. Using these, and correlating them with existing data, could show considerable insight into what is happening for hybrid workers and teams.

Managers need specific support though. Much of this can be provided through individual support. This would help each manager to build effective individual relationships with their hybrid employees, to help the development and performance of their hybrid teams, to consider the best options in terms of communication and collaboration, and how to best support the learning that their hybrid teams need. Doing this on an individual basis would enable the support to be tailored to each manager and their circumstances – because we know there is no one size fits all approach to hybrid working.

More support for managers can come from group approaches. Management development needs rebooting – the skill set and mindset that effective on-site, face-to-face, managers have had is unlikely to be a suitable match to the skill set and mindset needed to effectively manage hybrid employees and teams. Much of this should be provided through communities of practice and peer support.

The rest should be provided through more formal development, and there are themes that should be included in any hybrid management development programme that would give multiple options to build a bespoke programme. Themes include understanding the organizational approach to hybrid working; self-management for the hybrid manager; digital working; interpersonal skills for the hybrid manager; managing hybrid employees; managing hybrid teams; and meeting with hybrid employees. Tackling these themes but applying them to specific contexts will provide the right support for hybrid managers.

The longer read

Part One of this book focused on understanding the new world of work. Part Two examined how we need to make changes to ensure hybrid working is effective. In Part Three, beginning here, we will explore what practical support we need to give those working within our hybrid approach. Let's start with leaders and managers (and we will use managers to refer to both leaders and managers throughout this chapter).

Manager effectiveness is a key enabler of successful hybrid working. It can help to preserve and improve the culture, as well as keep productivity and engagement at best levels. But many struggle to adapt to a hybrid working environment. I often explain face-to face-management as a very sensory experience. Managers can see and hear (and perhaps even smell) what their team are doing. But in a remote or hybrid environment there is a sensory loss. This brings with it all the emotions and uncertainties that often accompany such loss. Much like with a sensory loss though, adapting one's practices, unlearning and relearning skills can be a way through such uncertainty, and managers who are used to face-to-face management must do precisely that. My own research, some of it anecdotal, suggests that newer managers who have become so since the Covid-19 pandemic often feel more comfortable than those who were managers prior to that pandemic. For the newer managers, the challenge may be simpler – learning about remote and hybrid management is all they have ever known. It is management to them, with nothing to unlearn.

Research by Microsoft shows the extent to which many managers are struggling:

- Eighty-five per cent say that the shift to hybrid work has made it challenging to have confidence that employees are being productive.
- Twelve per cent have full confidence that their team is productive, compared to 87 per cent of employees who feel they are productive (Microsoft, 2022b).

It is easy to see why Microsoft label this 'productivity paranoia', yet it is also understandable why managers may feel this given the lack of sensory information. As Microsoft also point out, these feelings risk making hybrid working unsustainable even though there is plenty of data (number of meetings, hours worked and more) to show that, if anything, employees are more active (Microsoft, 2022b). The world of work has changed drastically, and managers' mindsets – and skill sets – have not always kept pace. Nor are they suitable for a digitally connected, distributed hybrid workforce.

Managers' struggles

Managers could also be something of a 'squeezed middle' here, trying to reconcile the needs of their team with the views held by senior leaders in some organizations that only on-site working will work. Microsoft examined this and found that 35 per cent of managers had no personal preference about how often employees came on site but felt that they had to follow company policy regardless (Microsoft, 2021b). But such managers must follow the overall organizational hybrid approach. Managers must ensure that if they must get their hybrid employees to come on site that there is purpose to this. An on-site employee experience needs to be one that connects employees to each other and builds their social capital, while reminding employees of ways to keep connections going digitally in between the on-site time. Managers must create this, as well as creating the digital methods that build community among their team, keeping conversations going. This will be needed regardless of what the managers may feel about remote and hybrid working, or about the approach taken by their organization.

As a result of this, managers need to understand their role as the connection between the prevailing view about hybrid working in the organization and the employees themselves. They must be given the right support, and the right level of empowerment, to make this work. Managers could struggle with understanding this role, with seeing themselves as the main arbiters of team and, ultimately, organizational culture. Managers who have been used to being the main hub around which on-site working may revolve could find it difficult seeing asynchronous work and relationships between individual hybrid employees take a higher priority. Managers need to avoid being the bottleneck through which recognition and feedback between team members takes place but could equally struggle with letting go of such a function.

Managers may not fully grasp what asynchronous working (and, similarly, the alternative working week) offers to their team, but they need to do so to make hybrid working work better. Holding out for meetings seems unnecessary when group chats, and other collaborative methods, could achieve similar outcomes without the impact of bringing people together synchronously. Modern technologies could enable such asynchronous working, but managers need to be comfortable with using and promoting these.

As much as anything this is a mindset shift. From the work of the team only (or best) being done when on site, to distributed work that uses technology and asynchronous working to ensure work is done where and when it is best to do so. From only using sensory data, to using wider forms of data and evidence.

Data points to use

I have already mentioned in this book that a remote or hybrid worker generates more data points than an on-site worker. The main difference is that these are often digital rather than sensory data. They require a conscious effort on the part of managers to be aware of, look for and use them. Let's look at potential data points.

Every digital interaction between an employee and the organization generates potential data to look at, but few of these will be within the HR or L&D systems that we may think would be the first port of call for data about employees. Instead, they are spread across communications channels, interactions between employees, in emails and messages, in operational systems and lots of other places in addition to the expected systems.

Data on working habits, even if aggregated and anonymized, would be useful in learning health concerns and optimizing productive time. In-app tools can already supply some of this, such as Microsoft Viva for one, and can show us working hours distribution, effectiveness of time of communication and the impact of healthy or unhealthy working practices.

Employee monitoring tools could give you information, tracking, analysing and reporting on employee activities during or outside working hours. Whether or not you want to use such systems depends very much on your culture and the type of management you feel is right in your organization. Used in one way they supply surveillance data, but used in other ways they can supply insights about productivity and well-being also. This can be done by tracking behavioural data – application usage, working times, browsing patterns and more to understand more about the hybrid working experience (Gaffin, 2023). It could allow more insight into bottlenecks, pain points and inefficiencies as well as the emotional state and health of the hybrid employee.

Data will also be available about how often employees are on site, where they work when they are on site, and what resources and equipment they use. Combining this with some of the insight from monitoring tools could show some interesting patterns and trends, showing when and where peak collaboration happens. Looking at the same data for when employees are remote and analysing server and app usage could show where and when peak focused work happens too.

Communication platforms offer even more data to spot and analyse. Volume of traffic, type of communication, chosen platform, frequency and duration of use, impact of communication, can all be learnt from looking at the data available on the platform, whether through a formal report or informal 'listening'. Analysing available data about who communicates with whom, and the impact this has, could uncover useful information about team dynamics, individual training needs and where coaching conversations could be used best. It might also show a manager where more team-building or collaborative opportunities could be created based on where the communication flow is most impacted.

All this data could be correlated with data that exists within HR or L&D systems to provide further analysis – are the patterns happening in certain teams, or to employees with certain characteristics? Are the patterns restricted to new starters or to those with particular hybrid patterns? Are the pain points where employees are obviously seeking out support matched by use of available learning and training methods?

To make this work though, managers may need more help. In the rest of this chapter, we will explore what kind of help and how this can be delivered. We will look first at individual support, and then to close this chapter we will look at organizational approaches to leadership and management development.

Individual support for managers

Here we will talk about what individual support and guidance managers may need. The term 'coaching' is used to signify one-on-one conversations, as well as confidence building. Much of the support managers need can be effectively given on an individual basis, by other managers, more senior leaders or by people professionals. But what kind of things will managers need support on?

Individual relationships

Many individuals will want and welcome hybrid working, particularly if they can decide the precise arrangement to suit the work they are doing as well as their personal circumstances. But there is a need to manage hybrid employees, though as we will see in the next chapter this should be tailored heavily to everyone. Here are some questions to prompt this type of thinking in managers. They could be used by managers directly, or by you to help your managers to do this (through coaching or another method):

- How will you clarify the expectations that you have about keeping in touch, communications and working arrangements for each person, and then step back to allow them to feel comfortable and not micromanaged?
- What signs of poor well-being do you need to look out for in hybrid employees? How will you discern their emotional state from digital communications?

- What aspects of working habits and practices do you need to watch in hybrid employees, and how will you spot and act upon unhealthy working habits and practices?
- If an individual hybrid employee is showing signs of struggling with any aspect of work, what adjustments would you explore to help them get back to optimum levels of performance and well-being?
- What data will you need to gather to ensure that you are acting inclusively and not unduly favouring employees who are co-located with you more often?
- How will you ensure that you are judging performance of each hybrid individual by their outcomes and not by their on-site presence?
- When meeting with a hybrid worker, how will you ensure that you balance managing the human being with managing their work and outcomes?
- What coaching does each individual hybrid worker need on building better relationships with their team?
- How will you decide, and meet, the equipment and resource needs of each individual hybrid worker?

Team relationships

It is crucial that managers help the team to develop positive working relationships. We have already talked about the data that they could draw upon to help them understand what needs to be done. In Chapter 10 we will talk about the role that a team charter might play in solidifying ways of working among the hybrid team, but many of the questions for managers to consider are pertinent here:

- What expectations do you have of the team in terms of how they communicate and work with each other?
- What do you as manager need to do to check the effectiveness of team relationships?
- How do you expect the team to address conflict and solve problems? What involvement will you have in these things?
- What socialization elements will you build into team meetings and how will you encourage the team to use these effectively?
- What dedicated channels and mediums will you co-create with the hybrid team for people to talk about non-work activities and interests?

- How will you and the team review the effectiveness of hybrid working arrangements?
- How will you agree and share team priorities so that each person knows what matters to the team and what takes priority regardless of hybrid working arrangements?

Communication and collaboration

Managers must be effective communicators in a general sense, but hybrid working can create challenges for them. The proliferation of communications platforms and channels, and the growth in asynchronous communication, may give rise to more support needs from managers who could struggle to know what to do. Relevant questions to pose to managers include:

- How can you get across the point that replies to communication can be asynchronous? And how will you make it clear when communication needs to be synchronous?
- How will you give the right amount of time to communicate asynchronously?
- What team activities and tasks are best tackled synchronously, and which asynchronously?
- What aspects of your personality are shown through different methods of communication, and how can you use this to best effect?
- How will you check in with individual hybrid employees to ensure that they are up to speed on different communications?
- What communications channels do you need to 'listen' to, to be reassured that the team is working effectively, and decide where you may need to intervene?
- If you choose to work outside of traditional working hours, what use do you need to make of the scheduling function when sending communications?
- How will you encourage the team (and yourself) to change 'working out loud' from a solely verbal to a mostly digital and asynchronous activity?
- How and when can the team contact you for ad hoc queries and conversations, and how do they know that?

Learning

A key role for managers is to help their hybrid employees, individually and as a team, to learn effectively. There is an often-expressed view that learning from other people is best done on site. This is discussed in other parts of this book in more depth, but learning must be intentional. Learning won't just happen in a hybrid team; it must be planned and structured. Managers need to create this structure, and they will need support to do so. Relevant questions for managers to consider here:

- How can you build in time for hybrid employees and the team to reflect on and make sense of their experiences? When, where and how will this take place?
- How will you ensure that hybrid employees have the right connections to be able to learn effectively from other people?
- What specific support will new hybrid employees need in your team, and how will you ensure that the team itself provides some of this learning?
- How will you ensure equal access to learning opportunities and methods across the hybrid team?
- What will you do to support the learning of and by the hybrid team, so that knowledge is effectively shared regardless of hybrid working arrangements?

Put simply, those in management roles need to raise their game around what may previously have been termed 'soft skills', but which must now be regarded as essential managerial skills for success. We cannot assume that managers who have been good at on-site, face-to-face, management will automatically be good at managing remote and hybrid teams. The skill set and mindset requirements are different. It is a different world of work. We will also need to consider how we reboot management development for all our managers because of this. Let's do that in the rest of this chapter.

A framework for leadership and management development

Those in management positions in a hybrid working organization could be fine with no support. They could adapt on their own and thrive. They could be lucky and have the right skill set and mindset to be able to be effective hybrid managers. But what if they aren't fine, can't adapt or thrive, and aren't lucky enough to have the right skill set and mindset? Is this something that any organization wants to leave to chance? I suspect not. As with all other aspects of hybrid working, we must be intentional, conscious and deliberate about the way we approach management development. If we are serious about making hybrid working work, then the key people to develop will be managers, as they could make or break the overall approach.

I recommend rebooting leadership and management development. The learning, the skills and knowledge, and the mindsets that anyone who became a manager when on-site management was the only choice may have, are out of date. They will no longer be right for a hybrid working organization. We should look at the onset of hybrid working as a chance to reboot leadership and management development. If your organization is a hybrid one, and many are, then managers need a reset.

The well-known 70:20:10 model is based on the principle that 70 per cent of learning comes from experience, experiment and reflection, 20 per cent derives from working with others, and 10 per cent comes from formal interventions and planned learning solutions (Arets, Jennings and Heijnen, 2016). This could easily be used as a template for how we need to develop our hybrid managers and suits a hybrid model quite well. We will revisit this when we look at helping individual hybrid employees in the next chapter but will use it here to think about types of learning opportunities and methods that could help hybrid managers.

Critical to both the 70 and 20 per cent of the model is the creation and nurturing of a community of practice (CoP) among hybrid managers. We will see in one of the case studies in this chapter how this has been successfully done in one organization and can learn from this example. A well-thought-through CoP could allow for joint problem solving around hybrid working, reflection on what works and what does not, sharing of good practice and learning from mistakes. It could also foster the creation of peer-coaching arrangements, and two-way feedback about hybrid working arrangements. An action learning type approach would also be helpful for building trust and confidence. We could also make effective use of the coaching support mentioned earlier in this chapter. The CoP should have both digital and physical arrangements, making effective use of available technology and on-site resources to encourage closer connections and relationships between hybrid managers, enabling them to support each other better. Digital (and asynchronous) communities supported by on-site get-togethers are recommended, but careful management of this CoP is also needed. It cannot be left to self-manage in its initial stages. There is a need for facilitation, and I would recommend using a suitable selection of the types of questions explored in the individual support for managers section of this chapter to structure an agenda for discussion.

We can supplement these methods with aspects of the more traditional 10 per cent formal learning. There should be courses, workshops, thought leadership, self-study resources and more provided on hybrid management. We will explore some of these things later in this section and look at what the content of such things could cover.

But who should be included in this development? Should it be an exclusive arrangement, focusing only on those who are at a certain level in the organization? Or should it be an inclusive arrangement, allowing anyone who wishes to develop their leadership or management skills and mindset to be involved? The answer to this is highly contextual and there are pros and cons of both directions. Each organization must be clear on this to be able to manage expectations accordingly. My advice would be to consider anyone – whether they are an existing manager or an aspiring one – to be developed in line with the content below.

Content

Here we will look at recommended content to be included in the formal aspects of leadership and management development, designed to supplement the on-the-job and socialized learning that will be taking place. The recommendations in Table 8.1 are arranged into themes, rather than prescriptive content. Use these themes to find the right aspects to focus on within your context. The indicative content can be built into workshops, seminars, and other forms of training and learning. They can be delivered on site or virtually, or a mix of both. They appear in the table in no particular order. Collectively though, this is the bespoke help that your managers need to be able to thrive in a hybrid working environment. There are, naturally, other aspects of management skills that are not bespoke to a hybrid environment (like managing finance, managing projects, managing change and many more) – these are not included here but would sit alongside this indicative content to supply a more holistic development offering.

Is it enough to just develop the managers though? No. Individuals, and the teams they are part of, also need development. In the coming chapters we will look at what they need and how we provide that.

Both organizations featuring as case studies in this chapter have been anonymized. Both are UK public sector organizations employing several thousand people nationwide.

TABLE 8.1 Leadership and management development indicative content for hybrid working

Theme	Indicative content
Understanding hybrid	• What is the organizational approach to hybrid and how has this come about? What are its pros and cons and how is it being implemented and reviewed?
	• What are the wider implications of this approach for the organization, its real estate, technology and stakeholders?
	• What does agile and flexible mean for the organization in practice?
	• If there is a mandated hybrid approach, what decisions can managers take within this? If there is an individualized hybrid approach, what decisions can managers take within that?
	• What aspects of the organizational approach are not up for debate, and why?
	• What things can managers decide without reference to a more senior leader?
	• What changes will the organization make to its resource and equipment provision for on-site and remote workers and teams?
	• What changes will the organization make to its on-site locations to optimize them for diverse types of work?
	• What is the definition of leadership and management within the hybrid organization?
	• How will managers at all levels shift their own personal working arrangements to match the organizational approach more closely?
	• How will managers at all levels get more involved in cross-organizational asynchronous communication and different platforms?
	• How are the organizational values seen and embedded in the hybrid approach?

(continued)

TABLE 8.1 (Continued)

Theme	Indicative content
Managing self	• What aspects of management tasks need performing on site and which remotely? Which need doing synchronously with employees and which asynchronously?
	• How often could and should a manager be co-located with their employees? Why is this?
	• What are the signs in a manager that hybrid working is not working for them? How do we prevent or act on these?
	• What kind of support is available for managers who manage hybrid teams?
	• What aspects of the organizational hybrid approach does a manager need to role model, and which do they not?
	• What types of peer support are available for managers of hybrid teams? How can their community of practice help?
	• What data does a hybrid manager need to be able to access and analyse to avoid micromanaging?
	• What does a great hybrid manager do? What does a poor hybrid manager do?
	• How can a manager consciously experiment with new ways of working or behaving and get constructive feedback on these things?
Digital working	• What platforms does the organization supply and what is their intended use?
	• What other platforms do employees use and what for?
	• What is the level of digital literacy – reading and especially writing – in the hybrid team? What is the level among hybrid managers?
	• What does a digital employee experience look and feel like? How will that differ from those who had a more traditional on-site experience?
	• What are the limitations of digital forms of communication and collaboration? When should they not be used? How can we overcome the limitations?
	• What digital resources could a manager create to support a hybrid team?
	• How can artificial intelligence aid a hybrid manager, as well as help their hybrid teams?

(continued)

TABLE 8.1 (Continued)

Theme	Indicative content
People skills	• How can a manager strike a balance between connecting with and understanding hybrid employees, and enabling a focus on performance? • What does a hybrid manager have to do to be an active listener to a hybrid employee or team? How is that different to actively listening when on site or in person? • How can a manager build the right elements of emotional intelligence to know when to act or speak, and when not to, with a hybrid employee or team? What signals will help here? • What behaviours will a manager need to demonstrate to show reliability to the hybrid team and acceptance of their working arrangements? How can they get this in return? • What behaviours will a manager need to show to be open and authentic with their hybrid team, and encourage openness and authenticity in return?
Managing hybrid employees	• What are the most important conversations a manager can have with a hybrid employee? How are these structured? • How can a manager adopt 'little and often' checking-in methods with hybrid employees? (Note: see Chapter 9 for more on this.) • What are the signs of poor well-being in a hybrid employee or team? How can these be addressed or prevented? • How should a manager be inclusive of all hybrid employees within the team? What behaviours should be shown, and which avoided? • What specific support will a new hybrid employee need from their manager and the rest of their team? (Note: see Chapter 9 for more on this.) • What data generated by hybrid employees and teams will be useful for managers to have sight of, and why? • What analysis can be done, using the four-box model covered in this book, to show the right hybrid working approach for any individual or team? • What agreements does a manager need to make with each hybrid individual so that their performance and productivity is optimized, and their well-being promoted? (Note: see Chapter 9 for more on this.)

(continued)

TABLE 8.1 (Continued)

Theme	Indicative content
Managing hybrid teams	• How can hybrid teams hold each other accountable for certain tasks? How can we help them to learn the impact that their work has on others in the hybrid team and wider organization, including things like missing deadlines, skipping or being late for meetings and more? • How will the hybrid team keep each other informed of developments regardless of who is working where or when? • How do teams need to be helped through stages of development like in a model such as Tuckman's Storming-Norming model (MindTools, nd)? • What kinds of things should the team agree on around its ways of working in a hybrid environment? (Note: see Chapter 10 for more on this.) • What socialization opportunities do the hybrid team need to build closer connections with each other, both in and outside of work activities? What platforms and methods can be used for this? How would alternative working weeks affect this? • How can managers upskill the hybrid team to solve problems asynchronously (if needed) or without easy access to the manager? How would alternative working weeks affect this? • How will the hybrid team resolve conflict? How would asynchronous working and alternative working weeks affect this? • How will the hybrid team celebrate successes and share learning from mistakes, without attaching blame to them? • What aspects of the team's culture are suited to hybrid working? Which are not suited? How will the hybrid team keep a positive culture regardless of who is working where or when? • How will peer-to-peer recognition and feedback be encouraged among the hybrid team? What medium and method will be used? • Which are the preferred communication platforms for the team, and why? What things need to be discussed or shared on each platform? How do alternative working weeks affect this? • How will the hybrid team be engaged in reviewing processes and redesigning work so that it better suits all stakeholders?
Meeting with hybrid employees	• How can a manager plan, prepare for and chair a successful virtual meeting? What platforms and functionality are available to help? What behaviours are helpful to show during the meeting? • How can a manager design and deliver an impactful virtual training session? What platforms and functionality are available to help? What behaviours are helpful to show during the training? • How can asynchronous collaboration reduce the need for synchronous meetings? What does a manager need to do to make that work?

CASE STUDY ONE

'Organization A' launched their hybrid working approach in 2022, consciously following principles (co-created with staff) to reflect the needs of the organization with a focus on trust and empowerment. To arrive at the principles, a large period of carefully planned and extensive consultation and engagement exercises was carried out, starting with senior leaders, involving line managers and ultimately all employees across the organization. The organization wanted to ensure that the intentional adoption of hybrid ways of working, coming out of the pandemic, was grounded in ensuring an approach met the needs of the organization while recognizing the shift in employee needs. As part of the work to adopt principles, there was acknowledgement of the difference in culture of how the organization had worked in the past.

The people team knew that with such a departure from organizational norms, their managers would need lots of support, not just for themselves but for helping their teams to adapt to hybrid working too. They supplied a range of toolkits and explainer documents but are proud of one intervention – regular video meetings for their top 100 managers in the organization, which focused on how hybrid working was working. This allowed the sharing of good practice and discussions around consistency. It also allowed very senior leaders to admit where and why they were feeling vulnerable or struggling, and allowed the people team to notice where managers were trying to implement rules instead of following the principles. This created a community of practice around hybrid working where these managers could air their concerns and grievances about the principles and approach. Holding space for the organization leaders and managers in this way enabled a new mechanism of cross-organization engagement.

I asked the people team what the main concerns were that managers shared in this forum. They reported that it was around changes to habits and ways of working – for example managers were used to their staff going *to* work and being seen *at* work and were struggling to conceptualize how work could be done somewhere else without them having 'eyes on' the staff. Also, how to ensure new employees were successfully inducted into the organization, building team relationships and working to a common purpose. There was also concern around staff welfare, with some managers worrying how they could adequately support staff, for example well-being concerns may not be picked up as readily when working remotely.

'Organization A' then used this level of concern and forum to air worries as fuel. Posing the concerns to managers as problems to be solved, they encouraged managers to shape what they needed to solve the problems. They also encouraged managers to see the principles as the start point not the end point, and that the practice of hybrid working could and would evolve over time. The people team describe this as the implementation shaping the policy, rather than policy shaping the implementation. They were then able to steer the conversation around from addressing the concerns about hybrid working to assessing the impact of hybrid working. As the impact was undoubtedly a positive one in every measure, managers gradually became more confident and comfortable with the approach. What they could not do though was show that hybrid working was better than more traditional on-site working, because the latter had never been measured. But the principles followed became their enabler of success and not a barrier to it, as a more rigid policy could have. They allowed for agility, speed and open discussions where policies and rules may not have.

Since the implementation, 'Organization A' are seeing more staff come on site than previously, but this is a planned and coordinated development, with transparent information showing who is working where on any given day. Like the advice given in Chapters 4 and 5 in this book, they use the nature of the task to decide what needs to be done on site and what needs to be done remotely.

Within the people team, regular contact days have been implemented, such as anchor days where all staff are encouraged to be on site, for quarterly roadshows, team social events or more random days – for example anyone in or around a specific location should come on site on one specified day to see everyone else. More widely across the organization, teams are encouraged to be intentional about the spaces where work is best done and how they can effectively collaborate to deliver on organizational outcomes.

The people team also explained how the hybrid principles have been mapped into formal leadership and management development modules, as well as more specific development on hybrid working itself and a comprehensive package of well-being. The focus has been on strengthening the capability, understanding and skills of managers through interactive themed sessions, and these have been well received and led to an evolution of the organizational culture and internal relationships across the organization.

CASE STUDY TWO

Towards the end of the Covid-19 pandemic, 'Organization B' set up a project group to trial hybrid working. The group began by establishing some general principles to work to. Following this the group began to look at those job roles where it would be difficult to incorporate hybrid working. The aim was to rework on-site workspaces, provide employees with the right kit, and give protected time for things like learning and development as well as well-being support. They intended to encourage experimentation among employees to work out what worked well and what did not.

Part way through the group's work and trials, 'Organization B' decided to mandate on-site attendance for at least 40 per cent of working time. This was initially unpopular among most employees, but the people team were determined to make it work as best as possible and to develop managers to be able to work within this mandated hybrid approach. The group repurposed itself to look at what employees were struggling with around the mandated hybrid approach and to provide the right kinds of support.

A parallel project on asynchronous working has helped the organization to adapt, aided by increased adoption of technology such as Microsoft Teams. The project has helped employees and managers to think about how they share information, and how they ask for and answer requests for support. It has also begun to shift the perception of learning as something only done in a live environment (whether virtual or on site) to something that is more often done asynchronously.

'Organization B' have begun remodelling many of their on-site locations to allow for diverse types of work to be done, but many managers have found it difficult to move their teams to the right on-site locations based on the type of work being done. The people team report that it takes a lot of forward planning to make on-site work effective for employees, and this has led to increased development for managers who have found such things difficult.

As 'Organization B' did not measure productivity in a consistent way prior to the mandated hybrid approach they have been unable to assess whether productivity has been affected by hybrid working. The people team believe that it would show a positive impact on productivity and inclusion if it were measured but note that many managers were struggling to manage the performance of hybrid workers. They see that in most cases this was more about managerial capability and willingness to adapt their own style than any performance or skill gap from employees. They have worked to overcome this instead of focusing the debate on location.

The organization's approach is to encourage managers to be proactive about making hybrid working work, as opposed to being told how to do it or being made to follow rigid policies. The people team's work has been to provide development to managers on how to be intentional, conscious and deliberate about how they manage their team and its hybrid approach. They note that this may be a long journey, with some managers needing more frequent support, training and communications than others.

To help with this, the people team brought in my company, EPIC, to design and deliver sessions for managers on how to make hybrid working work more effectively. These sessions are part of a wider approach, which includes frequently asked questions documents, refreshed learning and development pathways, standards and expectations documents, and dedicated communities of practice to offer peer support. The sessions delivered have focused on how to manage the flow of work so that a 40 per cent mandated hybrid approach can be made easier, and how to engage employees in the redesign of work to better meet individual needs. The sessions have also looked at how to contract with individual employees based on that employee's hybrid pattern, and how to lead each person differently in a hybrid team. We have also given help and guidance on how to create team charters to establish the right expectations among the team. The organization have complemented this with other sessions on managing performance and managing learning in a hybrid environment.

The people team report that the mandated 40 per cent on-site attendance is neither being consistently met nor fully checked. The data shows that across the whole organization there is 40 per cent on-site attendance on average, but that this differs considerably between individuals. The organization has therefore begun with a mandated hybrid approach but been forced, through events, to realize that jobs are different, and individuals likewise. There is still a residual sense of inequity between employees whose jobs may have different hybrid capabilities, but a growing realization that this is driven by the tasks themselves as much as individual circumstances. This inequity is further reduced by offering distinct types of flexibility to those whose jobs require more on-site working.

Case study reflections

In our first anonymous case study, 'Organization A', the following points stand out for consideration:

- Co-creating the principles around how work is done, irrespective of whether that is hybrid or any other kind, is an effective way to explore what the organization and employees need.

- Adopting principles instead of more rigid rules and policies allows for the approach to be flexible and evolve as it goes.

- Showing managers that they can shape the eventual practice during the implementation by listening to their concerns will get them engaged and ensure that they do not feel as if the implementation and practice is imposed.

- Consciously deciding to treat hybrid work differently from how things are normally done makes it stand out as something bigger, more significant than other aspects of the employee experience.

- Encouraging senior leaders to express their own vulnerabilities will be heartening to other leaders.

- Creating a community of practice where concerns and grievances can be aired is critical at the start and will develop a more consistent and transparent approach.

- Providing a range of tailored support for managers is necessary for them to feel supported.

- Mapping the hybrid working principles into existing and bespoke leadership development is helpful and gives structure to the support and development.

In our second anonymous case study, 'Organization B', the following points stand out for consideration:

- Encouraging experimentation and learning from this is an effective way to work out the best overall approach to hybrid working and build on each iteration.

- Where a mandated hybrid approach is the chosen one in the organization, finding a way to work within this instead of fighting against it is a sensible move.

- Developing thinking and capabilities around asynchronous working is likely to be a tremendous help to managers of hybrid teams.

- Often if there are performance concerns about a hybrid employee, this can tell us as much about managerial capabilities as it can about the capabilities of the employee in question.

- Being intentional, conscious and deliberate in management action is crucial to making hybrid working work better. It cannot be left to chance, and this intentional action needs to flow through the entire organizational culture.

- Structured development for managers will allow them to explore good practice and share concerns about hybrid working, as well as giving them access to practical guidance and templates to implement in their hybrid teams. Supplementing this with other development, both formal and informal, is necessary to be able to embed the right mindset as well as skill set.

- Even with a mandated hybrid approach, there will be individual differences based on job requirements and individual needs. Recognizing this and working within the 'bottom line' mandated figure can allow the best of both worlds to be realized.

The action plan

If you are looking to improve the confidence and capabilities of your leaders and managers in a hybrid working environment, consider answering the following questions:

- What concerns do your managers have about hybrid working, and how will you address these?

- How bought in are your managers to the organizational approach to hybrid working?

- Where are the data points that your hybrid employees generate, and how can managers best access these?
- What value could employee monitoring tools provide for your managers?
- How can you build data analysis skills among your managers?
- What data can be correlated to supply added insights into hybrid working practices?
- Who is best placed to provide individual coaching to managers of hybrid teams?
- Which questions need to be posed to managers during coaching sessions to improve their confidence in managing hybrid workers?
- How can you assess whether newer managers are coping better with hybrid working than more experienced managers?
- How optimized for hybrid working is your current approach to management development?
- What communities of practice do you need to create and nurture for managers of hybrid teams?
- Will you develop an inclusive or exclusive management development programme, and why?
- How will you make the provided themes and indicative content to build a management development programme bespoke, and what help could you need with that?

References and further reading

aNumak & Company (2022) What should leadership development in the hybrid era look like? LinkedIn, 24 August, www.linkedin.com/pulse/what-should-leadership-development-hybrid-era-look-like-/ (archived at https://perma.cc/RJZ4-VLH5)

Arets, J, Jennings, C and Heijnen, V (2016) 70:20:10 Into Action, 70:20:10 Institute, https://702010institute.com/702010-model/ (archived at https://perma.cc/5KK3-GX3Y)

Birkinshaw, J, Gudka, M and Marshall, S (2023) What leadership development should look like in the hybrid era, *Harvard Business Review*, 1 June, hbr.org/2022/06/what-leadership-development-should-look-like-in-the-hybrid-era (archived at https://perma.cc/LHC6-EGFL)

CIPD (2023) Preparing your organisation for AI use, 30 June, www.cipd.org/uk/knowledge/guides/preparing-organisation-ai-use/ (archived at https://perma.cc/R2T6-SHTC)

CIPD (2024) People manager guide: Supporting hybrid working, 19 February, www.cipd.org/uk/knowledge/guides/line-manager-supporting-hybrid-working/ (archived at https://perma.cc/BM72-5KAA)

Clark, L (2021) Leader mindsets: New ways of thinking for a new hybrid world, GP Strategies, 11 August, www.gpstrategies.com/blog/leader-mindsets-for-a-hybrid-world/ (archived at https://perma.cc/L3BN-GJ6N)

Dalal, K (2021) Reinventing work: How your hybrid workplace can deliver on CX and EX, Reworked, 13 September, www.reworked.co/employee-experience/reinventing-work-how-your-hybrid-workplace-can-deliver-on-cx-and-ex/ (archived at https://perma.cc/N8KY-RMMY)

Gaffin, K (2023) How employee monitoring tools facilitate hybrid work through data analysis, 2 October, www.insightful.io/blog/employee-monitoring-hybrid-data (archived at https://perma.cc/REX8-XUXE)

Hallenbeck, G (2023) How to approach leadership in a hybrid work environment, Center for Creative leadership, 2 January, www.ccl.org/articles/leading-effectively-articles/how-leaders-should-approach-todays-new-hybrid-workforce/ (archived at https://perma.cc/V4US-YDZC)

Hancock, B, Schaninger, B and Weddle, B (2021) Culture in the hybrid workplace, McKinsey & Company, 11 June, www.mckinsey.com/capabilities/people-and-organizational-performance/our-insights/culture-in-the-hybrid-workplace (archived at https://perma.cc/GAC9-6CKC)

Marsh, V (2021) How to be a high-performing leader in a hybrid workplace, EY UK, 1 October, www.ey.com/en_uk/workforce/how-to-be-a-high-performing-leader-in-a-hybrid-workplace (archived at https://perma.cc/AEA5-L66U)

Microsoft (2021a) In hybrid work, managers keep teams connected, 30 March, www.microsoft.com/en-us/worklab/work-trend-index/managers-keep-teams-connected (archived at https://perma.cc/TU4B-XHSZ)

Microsoft (2021b) To thrive in hybrid work, build a culture of trust and flexibility, 9 September, www.microsoft.com/en-us/worklab/work-trend-index/support-flexibility-in-work-styles (archived at https://perma.cc/L4NW-XML3)

Microsoft (2022a) Great expectations: Making hybrid work work, 16 March, www.microsoft.com/en-us/worklab/work-trend-index/great-expectations-making-hybrid-work-work (archived at https://perma.cc/KSV3-CWJD)

Microsoft (2022b) Hybrid work is just work. Are we doing it wrong? 22 September, www.microsoft.com/en-us/worklab/work-trend-index/hybrid-work-is-just-work (archived at https://perma.cc/VTV6-RLUY)

MindTools (nd) Forming, storming, norming, and performing: Tuckman's model for nurturing a team to high performance, www.mindtools.com/abyj5fi/forming-storming-norming-and-performing (archived at https://perma.cc/74UU-83E8)

OpenLearn (2022) Hybrid working: Skills for leadership, 26 September, www.open.edu/openlearn/money-business/hybrid-working-skills-leadership/ (archived at https://perma.cc/69ZJ-WMQD)

Percy, S (2023) How can leaders make hybrid working work? *Forbes*, 25 April, www.forbes.com/sites/sallypercy/2023/04/25/how-can-leaders-make-hybrid-working-work/ (archived at https://perma.cc/BNQ4-UC86)

Robertson, J (2021) A hybrid workplace framework for the senior leadership team, *Medium*, 1 March, www.medium.com/digital-employee-experience-dex/a-hybrid-workplace-framework-for-the-senior-leadership-team-b4acb5c6e7ed (archived at https://perma.cc/9ULK-77R6)

Scharf, S and Weerda, K (2022) How to lead in a hybrid environment, McKinsey & Company, 27 June, www.mckinsey.com/capabilities/people-and-organizational-performance/our-insights/the-organization-blog/how-to-lead-in-a-hybrid-environment (archived at https://perma.cc/H2YV-ALYQ)

University of Leeds (nd) Hybrid working: Supporting our ways of working, OD&PL Leadership and Professional Practice, https://leadershipandprofessionalpractice.leeds.ac.uk/home/staff-development/hybrid-working/ (archived at https://perma.cc/D4MG-AW3G)

Vanderheyden, K and De Stobbeleir, K (2022) Seven ways leaders can develop their hybrid skills, *People Management*, 19 May, www.peoplemanagement.co.uk/article/1756509/seven-ways-leaders-develop-hybrid-skills (archived at https://perma.cc/HNL3-ARP6)

9

Helping individuals

The shorter read

If we are going to make hybrid working and alternative working weeks work, we know already that we must focus on personalizing work and the whole employee experience. This means also providing the right support for individual remote and hybrid workers so that they can overcome any struggles or issues.

Remote and hybrid workers face a risk of isolation. Facing reduced social contact can lead to more serious problems, and the nature of remote and hybrid work can worsen these issues if not tackled. This can be made worse through a lack of support from their team and/or manager. We must encourage socialization in digital interactions and encourage remote and hybrid workers to seek interactions elsewhere too.

Many can find it difficult to unplug when remote working and run the risk of working too long. It can be too easy to continue working because of the way that remote and hybrid working is often done in one's home. We must encourage these workers to build more structure and support into their routines and give guidance on how to minimize or resist the temptation to work more.

Working in your own home brings with it a range of potential distractions and difficulties in managing your own time. An individual remote or hybrid worker may struggle to manage these and achieve the work-related outcomes they want, while satisfying other stakeholders in their personal lives. We must help them to understand their own rhythms and energy levels, to manage their time more effectively, to use available technology to be more efficient, and to create the most appropriate working environment in their home. We must also give permission for them to make decisions about undertaking personal tasks, and devoting time to non-work activities also.

There could be complications in collaborating with other colleagues. These colleagues may be on site or may also be remote or hybrid workers. If left to chance, bad working habits and ineffective use of technology that should be helping and not hindering collaboration could develop. Asynchronous working has enormous potential but can get in the way if the right support is not given. We must encourage individual remote and hybrid workers to be clear on their working schedule and those of others to plan collaborative working more effectively. We must give guidance and support on how to use technology better.

The technology itself requires greater levels of technical ability but also greater digital literacy, and this can often be taken for granted. Developing technologies such as the metaverse and artificial intelligence offer considerable potential but only if used appropriately by the organization. Remote and hybrid workers may be working alone while using such technologies and may be ill-equipped to deal with problems that may occur. Again, guidance and support are necessary here.

Much of the above creates learning needs for an individual remote or hybrid worker. We must help them, but the way that such workers will learn means a change in the way we design and deliver content to them. Live sessions are helpful but will become a minor piece in the overall learning ecosystem. Greater use of planned on-the-job learning opportunities, access to dedicated communities of practice, and more encouragement of user-generated and audio/video content will enable the individual remote or hybrid worker to access learning content and knowledge in real time, at the point of need. Modern technologies such as artificial intelligence can aid learning for such workers too.

This points to a need to personalize the hybrid employee experience, but how? Contracting (agreeing how things will be done) with everyone is helpful, and there are specific questions that would be helpful to discuss with everyone to ensure that their experience is a positive one, and the one most likely to result in better outcomes for all.

Even then there is a need to increase the frequency, but decrease the duration, of check-ins with individual remote and hybrid workers. Just because we have put the required support in place, and just because we have set up a personalized relationship and experience, does not mean it will continue to work well. Regular check-ins will keep the momentum going and enable good adult–adult conversations about what works and what does not.

The longer read

So far in this book we have covered what organizations need to do to make hybrid working and alternative working weeks work more effectively, and in the previous chapter we have focused on how we help managers of hybrid individuals and teams. But what about the individual remote or hybrid workers themselves? In this book there have been lots of hints about the kinds of issues that those workers will experience – this chapter will explore these explicitly.

What individual remote and hybrid workers struggle with, and how to help them

The individual remote or hybrid worker may find the experience a pleasant and positive one, resulting in improved productivity and performance, and a healthier work–life balance. But we must not assume that simply providing remote or hybrid working will deliver these outcomes. Again, their experience is not something that should be left to chance. There are many potential areas where they could struggle and may need help.

Isolation

Working on site, assuming others are doing the same, offers lots of ad hoc serendipitous moments of interaction – the semi-mythical 'water cooler conversations'. A hybrid worker can be deprived of such opportunities when working remotely, and this sense of isolation can hit productivity and motivation. Unless hybrid workers make the effort to socialize with others (or are encouraged to), there is a danger they won't. This may lead to missed opportunities to form friendships with colleagues.

While many would dispute the claims around water cooler conversations, there can be reduced social interaction when working remotely. Things as simple as saying 'good morning', eating meals together or quick conversations about non-work matters all happen naturally when on site. When working remotely they need to be given structure and explicit encouragement.

Research from the BBC suggests that isolation can lead to overthinking situations, over-analysing conversations and interactions, and needing more regular reassurance that everything is OK. The lack of face-to-face communication increases ambiguity and uncertainty in communication signals (Lufkin, 2022). An individual remote or hybrid worker may feel as if they are invisible to others at work and that their work goes unnoticed. When on site, simple signals such as nods, smiles and quick verbal encouragers are easy to obtain and process, but remotely this can be more difficult. The absence of these signals can lead to a spiral of negative thinking if not checked or challenged and is a major drawback to asynchronous and digital forms of communication.

There could be many ways to address this. The suggestions below are not exhaustive, nor guaranteed to work for every individual and must be contextualized to each individual situation:

- Getting interaction elsewhere. When I work remotely and on work where I need to focus deeply, I can go many hours without human interaction. Consciously scheduling time during my day to have lunch with my wife, or go for a walk with her, or to do a school run, or go and see my dad all help me to get some human interaction. Even going to the shop or to get a coffee can bring human interaction and minimize feelings of isolation.

- Building socialization into digital interactions. In every meeting or live virtual training session I ensure that I spend time talking about non-work things for a few minutes before the main discussions begin. It helps me to feel as if I am dealing with human beings and not just dealing with business issues.

- Utilizing (internal or external) social media channels to have active work and non-work discussions with other people. This is something I will consciously do during the working day. It helps me to feel connected to the world outside of my remote workplace and have conversations about things that can build greater connections.

Unplugging and working too long

Personalizing work, for hybrid workers, could mean greater freedom over when and where to work. For many, this will mean difficulty unplugging from work and setting the proper boundaries between work and home. It is estimated that 22 per cent of remote workers have difficulty unplugging after work, though I would place that estimate much higher (Matyska, 2022). The absence of a physical commute is a big contributor to this – a lack of a boundary between work and home.

But overworking can be an issue too. Not having to leave an on-site location because everyone else is, or because the site is closing, or to catch a train or bus, may mean that there is less incentive for ceasing work. Allied to this is the ease of doing work remotely from one's own home, surrounded by the right environment and creature comforts. The lack of a strong signal to stop work may mean that some would simply continue to work. They may also be tempted to work longer because that might mean generating better results, or because of a fear that the remote worker's manager may equate being remote with lower productivity.

The comfort of working from home could mean that adequate breaks, in line with various pieces of legislation, are not taken. The day could have little structure without the visible signs of other workers breaking for lunch and moving away from screen-based work, and the day could become overly long and onerous as a result. This could be worsened if the work is too sedentary, leading to musculoskeletal problems as well as eye strain. Back-to-back meetings could make this even worse.

There can be further issues with the devices used to perform work. When work is done through a screen, that screen can be accessed anywhere and remains in the hybrid worker's home even when not being actively used. If the home is where work happens, then work is delivered there via the device. Sometimes that same device is also a personal one, though not always. Regardless, the intrusions from notifications and temptation to use apps is a real and often strong one.

Here are some suggestions on how to address this. Again, these are not exhaustive nor guaranteed to work for individual remote and hybrid workers, but are certainly worth considering:

• If there are others in the remote workplace, they could be asked to help the hybrid worker stop work. For me, this is easy – when my youngest children return home from school it becomes increasingly difficult to do any work, but others will need a more explicit prompt from a family member or other person. If these other people can be connected to an event or activity, such as going out somewhere, this can prompt a proper disconnection from work.

- Setting reminders to take breaks during the working day can be an effective way to encourage some physical activity, a screen break or reconnect with others in the household.

- Going for a walk or some other form of physical activity can help to create the same effect as a commute at the start and/or end of the day. I will very often drop my youngest children at school and then go for a run before starting work, and I find that this creates something of a physical divide between my two worlds. A lunchtime walk can be equally beneficial.

- Deliberately not stocking the fridge and cupboards with easy-to-eat snacks and meals may force a hybrid worker to leave the house during the day to get food, enforcing a break from work and reducing risk of burnout.

- Turning off notifications on work apps or devices when not working can be a helpful step to avoid being drawn back into work and away from personal matters. A step further would be to turn them off completely or place them on airplane mode, but this may not be possible for some.

- Where possible, a separate workspace at home that can be closed off when not working will create something of a physical barrier and reduce temptation to resume working once stopped for the day.

Distractions at home and problems managing time

A connected problem, but almost the opposite, can be the distractions a remote or hybrid worker may face in their home environment. It could be household tasks, caring responsibilities, people coming to the house and many more. These could reduce the ability to focus, in addition to other more universal distractions such as social media, the internet, television and so on.

One of my main distractions, leaving aside the times of the day when young children may be in the house, which I can largely manage, is my dad. He's on his own these days and lives close by. It is always great to see him, but he has never grasped that me working from home doesn't equate to complete freedom to see him whenever he wants. Several times a week he will drop by unannounced, only to find I'm in a virtual meeting or need to complete a task by a certain time. Or he might ring me, and I won't be able to take his call. This causes me some concern as he is elderly and there could be some problem, but he is usually ringing just to tell me about someone he has seen recently and what he has been talking about with them, or to ask me to pick him something up from the supermarket. Or he will turn up when I'm trying to get some quiet, focused work done. He will assume that I can stop work whenever I choose, which can be done sometimes but often cannot.

What I've begun to do is ask my dad to let me know if he wants to come round so that I can either tell him if it isn't convenient or can arrange my work so that I'm available when he does. I haven't gone as far as sharing my calendar with him as that would blow his mind, but I do talk to him now about what I'm doing and he can get a sense of how busy I might be, or not. So when my dad does come round, I can then spend time with him, and have moved tasks to other times of the day or week.

There may be other problems managing time due to the lack of an overtly structured working day for a remote or hybrid worker. Some suggestions here, aside from the things I have tried with my dad, include:

- Working out the body's natural circadian rhythms. Some people are more energetic and focused in the morning, and others in the evening. Some have completely different rhythms – a hybrid worker with very young children may not find a traditional working day or week is the best use of their energy and may struggle to focus, so working with them to find a more appropriate working pattern for their rhythms may improve their productivity and reduce their propensity to be distracted at home.

- Encourage remote and hybrid workers to track their time spend on different tasks (there are plenty of apps that will do this for you) and discuss the data with them to see what it reveals. It could be that scheduling blocks of time to complete specific tasks, with reminders, may create a more efficient way of working. This needs to be done in an open and transparent way to avoid people finding this intrusive and wondering about why they are being asked.

- Consider utilizing artificial intelligence to semi-automate or fully automate routine administrative tasks and integrate this with email and calendar apps to reduce time spent administering such things.

- Giving explicit permission for remote and hybrid workers to undertake personal tasks during the traditional working day might mean that they can consciously schedule time to do such things and let their work flow around them, reducing the chance that these tasks will distract them while working.

- Talking with a remote or hybrid worker about what their home environment looks like and how to minimize distractions while enabling them to lead a fulfilling personal life is a helpful step. This could be done as part of a contracting arrangement, which we will discuss later in this chapter.

- Encouraging remote and hybrid workers to experiment with and set working schedules may help to reduce distractions.

- Adopt the principle of 'leaving loudly' whether on site or remotely (via internal social media channels) so that immediate colleagues know that an individual remote or hybrid worker has finished for the day or week.

Difficulty communicating and collaborating

This is one of the common criticisms of remote and hybrid working and one of the main reasons cited by those who want to bring such workers back on site. As explored in an earlier chapter this is not necessarily the case but is likely to be if left to chance. If people work at contrasting times, it is perhaps inevitable that there will be difficulties in communicating and collaborating. Sixteen per cent of remote and hybrid workers chose it as their top problem, and this is an even bigger proportion among those who have only begun hybrid working since the Covid-19 pandemic, suggesting that those who consciously chose and have adapted to long-term remote and hybrid working have found more effective ways to communicate and collaborate compared to those who have had such things forced upon them in times of need (Griffis, 2022).

This is perhaps not surprising. If remote and hybrid working is left to chance, this could create extra work because of a lack of clarity in what people are supposed to do, or in the way expectations around work are communicated. Digital literacy and communication are often assumed to be at the right level but may not be for some workers and managers. And when the team is dispersed, there is a danger that this creates fewer opportunities to have conversations about work, leading to further difficulties. The effort needed to ensure that all are clear on what is happening could lead to some hybrid workers being left out of communications.

Working asynchronously may be a helpful solution in implementing hybrid working, but if workers are used to synchronous communication, then they may struggle. There could be delays between sending a message and receiving a reply, and this could create a feeling that hybrid working slows down communication or creates unnecessary delays. If teams have elongated working hours because of different working patterns, then this could create a feeling that hybrid workers need to be 'always on' to cope with the need to communicate to team members working different hours to them. Implementation of alternative working weeks could worsen this feeling.

It can be equally frustrating if individual remote and hybrid workers must come on site but the colleagues they need to collaborate with are not there at the time.

Some suggestions for overcoming these obstacles include:

- Ensure that each individual remote or hybrid worker keeps to a similar schedule once they have worked out what that needs to be. There will be exceptions, but knowing when and where someone is going to be working is helpful if there is a need to contact them or work synchronously on a task.

- Working out what the exceptions could be to this – for example if someone has some personal stuff to deal with in the short term, or may not be 100 per cent fit, or may have difficulties affording the commute.

- Actively build 'co-working time' where specific individual hybrid workers are going to be working at the same time as (though not necessarily in the same place as) other workers to encourage easier communication and collaboration.

- Encourage use of asynchronous communication tools but create the expectation that a response need not, and may not always be, immediate. Individual hybrid workers should thus plan to do other tasks in between waiting for responses from colleagues.

- Provide guidance and support on how to use text-based communication more effectively, raising the level of digital literacy among individual hybrid workers.

- Provide guidance on how to use video-based communication methods more effectively to ensure that collaboration is not only reserved for on-site working. Add to this with training on how to use other types of asynchronous collaborative software (from things as ubiquitous as MS

Teams and Zoom, to MS Planner and MS Viva, to more powerful and complex project management tools).

- Consider recording important meetings where there are those whose working pattern precludes their attendance and instigate follow-up discussions using internal social media.
- Encouraging individuals and their teams to consciously ask whether something could be covered in an email or channel discussion instead of a synchronous meeting.
- Giving clarity on what tasks are synchronous and how to plan for these.

Technological challenges

There could be technological challenges arising from remote and hybrid working. Access to technical support is among these. A remote or hybrid worker may be using their own equipment or may be using company equipment to perform company work. Regardless, they are remote and distant from immediately available support no matter how available virtual support may be. If using their own equipment this may limit the available support, and in most cases the individual hybrid worker will need to undertake some of their own checks on hardware and software before contacting technical support. This may be daunting for some, and some may also not have backup equipment in case of a failure.

Research from Microsoft suggests that 52 per cent of employees expect to be using digital immersive spaces in the metaverse in the coming year for meetings or team activities (Microsoft, 2023), posing challenges for those employees and their managers on how to best use such emerging technologies. Further Microsoft research points to how all pervasive the use of artificial intelligence could become – 76 per cent feel they will use it for administrative purposes, 86 per cent for finding answers to questions, 80 per cent for summarizing meetings and 77 per cent for planning their day (Microsoft, 2023).

To address these challenges, some of the following suggestions could be helpful:

- Provide guidance to individual remote and hybrid workers on what to do in case of equipment failure. This could involve using backup equipment, basic checks to do on the failed hardware or software, and a range of people they could contact for advice before contacting remote technical support.

- Provide guidance to employees on how to use artificial intelligence effectively and work iteratively with it, given that much of their interactions with it may come in the remote workplace.
- Provide guidance on how to troubleshoot issues with digital communications tools and platforms.

All of this suggests that there is a great deal for individual remote and hybrid workers to learn, and indeed there is. But how best to achieve that learning?

How to support learning for hybrid workers

Learning for individual remote and hybrid workers is different. Their work, and life, is already different than others – so we must try to personalize their learning experiences too. A wide range of different learning opportunities and methods could be used to do this.

Live training sessions

The main place where individual remote and hybrid workers learn should not be a live session, whether virtual or on site. Those will be a piece of the learning puzzle that will have started before the live session and will continue after the live session – if indeed a live session features at all.

Should a live virtual session feature then small group learning would be recommended for those individuals attending to allow for individual focus and attention. They should be as interactive as possible to help embed the learning and done in a psychologically safe way by the facilitator. The sessions should be shorter rather than longer to avoid digital fatigue, and training should be available on how to use the technology more effectively to learn. Training on digital literacy may also be helpful.

If a remote or hybrid worker has attended a live session then we must follow these up with opportunities to reflect and share, by discussing their learning with them individually and giving them a chance to discuss with their colleagues in more depth.

But simply doing more live sessions would not shift the culture around or perception of learning in the way we need it to for individual remote and hybrid workers. We must offer diverse types of learning opportunities.

On-the-job learning opportunities

As we noted in the previous chapter, for managers most learning opportunities come from working on the job and from working with others. The same will be true for individual remote and hybrid workers. Therefore, we need to ensure that these opportunities are provided, and utilized.

One of the biggest barriers to learning can be the time it takes to access it, taking people away from their day jobs. This reinforces how we must refocus learning as an aid to performance via bite-sized chunks of content, and opportunities to discuss work with colleagues, as well as challenging assignments with coaching and reflection opportunities. The challenging assignments may encourage (or even force) individual remote or hybrid workers to seek out other people to get new knowledge, develop new skills or build new connections.

Hybrid workers are likely to spend time working in various places. They will need access to learning content and opportunities regardless of where and when they work. If you look at the 10 most utilized tools for individual learning you will note that five are individualized learning tools, which can be accessed whenever and wherever a hybrid worker works (Hart, 2023). Three of the remaining five are collaborative tools for individuals to share knowledge and insights with colleagues. While these are personal learning tools, rather than workplace-specific tools, this offers an interesting point. Hybrid workers already have hybrid lives, as we have examined. They (or we) are already used to learning asynchronously on our own, and synchronously with others using technology, in our personal lives. Think back to the last time you taught yourself something by watching a YouTube video. You didn't wait for a live session on it – you needed knowledge and got it whenever and wherever you wanted it. How do we translate this mindset into the workplace for individual remote and hybrid workers?

In *HR for Hybrid Working*, I talked about breaking down recorded live sessions into bite-sized chunks – no more than five minutes in duration and categorized by topic. This would allow for searchable repositories of video-based discussions that can be accessed in a comparable way to how we search for YouTube videos in our personal lives. In a similar vein, we could replace text-based documents or updates with audio or video content from the creator of the document or update. This could be more time efficient for remote and hybrid workers, as they could speed up, pause and come back to, and generally access it quicker than reading a text-based document or update. Adding the ability to message the creator or author or chat asynchronously with others who have viewed the updates, as happens on YouTube, could facilitate new connections and sharing of tacit and explicit knowledge.

Live sessions take time out of people's day, but the above types of more accessible learning content may embed this into the flow of work. Some of them, particularly audio and video content, can be done while multitasking, listening or watching while working. In our personal lives we do this already – listening to podcasts while commuting, audio books in the bath or bed, music when we exercise or in the car. Providing these diverse types of content could help more efficient and effective learning for individual remote and hybrid workers. There are also pieces of technology that can help individuals to learn while working, and a quick internet search will reveal many.

Communities of practice (CoP)

We have mentioned CoP in other chapters already. Done well, they can help knowledge sharing, underpin innovation and have the potential to improve performance. While there can be downsides to them if they become cliquey or are overly controlled by power and authority, they could be an effective means for individual remote and hybrid workers to learn. If we look at the examples of touchpoints in the hybrid employee experience, and distinct types of hybrid workers, both discussed in Chapter 7, these offer obvious opportunities to create CoP at specific junctures. Other examples might include posing questions in a web chat for people to answer and share knowledge; bringing together smaller, virtual groups to make use of resources specific to them; and more (Dawson, 2023).

CoP provide individual remote and hybrid workers with significant opportunities to connect with others in similar positions, in or outside of their immediate team, and to reduce reliance on time-intensive learning opportunities. They will also bring benefits around the sharing of knowledge and the embedding of organizational culture.

User-generated content

User-generated content, based on where remote and hybrid workers feel their main pain points and performance issues are, can often lead to higher engagement and the more effective sharing of tacit knowledge but in smaller chunks.

Allied to this, we could reward knowledge sharing through recognition and performance management, making it worthwhile for people to gain new skills and share their knowledge by creating their own content. This could be done through providing an accessible and usable organizational wiki, or dedicated internal social media channels where quick, casual communication can lead to knowledge sharing and user-generated content that can be accessed by all.

There may be a need here for someone within the organization to take on a quality control role and ensure that the user-generated content is more than just links to external websites and is genuinely useful in resolving performance issues.

Using artificial intelligence (AI) and other technologies

There are plenty of distinct aspects to discuss here. Starting with wearable technology, it is startling to think how this has evolved even in our lifetime. My own early experiences involved simple wristwatches that told me about the time in various cities, in real time whenever I wanted the knowledge, just in time. Now such devices provide a richer variety of knowledge and information along with connectivity to other systems. While this could and will evolve further, wearable technology could be useful assets for individual remote and hybrid workers who may be more in need of portable technology and more convenient access to systems, connections and knowledge. How much of your own organization's IT systems can be effectively accessed and used through wearable technologies?

There are other, more dedicated books covering the growth of AI and its potential in learning. Donald Clark's *Artificial Intelligence for Learning* is a good start point, but there are others as well. I do not aim to summarize these significant pieces of research here or to be comprehensive, but to prompt some thinking based on principles they explore, particularly for remote and hybrid workers. To learn more, you may need to access the more specific research though.

The metaverse, or a version of it, may offer us interactions with other people regardless of location or working arrangements, as well as on-screen snippets of knowledge and insights into what those people are doing and talking about, easing the acquisition of knowledge, and building more connections. Augmented and virtual reality programmes may provide realistic alternatives to on-site training sessions that can be replayed, retaken and completed asynchronously or synchronously.

Intelligent chatbots could help individual remote and hybrid workers understand difficult concepts while working, combining learning with work. They could signpost to other resources or people with more knowledge. They could link to the organizational wiki or internal social media channels or could guide a worker through an interaction using augmented or virtual reality.

Machine learning and AI can generate content suggestions based on search history and other interactions from remote and hybrid workers, giving them the information they need more quickly. This already happens in our personal lives. We already use search engines in our personal lives multiple times a day, whether that be Google, YouTube or social media searches. We harvest such sources for information and knowledge, and we do the same with other people too (Looop, 2022). We use smart devices to give us information and knowledge in our personal lives, but not so much in the workplace. Our remote and hybrid workers will need AI in the workplace because they already use it in their personal lives – in the household that has become their remote workplace. We have much to catch up on at work.

Given what we have discussed in this section, we may not be able to rely on individual remote and hybrid workers voluntarily accessing the right content and learning opportunities in the right way. Perhaps we need to make individual learning and development plans mandatory – an expectation that people will learn and develop, with mandatory discussions about growth and development. There could be too much to leave it to chance.

Ultimately though, how this is all achieved will be contextual to each individual remote or hybrid worker, and managers need to personalize their approach so that the learning opportunities are aligned with how each person is managed.

Contracting with remote and hybrid workers

There are several areas where managers could make explicit agreements and arrangements with individual remote and hybrid workers to ensure that the management relationship and the overall employee experience is a positive one. It would also speak to the concept of personalizing work, which we covered in Chapter 5. The process is called contracting and sounds very formal but need not be. The key is the conversation and not the formality.

What kinds of things would be covered? Here are some suggestions, though this is not an exhaustive list. The questions are phrased from a manager's perspective, to give managers some prompts on how they can best get optimum performance from the individual remote or hybrid worker:

- What will you do to encourage and agree healthy working practices for everyone? What times can they choose to work, and where may they have no choice?
- How will you agree how flexible individual working arrangements are, and what would change those?
- What might be circumstances where the individual may need to make themselves available for other team members or customers?
- What do you need to agree about forms and mediums of communication with everyone?
- How will you get updates from and give feedback to everyone about their work? How will this differ according to specific tasks they undertake?
- How will you give recognition and appreciation to everyone?
- What coaching does each individual need on building better relationships with their team?
- What equipment does each individual need in their remote or on-site workplaces?
- How will you ensure that each individual feels included and has a voice at work?

Of course, some or all of this could be done via a policy and applied to the entire organization or all its remote and hybrid workers, but this runs the risk of generalizing the hybrid employee experience and not personalizing it. But it doesn't always.

North Somerset Council is a local authority based in the UK. They have a hybrid working policy that aims to set out the principles by which individual remote and hybrid workers will be managed, and they encourage individualized agreements on how relationships and the entire arrangement will work.

The policy covers examples of circumstances where individual hybrid working arrangements would need to be flexed and the individual may be needed on site at a time they would usually work remotely. These include being on site to collaborate with colleagues; to attend training; to provide support and training for new colleagues; to cover for a colleague who is sick; or in case of equipment or system failure.

It also explains what healthy working practices could look like and encourages everyone to agree these with their manager. Practices covered include: not creating extra work for colleagues by working at unusual times; being courteous and respectful to colleagues if choosing to work at unsociable hours; checking in with a manager if working long periods alone; safety arrangements when working remotely; taking regular rest breaks from work and from screen-based work; avoiding working longer hours; and connecting with colleagues to maintain a sense of belonging.

Also covered are how teams should manage their own arrangements, with guidance given on what should be agreed but the detail encouraged to be decided upon by the teams themselves. Items include what effective communication looks like; the need to hold regular team meetings and for these to be used to coordinate office cover and check work programmes; and to keep electronic diaries up to date and for them to reflect working routines.

Within the local authority, individual jobs are allocated to a work type, with typical arrangements and personas in place for each of these:

- **Flexible worker** – someone who spends two to three days on site, with the precise detail decided by the task undertaken. Training is given to these individuals on work–life balance, timekeeping and building travel time into schedules, and ensuring effective communication with colleagues.

- **Mobile worker** – someone who may only be on site one day per week or less for specific meetings. Guidance is given around giving these individuals very portable technology, and how to use virtual communication to keep team relationships effective. Training is given to these individuals around display screen equipment assessments, good practice physical and mental health, and work–life balance.

- **Fixed worker** – someone who spends almost all their time on site, whether because of their role or because of the unsuitability of their remote working arrangements. They are given training on how to treat the on-site workplace as a shared space.

- **Field worker** – someone who is hardly ever on site, and who is supported by touchdown spaces when they do come on site.

The use of such personas has been covered in an earlier chapter but here it is combined with how to manage each individual and remote hybrid worker more effectively by contracting with them in the most appropriate way. Much is still left to the individual and their manager to agree, and there is a clear need to continue to check in often with individual remote and hybrid workers.

Checking in with remote and hybrid workers

How is it best, given what we have discussed, to check in with individual remote and hybrid workers? How best to strike the balance between managing their engagement and checking their well-being, and ensuring that they are performing in role?

The phrase little and often comes to mind. Compared to an on-site worker, I recommend the frequency of contact is increased for a remote or hybrid worker, but that the duration of contact is decreased. But the content of the contact will change. This is because much of what a remote or hybrid worker does in terms of performance can be assessed asynchronously by analysing data or running a report (see Chapter 8 for examples of the types of data that a manager could analyse, and that's even without thinking about performance data). Done well, a contact with a remote or hybrid worker won't need to focus heavily, or at all, on how that individual is performing. The manager should be able to assess the level of performance and productivity from the data. This means that gone are the days when an individual worker needed to produce a report on their performance and present it or talk it through with their manager.

But what takes its place?

A good example featured in Chapter 8 of *HR for Hybrid Working* where Anna Edmondson from PowerONPlatforms talked about their use of the Weekly10 model:

- Successes – what has worked well, what are you proud of?
- Challenges – what has been difficult, how can we make this better?
- How are you feeling?
- Giving thanks – who do you want to recognize for good work?
- Learning – what have you learnt this week? What future learning do you need? (Cookson, 2022)

While the Weekly10 model is a paid-for platform, an informal approach using similar principles is likely to prove successful too. The focus on the five areas gives both manager and individual worker a chance to discuss issues related to work, personal life and more besides. There should be little in the way of formal preparation, and the focus should be on the quality of the conversation using the structure rather than producing data and reports around performance and productivity.

Our focus is on managing the human being, not the performance. If we do that well enough, the human being will take care of the performance. A structure like the Weekly10 one above offers a good balance of issues that are relevant to remote and hybrid workers without being too onerous.

The manager should agree, via the contracting process described earlier in this chapter, how such check-ins are done logistically, and how other updates will be provided about both work and how the individual is feeling at any given time.

In addition to this regular individual check-in, I also recommend a team version of this to allow teams to express their views on what is working and what is not. In our next chapter we will examine this in more detail.

CASE STUDY ONE

Stuart Cavanagh is the Associate Director of People and Happiness at University Academy 92 (UA92), a Higher Education institution founded in 2017 in the UK to provide degree-level study with a particular focus on preparation for the workplace. They have around 120 staff based in Manchester, UK, but have plans to grow their global reach over the next few years. Cavanagh's job title, including the word 'Happiness', speaks volumes about the overall approach to hybrid working and employee engagement at UA92.

UA92 have a hybrid working approach that encourages, but does not mandate, on-site attendance three days a week for most people. UA92 aim to treat employees like adults and let them make their own decisions about where and when to work. Some jobs, such as lecturing positions, will naturally spend a greater amount of time on site but UA92 have implemented 'online Wednesdays' where all teaching takes place remotely – this is a conscious decision to allow lecturing staff to benefit from remote working. They have also implemented 'free from Fridays' where no formal, planned meetings take place. This move enables individuals to plan their time more effectively and to do tasks that could be done remotely or could be done on site – the choice is theirs. Lecturing staff can request to reduce their teaching load in exchange for other duties, which changes the balance of their on-site attendance requirements, again to suit individual choices. Remote and hybrid working is encouraged at all levels of the organization, with the CEO adopting a healthy balance of remote and on-site attendance.

UA92's main on-site location is consciously designed to give individuals the right support. It has a plethora of shared spaces and social spaces. Hot-desking and touchdown facilities are available, along with individual and paired booths for more focused work and communication. All these spaces are bookable in advance except for the social spaces. At numerous hot desks and touchdown spaces there are desks that can be raised into standing desks, and treadmills or indoor cycle facilities can be added to each desk to encourage physical activity while performing sedentary tasks. Many staff rooms have flexible equipment with chairs and tables on wheels to allow for the creation of ad hoc collaborative spaces. There are several on-site gyms, and contemplation and prayer rooms, shared with students. Renting out these and other spaces within the building supplies a valuable and sustainable source of secondary income for the organization, which it reinvests into the student and employee experience.

Cavanagh told me that UA92 actively encourage flexibility in working patterns to suit individual lifestyles and needs. He gave examples of people requesting flexible working, or returning from maternity leave, being asked to design what their working pattern looks like. The organization also offers generous family-friendly leave arrangements, and a considerable amount of annual leave – around 45 days in total, which includes a day off for employees' birthdays and two full weeks over Christmas. The aim here is to provide support for whatever individuals may be prioritizing and dealing with in their personal lives. Where individuals do need to do added work in evenings or at weekends, there is time off in lieu granted in recognition of the impact that the added on-site work may have on individuals and their personal lives.

UA92 have a unique philosophy as a higher education institution and focus on what they call character development alongside more traditional professional development. Their '92 Programme' offers several modules that students must complete as part of their studies, and Cavanagh has recently mirrored this almost entirely as part of the onboarding and induction process for new staff. He recognizes that it can be hard to acclimatize to a new organizational culture, particularly with elements of remote and hybrid working, and feels a staff version of the 92 Programme helps to embed culture and build individual character in the first stages of employment. The elements of character reflect UA92's values, which Cavanagh is ensuring are embedded into every aspect of the hybrid employee life cycle. There are a range of both virtual and on-site socialization opportunities, focusing on things that UA92 does well – such as media/movie nights, sports events, lunch and learn events, and similar.

Cavanagh's team is small, and all work in a hybrid way. To enable good visibility for all about the team's activities, Cavanagh uses kanban boards to plan and structure work. Shared email accounts ensure that queries are effectively dealt with regardless of who is working where or when, and FAQ documents are created to help asynchronous working. Cavanagh's team have 'Collaborative Wednesdays' where the entire team are on site. These days begin with a stand-up team meeting where each person has up to 15 minutes to discuss what they are working on, focusing specifically on the reds and ambers in their red/amber/green status on the kanban boards. The team also uses Yammer, and Sharepoint, to discuss issues and provide information to the rest of the organization. It has been using video content related to organizational policies to provide easier and clearer access to information critical to the hybrid employee experience for those working remotely.

The organization is aware of what makes it unique both as a university and as an employer. It aims to tackle deprivation in its local area and sees this as a major talent attraction point. It offers performance-related pay increases (alongside cost-of-living rises) rather than annualized length-of-service-based incremental rises, as it wishes to reward individual progression and performance. Inclusivity is a key area of focus also, and Cavanagh has overseen small but effective changes to how the organization promotes this – UA92 believes that every member of staff, whether on site, hybrid or remote, has the potential to have an impact on the organization. It aims to treat staff like adults, and encourage both flexibility, common sense and informality in the hybrid employment relationship.

CASE STUDY TWO

Fran Manca and Kelly Roskell are co-founders of Clockwork Studios, a community interest company based in Prescot, near Liverpool in the UK, which provides co-working spaces for remote and hybrid workers based in that location. They founded Clockwork Studios after realizing that they were both beginning to work from the same locations, without much of the support that remote and hybrid workers could really benefit from. They realized there was no suitable space in Prescot, so set up their own.

Both of Manca and Roskell's children have special educational needs, meaning that a traditional working week was a tricky thing for either to stick to. Remote working or at least the avoidance of a fixed commute became something both valued. Their co-working space and community hub is designed to support workers with managing their personal circumstances and providing the right environment for their work (and by extension their businesses) to be more effective. Manca and Roskell both thrive on supporting business owners and new businesses and help these to think about how to support the individuals who work within those businesses.

Clockwork Studios provide a range of distinct types of spaces within their building to allow distinct types of work to take place. People use the spaces for varied reasons – some for quiet, focused work if their remote workspace is not suitable or right; some for client meetings; some for social connections with other people and the desire to be where others are working. There are spaces to hold video calls, record podcasts and edit videos. Free learning resources and events focused on how to run businesses and leadership skills are also provided and are well utilized.

Clockwork Studios find that those who use their co-working space often are hybrid workers, with on-site attendance on some days of the week but who choose to spend their remote working time at the co-working space surrounded by like-minded individuals. While one could question why these people don't simply go on site to their own organizations more often, this downplays the sense of community and connection that Clockwork's co-working space offers.

The organization is located close to both a theatre school and a dance school. The co-founders have noticed that remote and hybrid workers will often collect their children from mainstream schools around 3 pm each afternoon, drop them at the theatre/dance schools, and then come to work in the co-working space for up to two hours before collecting their children from the respective nearby schools. Children do occasionally end up being in the co-working space also, and Clockwork hire out their spaces to other community groups, so the space has a genuine community hub feel. The space is open from 8 am until 5.30 pm, Monday to Friday, through the choice and availability of the co-founders, but both believe that remote and hybrid workers would use the co-working space outside of these times if it were available.

I asked Manca and Roskell if there had been issues in setting up an etiquette around how to use the co-working facility. They reported that when they first set up, in 2018, there had been lots of issues, but having worked to address them and set up rules and boundaries since, there are now none. The co-working space has become self-regulated now that the individual remote and hybrid workers have the right tools, the right environment and the right support.

Case study reflections

In our first case study, UA92, the following points stand out:

- A focus on what makes individuals happy or happier at work may give rise to some interesting debates about how to lead and manage them.
- Consciously redesigning some tasks to allow greater flexibility about where and when they can (or cannot) take place can enable hybrid working in diverse ways, as can allowing individuals to request different tasks.
- Building design is critical for a good on-site experience. Focusing on socialization and well-being is important for individuals.
- Flexibility in working patterns matters too, and giving the design of working patterns to interested individuals could make them really think about how it can work, as opposed to them expecting their manager to do that for them.
- A focus on character development (or behaviours and values) is a good thing during the early parts of the employee life cycle and will help individuals to work out what they need to flourish in the organization – and how much they feel included by and in the organization.
- Embedding the organizational values in each part of the hybrid employee life cycle will enable an individualized approach to be further developed.
- Using asynchronous communication and collaboration tools allows for hybrid working for everyone without forcing that to be the case.
- Allowing each individual the time and space to focus on their main priorities without the pressure to talk about everything is helpful. Treating individuals like adults is also a positive step.

In our second case study, Clockwork Studios, the following points stand out:

- Remote and hybrid workers need tailored support. Leaving this to chance isn't really an option.
- Remote and hybrid workers need connection and socialization opportunities with like-minded people. Giving them this in the on-site location is good, but their personal circumstances may not suit full-time on-site attendance, so finding ways to get this to them in their remote workspace is important.

- Individual remote workspaces may not be right for all types of work or may only offer one fixed type of workspace. Considering where other workspaces may be locally that could offer a more conducive environment for a task may unlock more productivity.

- Remote and hybrid workers will likely have their own working patterns, perhaps arranged around caring responsibilities. Finding spaces where they can work during breaks from these things may again unlock more productivity.

- Eventually a workplace can self-regulate but guidance is needed on how individuals must relate to and behave towards each other. Otherwise, there is a risk that things could deteriorate.

The action plan

If you want to provide the right support to individual hybrid workers, consider how you would answer the following questions:

- What actions will you recommend to help your employees to deal with the risk of feeling isolated?

- What guidance will you provide for your employees to help them to unplug from work and avoid working too long?

- What conversations will you encourage to take place between employees and their managers about managing distractions at home and making more effective use of their time?

- How will you ensure that employees plan collaborative time more effectively?

- How will you ensure that employees make best use of available and developing technology to collaborate and communicate more effectively?

- How will you assess the level of technical skills and digital literacy among your employees?

- What guidance will you provide for your employees on how to cope with technological problems?

- How will you ensure that your employees can use artificial intelligence in a suitable way?

- How will you change your live training sessions so that they fit better with other learning methods in the wider ecosystem?

- How will you guide employees to learn from on-the-job tasks and collaboration with others?

- What distinct types of learning content will you create for employees that they can more easily access in the flow of work?

- How will you consciously create and encourage use of specific communities of practice to build socialization and learning opportunities for employees?

- How will artificial intelligence help your employees to learn more effectively?

- How will you implement and encourage contracting between managers and employees to personalize their hybrid working arrangements and experiences?

- What structure and guidance might managers need to make check-ins with individual remote and hybrid workers more effective?

References and further reading

Clark, D (2024) *Artificial Intelligence for Learning: Using AI and generative AI to support learner development*, 2nd edn, Kogan Page, London

Conway, K (2022) How to leverage the benefits of hybrid learning and development, *Chief Learning Officer*, 9 December, www.chieflearningofficer.com/2022/12/09/how-to-leverage-the-benefits-of-hybrid-learning-and-development/ (archived at https://perma.cc/9K5Y-TA5M)

Cook, J and Daly, J (2022) Through the Lens of Research: Amplifying human focus in virtual and hybrid learning, Virtual Research Insights, www.virtualresearchinsights.com/report2022/ (archived at https://perma.cc/DC8Q-HR6J)

Cookson, G (2022) *HR for Hybrid Working: How to adapt people practices to support employees and the organization*, Kogan Page, London

Davis, M C et al (2022) Where is your office today? New insights on employee behaviour and social networks, University of Leeds, October, https://futureworkplace.leeds.ac.uk/wp-content/uploads/sites/86/2022/10/Where-is-your-office-today-Oct-2022-2.pdf (archived at https://perma.cc/7KTZ-LYU8)

Dawson, A (2023) Five ways to engage remote employees in learning, *People Management*, 28 April, www.peoplemanagement.co.uk/article/1821215/five-ways-engage-remote-employees-learning (archived at https://perma.cc/DEQ5-JNSH)

Griffis, H (2022) The 3 biggest struggles of the remote worker – and how to fix them, Built In, 13 July, www.builtin.com/remote-work/remote-work-struggles (archived at https://perma.cc/3GUM-HXS4)

Haas, M (2022) 5 challenges of hybrid work – and how to overcome them, *Harvard Business Review*, 15 February, www.hbr.org/2022/02/5-challenges-of-hybrid-work-and-how-to-overcome-them (archived at https://perma.cc/GEL7-4ZMD)

Hart, J (2023) Top 100 tools for learning 2023, 4 September, www.toptools4learning.com/ (archived at https://perma.cc/9993-WSEA)

Herrity, J (2023) 7 challenges of working remotely and how to overcome them, Indeed, 13 January, www.indeed.com/career-advice/career-development/working-remotely (archived at https://perma.cc/LW54-D687)

Kojic, M (2023) Overcome remote work challenges – expert insights, Clockify blog, 7 December, www.clockify.me/blog/remote-work/challenges-remote-work/ (archived at https://perma.cc/TT2A-FKMD)

Looop (2022) AI in L&D with Donald Clark, *The Learning & Development Podcast*, 14 June, www.looop.co/podcast (archived at https://perma.cc/X7BF-N3KW)

Lufkin, B (2022) Why overthinkers struggle with remote work, BBC, 9 August, www.bbc.com/worklife/article/20220803-why-overthinkers-struggle-with-remote-work (archived at https://perma.cc/XX8A-NLJR)

Matyska, K (2022) The challenges of working remotely, Timeular, 19 September, www.timeular.com/blog/challenges-working-remotely/ (archived at https://perma.cc/KT95-5R8E)

Microsoft (2022) Here's how you can work flexibly, have an impact on your team and keep your boss happy, 19 April, https://ukstories.microsoft.com/features/microsoftstories-podcast-season-2-episode-5-heres-how-you-can-work-flexibly-have-animpact-on-your-team-and-keep-your-boss-happy/ (archived at https://perma.cc/4AJZ-8ZWB)

Microsoft (2023) Will AI fix work? (2023) Work Trend Index, 9 May, www.microsoft.com/en-us/worklab/work-trend-index/will-ai-fix-work (archived at https://perma.cc/KC3W-39QM)

NHS Employers (2021) Implementing a just and learning culture, 23 February, www.nhsemployers.org/case-studies/implementing-just-and-learning-culture (archived at https://perma.cc/K6PW-Z7DQ)

Sinelnikov, D (2023) Strategies for staying connected and motivated while working remotely, *Forbes*, 24 April, www.forbes.com/sites/forbesagencycouncil/2023/04/24/strategies-for-staying-connected-and-motivated-while-working-remotely/ (archived at https://perma.cc/CSH8-GXYP)

Tirbutt, E (2022) The secret ingredients of effective hybrid L&D, *HR Magazine*, 26 August, www.hrmagazine.co.uk/content/features/the-secret-ingredients-of-effective-hybrid-ld (archived at https://perma.cc/2BYB-6D7U)

Workable (2023) The challenges of remote work (and how to overcome them), December, https://resources.workable.com/career-center/the-challenges-of-remote-work-and-how-to-overcome-them/ (archived at https://perma.cc/B9JC-RJZY)

10

Helping teams

The shorter read

We need to ensure that hybrid teams are given the support they need to work effectively in their environment. As with other aspects covered in this book, this support must not be left to chance.

Teams need access to the right technology and equipment otherwise hybrid working could become difficult for them. They need to know *how*, *when* and *where* each team member is working, or this too will be frustrating and confusing. Collaboration needs to be optimized for hybrid working to avoid conflict and inefficient work practices. And we must enable connections between team members, and with the wider organization, to combat isolation and to build stronger bonds. Productivity needs to be reframed and fully understood by all.

Hybrid teams can usefully adopt a remote-first approach by creating digital, rather than purely physical, communities. These can provide safe spaces to communicate, collaborate and to socialize. A range of different apps and pieces of technology will be needed to help them focus on the right work or things at the right time.

Effective asynchronous working is key to making hybrid working work, and teams must grasp the opportunities this provides while navigating clear of the risks. Training and support for asynchronous working is needed, so that managers can avoid micromanaging and productivity paranoia, and time is better spent being productive than talking about how to be productive. Meetings will still be needed but should be with purpose and clearly established goals, allowing the entire team to effectively contribute. New team members need to quickly embed themselves into the team and learn about its hybrid approach without undue delay or frustrations.

The way a hybrid team works lends itself to a team charter or equivalent – an agreement that sets out how, when and where the hybrid team works. These are a clever idea for any team, but for a hybrid team where its members are not always co-located on site and cannot see or notice team rituals, beliefs and ways of working, they are critical. There are numerous things that could be included in the charter, from communication preferences and etiquette to ways of working together, to providing role and task clarity and more.

The longer read

To this point in the book, we have looked at what managers struggle with in hybrid working and how to help them, and what individuals struggle with and how to help them too. In this last chapter our attention turns to teams, perhaps the most important part of the organizational system to address and get working effectively. Almost everyone in an organization belongs to a team, and while it is essential to get individual circumstances reflected in the ways of working, these will only be effective if they are aligned with the rest of the team and if the team knows how to operate smoothly and efficiently as a hybrid team. Much like other aspects of hybrid working, if left to chance, team dynamics and ways of working can be problematic. But if given conscious, deliberate thought, a hybrid team could be more effective than its face-to-face on-site equivalent.

What do teams struggle with?

A team working in a hybrid way may have access to a wider range of technology and equipment than an on-site team would. In Chapter 6 we examined how this could be confusing for individuals not knowing which piece of technology to use for which purpose, and in the new skills and knowledge needed to effectively use modern technologies and equipment. This could lead to a fragmentation of team culture if individuals do not have full understanding of how to communicate and collaborate with their teams. And while there will be some equipment and technology that is common across both on-site and remote working, there could be those that are only suitable for one or the other – again this could be confusing. But technology plays a crucial role in creating connections within a hybrid team, and the ability to communicate effectively using technology is cited by 95 per cent of employees as the most critical skill they will need in the years ahead (Microsoft, 2022b).

A hybrid team may not be co-located together much, if at all. Different individual working arrangements may mean that some team members see a lot of some people, and hardly anything of others. Finding where and when people are choosing to work in a hybrid team is important if there is synchronous work and collaboration to be done. As we explored in Chapter 7, there are types of hybrid workers for whom these things could matter more than for others. If any hybrid worker needs to see a colleague on site, there needs to be visibility of when that colleague may be on site. Likewise, if there is virtual collaboration to be done, knowing where and when one could connect to a colleague is also important. Teams could struggle with this visibility if they do not openly communicate or agree how the team will be practically administered based on who is working when and where.

Collaboration could become more difficult. When an individual's tasks don't involve close collaboration with colleagues, then remote and hybrid working is likely to have a neutral effect, but where such close collaboration is needed, then support needs to be provided to the team to ensure that this works effectively. The team needs to know who must work with whom and on which tasks, and how this needs to be done. Left alone, a team and its members should eventually work that out for themselves, but there is a chance that they won't, or won't land upon the most effective ways of working together.

Microsoft data suggests that hybrid workers are attracted to work on site to recapture social connection with other people and to rebuild their social capital – 84 per cent are motivated to come on site by the promise of socializing with co-workers, and by rebuilding team bonds, and 73 per cent would go on site more frequently if they knew their direct team members were there (Microsoft, 2022b). These bonds matter, and close friendships can be helpful in creating ties to an organization and in combating loneliness. This is a risk for remote and hybrid workers as we examined in Chapter 9. While virtual get-togethers can be helpful, unless a team and its members see each other in person at regular intervals (whether on site or elsewhere) it may struggle to be an effective and productive team. Geographically distributed teams can often be highly effective and productive, but also need help getting to that point.

Productivity itself can be problematic for hybrid teams, with some managers (as we have examined already in this book) having trouble believing that people are working unless they can see them. Teams need to fully understand what productivity looks like in their work and agree with their manager how this will be measured, checked and interpreted. If they do not, the manager could be tempted to adopt unhelpful management techniques such as micromanagement and managing through presence rather than by outcomes.

Kate Maddison-Greenwell is the founder of People Efficient and specializes in training leadership teams to use agile methodologies to improve collaboration and communication, and respond to change at pace. During her career she has led dispersed teams, and in her earlier years as a manager found herself micromanaging her team due to the lack of training and a framework to communicate with and support them. All she had was the desire to insist work was done and to regularly check that it was – both of which were unhelpful behaviours.

These behaviours had a negative impact on both Maddison-Greenwell and her team – with Maddison-Greenwell suffering from burnout because of trying to over-manage them. There was regular conflict within the teams and between the teams and their clients with no obvious way to resolve the conflict. Information-sharing meetings were dominated by one or two individuals. There was little clarity about which communication methods and mediums should be used for work and which for social chat. Individuals in the team began to vocalize their frustrations about the way the team was working, feeling that they could not resolve issues if they were not co-located together.

These experiences led Maddison-Greenwell to research and become proficient in using agile methodologies, as these gave her the frameworks she needed to manage her team and encouraged trust and psychological safety to be built with and within the team. She developed charters within the team to set up conflict-resolution methods, and structured ways to share updates on progress on tasks (considering individual preferences and ways of working too). She encouraged the teams to brainstorm how to address the frustrations individuals had voiced. The teams developed their communications etiquette and preferences for the use of different technology and channels. The teams were supported to feel more comfortable with asynchronous working and using technology to address issues and focus on collaborative working.

Maddison-Greenwell's experience is no doubt reflective of the help and support that teams need to set up so that their experience is not left to chance.

What help and support can we give teams?

Digital communities

A hybrid team cannot rely solely on physical communities as a way of communicating, connecting and collaborating. There will be times when it will use physical communities, but it will only be effective if it has a strong digital community used in combination with the physical community. This digital community should have effectively used communication tools, genuine and honest conversations and presence from both leadership and team members alike. A well-thought-out digital community will supply a safe space and time for employees to connect in non-work ways, sharing vulnerabilities and providing support on a wider range of issues. This moves beyond just emailing – in their study, Microsoft say that 48 per cent of employees want to spend less time on such things and more time networking (Microsoft, 2022a), suggesting that such digital communities need to focus on much more than just transactional work-based activities and discussions. And while virtual team social events have their place, a supportive digital community may not need them as much if it is a safe space and one where people feel connected to each other. The recognition of achievements and passing on of praise should also be encouraged within this digital community. The digital community need not be on the most up-to-date platform or use a wide range of available functions – accessibility and ease of use is what matters. Ideally it could be integrated into work apps and systems and not kept entirely separate.

The right technology and equipment

Earlier in this chapter we looked at ensuring that teams had the right technology and equipment, and what could happen if they don't. The right technology, used the right way, can make a significant difference. Most of the tools discussed in this section can be adapted for use on a range of budgets. Managers need to talk to teams about their views and opinions on the technology and equipment they use on site and those they use remotely. We must remember that there are lots of available technologies and each was created for a specific purpose that may not suit other purposes. Such as:

- Project or portfolio management software may help in updating task completion and status updates, with clarity about what each team is tasked to deliver. Microsoft Planner, Asana and Monday.com can all allow the easy assignment of tasks and manage the organization of work and delegation of responsibilities.
- Shared calendar access may help in increasing visibility and improving transparency of who is working where and when.
- Digital workflows may help in assessing bottlenecks caused by ways of working, and the reports from these may help in balancing both the autonomy that hybrid teams need with the assurance that their manager needs that outcomes are being achieved. Some of the tools mentioned in the first point would be relevant here too.
- Various topic-specific channels on internal social media and communications apps can keep social chat separate from work chat but can also provide dedicated places for sharing and discussing ideas, so as not to overload email traffic. Whiteboarding apps can achieve the same end with ideas and discussions.
- Document management or knowledge management systems can provide easy access to shared documents and enable joint working on such items. These can function as the 'single source of the truth' for the entire team.
- First-class video and audio conferencing facilities in the workplace, and portable versions of these for individuals who are remote, can make meeting and communicating synchronously easier.

Anna Edmondson is Chief People Officer at PowerONPlatforms, who featured as a case study in *HR for Hybrid Working*. Edmondson told me how PowerONPlatforms support their hybrid teams. They encourage short, regular and scheduled team touchpoints – usually morning meetings, whether daily or less frequent. These meetings last a maximum of 15 minutes where team members share information about workloads, where they need support from each other and have some social connection time.

Teams have near-constant communication using MS Teams, which is used for dynamic information sharing and problem solving among the team. This helps less experienced team members gain access to support from more experienced colleagues without needing to rely on synchronous meetings or know specifically who is free or available. In each team there are more senior individuals who have responsibility to keep an eye on these chats and ensure that questions are answered by the expert, who often is someone other than the manager of the team. Edmondson also said that teams make effective use of Loop, which integrates into Microsoft apps to create meeting notes and support asynchronous collaborative working.

Asynchronous working

The work that Edmondson's organization is doing is designed to aid asynchronous working, which is a key skill for hybrid teams to master. There is a risk that teams, left to chance, will fragment because of working patterns that are too different or separate. Many teams will need to schedule some synchronous working so that team members can overlap with each other or hand over tasks. A good example of doing this virtually is to arrange some time when the entire team is logged in to a specific app while completing their respective tasks. Too much reliance on synchronous work could lead to inefficient use of time, more stress and potentially burnout due to more meetings than are necessary. Too much reliance on asynchronous work could heighten misunderstandings and limit innovation and creativity (Workplaceless, 2021). Striking the right balance is important. As we will see in our case studies, an effective way to enable good asynchronous working is to begin with the end in mind – decide the desired outcome from the task or project and decide the most appropriate ways of working to achieve that while respecting individual preferences and team characteristics.

Effective asynchronous working can allow team members to better control interruptions from notifications and to schedule time to respond in and around other workflows. It can also support better allocation of time to what could be called 'deep work' where fewer interruptions achieve better outcomes. Apps such as MS Teams, and Google Suite software, can make it clear to colleagues when someone is engaged in work that means they should not be disturbed. They also allow for notifications to be muted during such times. Documentation and other resources that can be made available reduce reliance on synchronous communication with other team members. This may lead to greater efficiency in work completion and improved quality.

The team needs to learn how to manage asynchronous work so that they can learn how to make decisions without holding out for synchronous meetings. They must be given support to be able to know how detailed their responses to messages should be, what input should be looked for from which team members, and how to document and record decisions. These things in turn should enable the managers of the team to have greater visibility of what work is happening in the team without being viewed as micromanaging or having to check up on work regularly. Managers can then use their time more effectively to foster connections, remove blocks, provide support and address team members' issues (Workplaceless, 2021).

Meetings and purposeful communication

Hybrid teams will need to meet, but setting up how to do this effectively is important. The purpose of each meeting needs to be clearly established – who needs to attend and why, and what the style of meeting might be (information sharing, socialization, collaboration, brainstorming, etc). To support asynchronous working teams should be asked not to meet for meetings' sake, but to explore other avenues and mediums for what they need to achieve. Where there are meetings, a rhythm and pattern familiar to them is helpful – same time slots, same frequencies, similar agendas shared in advance, same mediums used. Teams should also agree when these arrangements could and should be varied – when different working patterns take effect, or when on-site presence is more appropriate. Some team activities will be better done on site, and others remotely – the team should be supported to better understand the distinctions and create the right routines and structures. Teams need to be encouraged to find time within meetings to share ideas and talk about strategy rather than just about operational issues, things previously done in passing or at the sides of desks (Hall, 2023). Without such dedicated, explicit focus these things could be lost with asynchronous working.

Integrating new team members

Regardless of whether a new team member is brand new to the organization or is simply new to the team itself having moved from elsewhere in the organization, they will need specific support to understand how to integrate with their new colleagues. Consider sharing with them:

- What the team working patterns are – who works when and where.

- What time each person in the team is having lunch, and what other times are protected (e.g. no meetings).
- How the team share updates and progress and how they should do the same.
- Who does what in the team and what each person is accountable for – including what types of things each person can help the new starter with.
- Who they need to spend time with on site and how to arrange this.
- Why the team communicate in the ways they do, and how this works in practice.
- Where to find information and answers to questions without having to meet synchronously with anyone else.
- What connections they may already have with team members and wider stakeholders in the organization.
- What the team's rituals and experiences may be and how they can learn about and take part in them.

When you consider all these things for new team members, it may prompt you to reflect on whether the rest of the team understand these things too and whether it is worth explicitly saying these. It is!

Team charters

This section explores what a team charter is and what kinds of things need to be considered as part of one. You may be wondering why a team charter wasn't required when working on site. That's because the way a team works could be more easily observed or picked up through non-verbal communication, but with remote and hybrid working it isn't so easy – explicit agreement, whether verbal or (ideally) written, is needed.

A team charter is an agreement that defines the purpose of the team, how it will work and how it will achieve its outcomes. They give clarity on how the team works not just to team members but its wider stakeholders, and supply guidance when problems arise within the team. But what could go into one? The suggestions in Table 10.1 are not exhaustive but give an indication of some of the things that your hybrid teams may need to agree to be more effective within the hybrid approach.

TABLE 10.1 Indicative content for a hybrid team charter

Item	What this could cover
Communication	• What does everyone need to know? What would it be nice to know? • What communication is optional for team members to access? • What communication gaps and challenges do we have and how do we address these? • What is an acceptable reply time to non-urgent messages? • When should we tag individuals in team messages? • Which platforms should we use and for what? • How will we communicate with each other about work, and non-work, matters? • How do we connect with and keep stakeholders informed of what we do?
Meeting management and etiquette	• What is the expectation around limiting background noise and/or side conversations in virtual meetings? • How do we ensure that meetings are inclusive? • How often will we meet and for what? • How will we meet, and what decides that?
Team purpose	• Why does the team exist? What work does it do? What work does it not? • How do we contribute to the wider organizational strategy? • What shared values define the team? How do these relate to the organizational values? • What links exist between the team and others in the organization? How do we interact with them? What do they need from us and vice versa? • What outcomes does the team deliver and how are these proven?
Working together	• What skills and perspectives does each team member bring to the team? • What sub-groups exist in the team and for what purpose? • How will we share information among the team? • How will we make decisions as a team? • How will we solve problems when they occur? • How will we resolve conflict if it occurs? • Who should team members contact if they need help, and how should they do this?

(continued)

TABLE 10.1 (Continued)

Item	What this could cover
Role and task clarity	• What processes are we responsible for as a team? How will we optimize these for hybrid working (to allow greater autonomy and fewer bottlenecks around decision making)? • What decisions can team members make on their own, and which need input from others or from the team's manager? • What is each team member responsible for and how are they expected to do that either alone or with others?

Throughout this chapter we have focused on how to support hybrid teams, complementing what we have already covered about supporting hybrid managers and hybrid individual employees. I have aimed to give practical guidance and advice on how to do these things, but the devil is in the detail. It is now up to you to put these things, and the wider advice and thinking from this book, into practice.

I wish you well in doing it. I have spent a long time – nearly 25 years – doing it. I have enjoyed being able to share my thinking and good practices with you. If you feel I can help you in your organization to make hybrid working work, track me down – I'm not hard to find.

Good luck.

CASE STUDY ONE

This case study covers Watford Borough Council, a local authority in the UK employing around 250 people. I spoke with Donna Nolan (Chief Executive Officer), Lee Pound (Head of HR & OD) and Ishbel Morren (Executive Support, but also a pathfinder for the project we discussed here). All work in a hybrid way, as does most of the organization.

Nolan joined the organization as the Covid-19 pandemic hit. In other roles in other organizations, she had been used to much greater flexibility and agility than she found when she arrived as Watford's new CEO. She found that Watford was a very traditional organization at that point, with a lot of redundant real estate even before remote and hybrid working became normalized. She used the pandemic to push the boundaries of what was possible at Watford, to modernize the organization. She sought to consider changing expectations about work and to reflect that in the way Watford worked.

During the pandemic Watford gave their teams complete freedom and autonomy, with little structure about how, when or where work needed to be done. Consequently, they saw big increases in engagement and maintained productivity. Nolan and Pound equated this period to the unfreeze part of Lewin's change model, getting teams ready for a more meaningful change to how work was done and showing them what was out of date about traditional working models.

As the Covid-19 pandemic receded, Nolan and Pound launched Project Reimagining Watford. Morren became a pathfinder (a change champion) of this project along with around 20 others. Nolan explained that the project worked based on 'accountable freedom' – consciously not dictating ways of working to teams and creating a bottom-up approach where teams could decide their own ways of working. Nolan and Pound believe that teams have the best insight to be able to decide the best approach to service delivery while protecting the autonomy and freedom that they had got used to during the pandemic.

Each team was given the freedom to decide how, when and where it worked. This meant that some teams could decide to work entirely on site, or entirely remotely, or in a hybrid manner. Each team was asked to create its own team charter, using standard headings devised by the organization, and to complete the details under each heading of how they were going to deliver their service. Each charter was then placed on Watford's intranet so that the rest of the organization could read and comment on it. Nolan reported that this visibility led to some interesting and productive conversations between teams. The pathfinder community that Morren was part of were tasked with easing the development and agreement of the charters.

Teams were asked to ensure that if they chose to work on site that it was with purpose, and this helped Watford to redesign their on-site locations once the on-site requirements were clarified by teams. There is now much greater visibility about which teams are on site and which are not on any given day, and who is working remotely – Nolan and Pound both commented that the clarity around working arrangements makes it much easier to find people if they need them as everyone knows where each team will be, whether on site or remote.

Nolan and Pound consciously placed focus on teams rather than individuals in this project. The organizational belief is that teams deliver the services to residents, not individuals, and therefore the way that services are delivered need to be focused on team ways of working, not individual ways of working.

Following the pandemic and its later impact on ways of working, it became clear that the organization's values and behaviours needed to evolve to best reflect the organization in an agile working world. Like the development of team charters, Nolan and Pound took a bottom-up approach with staff – again supported by agile pathfinders – driving the development and implementation of these.

The effect of this piece of work is the need to review each team charter to ensure they accurately reflect the Council's new values and behaviours. In addition, to assess how well each team is upholding the organizational values and behaviours and to ensure the charters are still a practical tool for fostering unity and innovation, the Council have introduced a minimum annual review to be led by the teams. Nolan believes that there will be some shift required by teams who have got very used to a way of working that may not be wholly aligned with the values, and where new staff have arrived in the team. The organization is planning some added development for teams around aligning ways of working across different teams to allow for cross-organizational working.

I asked how this had affected what the organization does for its service users. Nolan reported that there have been fewer service delivery issues because of handing over accountability to the teams themselves. Each team has some level of face-to-face resident interaction that is needed but can design how that happens within the team in an outcome-focused way. Each team is empowered to look after its members in a way that delivers their outcomes. Each team member is accountable to the others for delivering their parts of the service as well as looking after their own needs. This in turn feeds into the corporate performance reporting structures in place to support the delivery of the Council plan and check outcomes for customers. Watford also have a staff group that mirrors the corporate management board and looks at the same issues but offers a team-based perspective on work and operational issues, which helps keep the focus on teams and their outcomes.

Nolan believes that conversations about working arrangements and individual/team rhythms has expanded and given more flexibility to service delivery in a very adult–adult way that could not have been achieved in a top-down approach. Watford is now able to deliver more to its residents than when its teams worked in a traditional way.

CASE STUDY TWO

Liz Dowling is Chief People Officer at VIOOH, a leading global digital out-of-home marketplace, who featured as an example in *HR for Hybrid Working*. VIOOH have 180 people, and their overarching hybrid approach is termed 'Future VIOOH – led by teams, measured by outcomes'. It sets out their main principles around hybrid work where teams are expected to spend 20 per cent of their time each quarter on site, with the rest a blend of office and remote, which is decided by the teams themselves based on their goals, customer needs and individual preferences.

Future VIOOH is underpinned by a VIOOH Essentials programme that each employee, whether new or not, must complete within a 90-day period to transition to hybrid working. This programme includes a range of self-study and gamified modules that seek to embed the culture of VIOOH as a hybrid (not remote) company, with a flexible approach but one that seeks to keep its unique organizational culture.

Dowling explained that the approach aims not to mandate how teams should work, but to create both accountability and autonomy with a focus on achieving goals. The VIOOH values and shared beliefs are the main guidance teams must work within. Cultural ambassadors function as champions to ensure that each team's voice is heard and listened to with the organization, and who shape each team's 'connected day' (a monthly on-site get-together, planned well in advance and designed to further the team's goals and projects).

VIOOH have a list of defined activities that take place on site, and teams are encouraged to increase their on-site presence during onboarding and induction phase for new starters, and a similar principle helps those moving within the organization to learn about their new teams. Otherwise, teams are free to decide when they work together on site, but the baseline is 20 per cent of time per quarter. There are no exceptions granted to this requirement, but teams are instructed to plan their on-site presence with purpose. Some teams have implemented more frequent 'anchor days' which are reflective of the rhythm and cadence of their work and projects. Not every team has these, but some have weekly anchor days. VIOOH use an app to manage on-site presence on any given day, which also increases visibility about who is working where and when.

There are quarterly all-company events and an annual VIOOH week in January where all employees are on site for an entire week, taking part in team building, organizational development and planning activities. Dowling also uses these weeks to consciously shape the organizational culture and to realign teams to organizational values and goals. Dowling commented that VIOOH see on-site working as like a trip to a marketplace – something planned in advance, to obtain things and to see particular people.

Dowling's team have deliberately created 'templates for everything' to enable teams to work together both synchronously and asynchronously. One such template is for teams to occupy digital space on the organizational systems to alert other teams about their purpose, team members, goals and outcomes, working patterns and useful things to know about the team, and answer frequently asked questions about the team's work.

Teams are also encouraged to explicitly state their rituals. These can be as simple as figuring out the frequency, duration, content and medium for team meetings, but can be more complex such as team norms, knowledge-sharing activities and processes, and how to update systems and information. Dowling's people team have a daily 15-minute meeting where each person shares what they worked on the previous day, what they are working on that day and any help they need from the rest of the team. Teams are also asked to consider their shared beliefs and values and to use those to guide their behaviours.

Each team is given support to work asynchronously, with systems and templates supplied to help. Dowling's people team begin their asynchronous work planning by looking first at the outcome required from a task or project and then working backwards to plan out how the team needs to get to that point, and consciously designing tasks and ways of working to deliver these outcomes while respecting individual and team preferences.

I asked Dowling whether this had worked for VIOOH. She said it had. She said that if VIOOH relied on teams being on site and working synchronously then they would lose their competitive advantage – 'some things can only be done in a hybrid way'.

Case study reflections

In the first case study, Watford Borough Council, the following points stand out for consideration:

- Changing the way that accountability has normally been controlled can empower and enable the teams that deliver services to make improvements.

- A bottom-up approach can be more effective and sometimes more innovative than a top-down approach.

- Using change champions to work with and within teams to embed practices and values is a helpful step.

- Team charters, or variants of them, are powerful tools to explore and agree ways of working.

- Sharing team charters in an accessible place can lead to useful conversations and greater consideration of organizational requirements.

- Focusing on teams, rather than individuals, as the main service delivery vehicle within organizations encourages open and honest conversations about how work needs to be done, and accountability to each other rather than siloed individual thinking.

- There is still a need to coordinate the organizational requirements and to regularly revisit team charters, particularly where there is turnover in teams or other impactful changes.

In the second case study, VIOOH, the following points stand out:

- Allowing teams to work out their own hybrid approaches but based on guiding principles and shared organizational values and beliefs is a helpful and empowering step.

- Supporting the hybrid approach with mandatory training about how it works and asking all employees to undertake this training will create consistency.

- The use of change champions is again shown to help embed new ways of working.

- Allowing teams to set what they use their on-site presence for and/or to increase it allows for different rhythms and cadences of teams' work to be reflected in the hybrid approach.

- Supplying templates for teams to use in planning their work can help create consistency too and support the team in that work.

- Team rituals – things that matter to the team or that the team tend to do regularly – are important. Explicitly stating these will help not just those in the team, but its wider connections also, to understand why the rituals exist and how they work.

- Asynchronous working offers many benefits, and some organizations can achieve greater things because of that, but teams need support on how to do it.

The action plan

If you are wanting to look at how to better support teams to work in a hybrid environment, consider the following questions:

- What pieces of equipment would a hybrid team need at your organization? Would that be the same for all hybrid teams?

- What is the range of technology and apps that would enable hybrid teams to be effective in various aspects of their work together, and how will they know how and what to use them for?

- How will you make it easy for hybrid teams and their members to see who else is on site or remote on any given day?

- What types of on-site get-togethers will you encourage hybrid teams to have?

- How does each hybrid team define productivity in its context?

- What digital communities are available to hybrid teams in your organization, and which do they need to create for themselves?

- What guidance and support will your hybrid teams need to embrace and be more comfortable with asynchronous working?

- How will you guide teams to redesign and perfect their processes for asynchronous working?

- What purpose do team meetings serve, and how can this be better realized for hybrid teams?

- How should your hybrid teams integrate new team members into their ranks?

- What use could be made of team charters to help hybrid teams, and what would the headings for these be in your organization?

References and further reading

CCL (2022) What's a team charter, and how can it keep your team on track? 25 February, www.ccl.org/articles/leading-effectively-articles/what-is-this-team-for-and-why-am-i-here/ (archived at https://perma.cc/QB6R-4SJ7)

Culturate (2022) How to create an effective hybrid team dynamics, 25 July, www.weareculturate.com/post/hybrid-team-how-to-create-an-effective-hybrid-team-dynamics (archived at https://perma.cc/6VYA-7HCE)

Davis, M C et al (2022) Where is your office today? New insights on employee behaviour and social networks, University of Leeds, October, https://futureworkplace.leeds.ac.uk/wp-content/uploads/sites/86/2022/10/Where-is-your-office-today-Oct-2022-2.pdf (archived at https://perma.cc/MVM5-DSNT)

Delaney, K J (2021) How to shift mindset and practices for hybrid work, Charter, 1 May, www.charterworks.com/robert-pozen-hybrid-work-remote-how-to-shift-mindset-and-practices/ (archived at https://perma.cc/8VVV-AVB2)

Gangnes, J T (2022) Building culture in a remote & hybrid workplace, ThoughtExchange, 29 April, www.thoughtexchange.com/blog/building-culture-in-a-remote-hybrid-workplace/ (archived at https://perma.cc/FUT3-QWW3)

Hall, J (2023) How to avoid productivity paranoia in hybrid teams, *Forbes*, 6 November, www.forbes.com/sites/johnhall/2023/06/04/how-to-avoid-productivity-paranoia-in-hybrid-teams/amp/ (archived at https://perma.cc/7VHL-KV4T)

Let's Grow Leaders (nd) 6 habits of highly successful virtual and hybrid teams, www.letsgrowleaders.com/6-habits-of-highly-successful-virtual-and-hybrid-teams/ (archived at https://perma.cc/B37Y-BNP5)

Lucidchart (nd) How to keep processes efficient across hybrid teams, www.lucidchart.com/blog/how-to-keep-processes-efficient-across-hybrid-teams (archived at https://perma.cc/W2DJ-GK4G)

Microsoft (2021a) In hybrid work, managers keep teams connected, 30 March, www.microsoft.com/en-us/worklab/work-trend-index/managers-keep-teams-connected (archived at https://perma.cc/4R3G-E7NS)

Microsoft (2021b) To thrive in hybrid work, build a culture of trust and flexibility, 9 September, www.microsoft.com/en-us/worklab/work-trend-index/support-flexibility-in-work-styles (archived at https://perma.cc/85VF-PEVB)

Microsoft (2022a) Great expectations: Making hybrid work work, 16 March, www.microsoft.com/en-us/worklab/work-trend-index/great-expectations-making-hybrid-work-work (archived at https://perma.cc/JZ7D-PEAT)

Microsoft (2022b) Hybrid work is just work. Are we doing it wrong? 22 September, www.microsoft.com/en-us/worklab/work-trend-index/hybrid-work-is-just-work (archived at https://perma.cc/WFJ7-6VWN)

MindTools (nd) Team Charters, www.mindtools.com/awmtnvc/team-charters (archived at https://perma.cc/CS8G-LZKQ)

North, J (nd) Hybrid working: A guide for teams, The Big Bang Partnership, https://bigbangpartnership.co.uk/hybrid-working-a-guide-for-teams/ (archived at https://perma.cc/XBF2-FY6D)

People Management (2023) Wellbeing in the workplace of now: How hybrid has created work-life balance concerns, 23 January, www.peoplemanagement.co.uk/article/1810964/wellbeing-workplace-now-hybrid-created-work-life-balance-concerns (archived at https://perma.cc/75HP-4JFH)

Smith, W (2023) Hybrid teams and how they're shaping the future of work, Multiplier, 23 February, www.usemultiplier.com/blog/hybrid-team (archived at https://perma.cc/WZ7Q-8ELM)

University of Leeds (nd) Hybrid working: Supporting our ways of working, OD&PL Leadership and Professional Practice, https://leadershipand professionalpractice.leeds.ac.uk/home/staff-development/hybrid-working/ (archived at https://perma.cc/PX9N-NSW6)

Viewsonic (2022) Virtual collaboration: 7 best practices for hybrid teams, 17 May, www.viewsonic.com/library/business/hybrid-work/virtual-collaboration-7-best-practices-for-hybrid-teams/ (archived at https://perma.cc/MT6J-EQG4)

Vogel, K (2024) Effective hybrid teams: 9 ways to work smarter, RingCentral blog, 29 May, www.ringcentral.com/us/en/blog/effective-hybrid-teams/ (archived at https://perma.cc/ZW7V-2AC6)

Watkins, M D (2013) Making virtual teams work: Ten basic principles, *Harvard Business Review*, 27 June, www.hbr.org/2013/06/making-virtual-teams-work-ten (archived at https://perma.cc/3CMP-DKJN)

Workplaceless (2021) Building productive hybrid teams: 10 key practices, 19 September, https://www.workplaceless.com/blog/practices-of-productive-and-inclusive-hybrid-teams (archived at https://perma.cc/HWP9-QGX3)

Sketchnote summary for Part Three

Part 3: Help and Support

Effective managers enable successful hybrid working

Managers are key

Hybrid Working

1-to-1 support

Mindset shift

Manager

group support

Help managers to adapt through:

DATA

There are many challenges to be addressed to make hybrid working successful

isolation

feeling unable to unplug

My home + my office?

Wooo!!!

Technology

Help!

Skills + Support

Collaborate effectively

Individuals can be helped by:

Learning
using a mix of methods

Contracting
Based on conversations with manager + hybrid worker

Regular check-ins with hybridworkers
e.g.
successes
challenges
how are you feeling?
giving thanks
what have you learnt?

Teams can be helped by considering:

What does productivity look like for our work?

Does the team have the right technology for hybrid working?

Productivity
And how will it be measured, monitored + interpreted?

Tasks | Doing | Done

A team charter

Team Charter
Purpose
How
When
Where

INDEX

Looking for another book?

Explore our award-winning
books from global business
experts in Human Resources,
Learning and Development

Scan the code to browse

www.koganpage.com/hr-learning-
development

More from Kogan Page

ISBN: 9781398605725

ISBN: 9781398604230

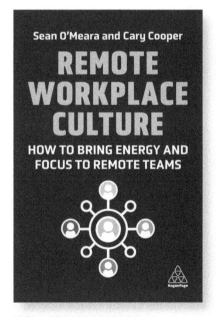

ISBN: 9781398603868

ISBN: 9781398600362

www.koganpage.com